THE ART OF DEBUGGING

THE ART OF DEBUGGING

DEBUGGING

with GDB, DDD, and Eclipse

by Norman Matloff and Peter Jay Salzman

no starch
press

San Francisco

THE ART OF DEBUGGING WITH GDB, DDD, AND ECLIPSE. Copyright © 2008 by Norman Matloff and Peter Jay Salzman.

12 11 10 09 08   1 2 3 4 5 6 7 8 9

ISBN-10: 1-59327-002-X
ISBN-13: 978-1-59327-174-9

Publisher: William Pollock
Production Editor: Megan Dunchak
Cover and Interior Design: Octopod Studios
Developmental Editor: Tyler Ortman
Technical Reviewer: Daniel Jacobowitz
Copyeditor: Neil Ching
Compositor: Riley Hoffman
Proofreader: Rachel Kai
Indexer: Fred Brown, Allegro Technical Indexing

For information on book distributors or translations, please contact No Starch Press, Inc. directly:
No Starch Press, Inc.
555 De Haro Street, Suite 250, San Francisco, CA 94107
phone: 415.863.9900; fax: 415.863.9950; info@nostarch.com; www.nostarch.com

Library of Congress Cataloging-in-Publication Data
Matloff, Norman S.
  The art of debugging with GDB, DDD, and Eclipse / Norman Matloff and P.J.
Salzman.
      p. cm.
  ISBN-13: 978-1-59327-002-5
  ISBN-10: 1-59327-002-X
  1. Debugging in computer science. 2. Computer software-Quality control. I.
Salzman, P.J. II. Title.
QA76.9.D43M35 2008
005.1'4-dc22
                        2003017566

BRIEF CONTENTS

CONTENTS IN DETAIL

3
INSPECTING AND SETTING VARIABLES
95

4
WHEN A PROGRAM CRASHES
117

5
DEBUGGING IN A MULTIPLE-ACTIVITIES CONTEXT 145

6
SPECIAL TOPICS 185

7
OTHER TOOLS 205

8
USING GDB/DDD/ECLIPSE FOR OTHER LANGUAGES   235

PREFACE

"Hey, this thing really works!" So said one of our students, Andrew, after he made serious use of a debugging tool for the first time. He had learned about debugging tools three years earlier in his freshman programming courses, but he had dismissed them as just something to learn for the final exam. Now as a fourth-year student, Andrew's professor urged him to stop using print statements for debugging and make use of formal debugging tools. To his delight and surprise, he found that he could greatly reduce his debugging time by making use of the proper tools.

There are many "Andrews" out there, among students and among working programmers, and we hope this book will trigger an "Andrew-like" epiphany for them. But even more so, we hope to reach the many people who do use debugging tools but are not sure what can be done in specialized situations and who would like to learn more about debugging tools and the philosophy behind them.

As this book's copyeditor pointed out, much knowledge of debugging exists in some communities as kind of folklore, but it is not written in books. Well, this book will change that. We'll address questions like the following:

- How do you debug threads code?

- Why do breakpoints sometimes end up at slightly different locations than where you set them?

- Why does the GDB until command sometimes jump to a "surprising" place?

- What cool tricks can be done with DDD and Eclipse?

- In today's GUI age, do text-based applications such as GDB have any value?

- Why didn't a segmentation fault occur when your erroneous code exceeded the bounds of an array?

- Why is one of our example data structures named nsp? (Sorry, that's an inside joke with our publisher.)

This book is neither a glorified user's manual nor an abstract treatise on the cognitive theory of the debugging process. Instead, it is something intermediate to these two genres. On one hand, we do indeed give information on the "how-to" for specific commands in GDB, DDD, and Eclipse; but on the other hand, we do set forth and make frequent use of some general principles for the debugging process.

We chose GDB, DDD, and Eclipse as our illustrative tools because of their popularity in the Linux/open source communities. Our examples slightly favor GDB, not only because its text-based nature makes it more compact to present on a page but also because, as alluded to above, we find that text-based commands still play a valuable role in the debugging process.

Eclipse has become quite widely used for much more than simply the debugging role we treat here, and it does provide an attractive, versatile tool for debugging. On the other hand, DDD has a much smaller footprint and includes some powerful features not found in Eclipse.

Chapter 1, "Some Preliminaries for Beginners and Pros," is an overview. Many experienced programmers may be tempted to skip it, but we urge them to read through it, as we do set forth a number of simple but powerful general guidelines that we recommend for the debugging process.

Then Chapter 2, "Stopping to Take a Look Around," covers the workhorse of debugging, the breakpoint, discussing all the ins and outs—setting, deleting, and disabling breakpoints; moving from one breakpoint to the next; viewing detailed information on breakpoints; and so on.

Once you arrive at a breakpoint, then what? Chapter 3, "Inspecting and Setting Variables," addresses this question. Our running example here concerns code that traverses a tree. The key point is convenient display of the contents of a node in the tree when we reach a breakpoint. Here GDB really shines, providing some very flexible features that enable you to effectively display the information of interest each time the program pauses. And we present an especially nice DDD feature for graphical display of trees and other linked data structures.

Chapter 4, "When a Program Crashes," covers the dreaded runtime errors arising from segmentation faults. We first present material on what is happening at the lower levels, including memory allocation for a program and the cooperative roles of the hardware and the operating system. Readers with a good systems knowledge may skim through this material, but we believe that many others will profit by acquiring this foundation. We then turn to core files—how they are created, how to use them to perform "post mortems," and so on. We finish the chapter with an extended example of a debugging session in which several bugs produce seg faults.

We chose "Debugging in A Multiple-Activities Context" for the title of Chapter 5 to make the point that we cover not only parallel programming but also network code. Client/server network programming does count as parallel processing, with even our tools being used in parallel—for example, two windows in which we use GDB, one for the client, one for the server. Since network code involves system calls, we supplement our debugging tools with the C/C++ errno variable and the Linux strace command. The next portion of Chapter 5 involves threads programming. Here again we begin with a review of the infrastructure: timesharing, processes and threads, race conditions, and so on. We present the technical details of working with threads in GDB, DDD, and Eclipse and again discuss some general principles to keep in mind, such as the randomness of the timing in which threads context switches occur. The final part of Chapter 5 concerns parallel programming with the popular MPI and OpenMP packages. We end with an extended example in the context of OpenMP.

Chapter 6, "Special Topics," covers some important miscellaneous topics. A debugging tool can't help you if your code doesn't even compile, so we discuss some approaches for dealing with this. Then we treat the problem of failure to link, due to missing libraries; once again we felt it was useful here to give some "theory"—types of libraries and how they are linked to your main code, for example. And what about debugging GUI programs? For simplicity, we stick to a "semi-GUI" setting here, that of curses programming, and show how to get GDB, DDD, and Eclipse to interact with the events in your curses window.

As noted earlier, the debugging process can be greatly enhanced through the use of supplementary tools, several of which we present in Chapter 7, "Other Tools." We have additional coverage of errno and strace, some material on lint, and tips on the effective use of a text editor.

Though the book focuses on C/C++, we have coverage of other languages in Chapter 8, "Using GDB/DDD/Eclipse for Other Languages," treating Java, Python, Perl, and assembly language.

We apologize if we have somehow missed the reader's favorite debugging topic, but we have covered the material that we have found useful in our own programming.

We owe a great debt of gratitude to the many staffers at No Starch Press who assisted us on this project over its long duration. We especially thank the firm's founder and editor, Bill Pollock. He had faith in this offbeat project from the beginning and was remarkably tolerant of our many delays.

Daniel Jacobowitz did a truly stellar job of reviewing the manuscript, providing many points of invaluable advice. Neil Ching, ostensibly hired to do copyediting, turned out to actually be a "ringer" with a degree in computer science! He brought up a number of important points concerning the clarity of our technical discussions. The quality of the book was greatly enhanced by the feedback we received from both Daniel and Neil. Of course, the usual disclaimer must be made that any errors are our own.

Norm says: I wish to say *xie xie* and *todah rabah* to my wife Gamis and daughter Laura, two amazing people whom I feel lucky to be related to. Their approach to problem solving, sparkling humor, and *joie de vivre* pervade this book in spite of their not having read a word of it. I also thank the many students I have taught over the years, who teach me as much as I teach them, and who make me feel that I chose the right profession after all. I've always strived to "make a difference," and hope this book will do so in some small way.

Pete comments: I thank Nicole Carlson, Mark Kim, and Rhonda Salzman for spending many hours reading through chapters and making corrections and suggestions, for no reason other than what you're reading at this very moment. I'd also like to thank the people of the Linux Users Group of Davis who have answered my questions over the years. Knowing you has made me smarter. *Todah* goes to Evelyn, who has improved my life in every way. Special mention goes out to Geordi ("J-Train" from San Francisco) who selflessly used his own feline body weight to make sure pages didn't blow away, always kept my seat warm, and made sure the room was never empty. You are deeply missed each and every day. Purr on, little one. Hi, Mom! Look what I did!

Norm Matloff and Pete Salzman
June 9, 2008

1

SOME PRELIMINARIES FOR BEGINNERS AND PROS

Some people, especially professionals, may be tempted to skip this chapter. We suggest, though, that everyone at least skim through it. Many professionals will find some material that is new to them, and in any case it is important that all readers be familiar with the material presented here, which will be used throughout the remainder of the book. Beginners should of course read this chapter carefully.

In the first few sections of this chapter, we will present an overview of the debugging process and the role of debugging tools, and then walk through an extended example in Section 1.7.

1.1 Debugging Tools Used in This Book

In this book we set out the basic principles of debugging, illustrating them in the contexts of the following debugging tools:

GDB

The most commonly used debugging tool among Unix programmers is GDB, the GNU Project Debugger developed by Richard Stallman, a prominent leader of the open source software movement, which played a key role in the development of Linux.

Most Linux sytems should have GDB preinstalled. If it is not, you must download the GCC compiler package.

DDD

Due to the more recent popularity of graphical user interfaces (GUIs), a number of GUI-based debuggers have been developed that run under Unix. Most of these are GUI *front ends* to GDB: The user issues commands via the GUI, which in turn passes them on to GDB. One of these is DDD, the Data Display Debugger.

If your system does not already have DDD installed, you can download it. For instance, on Fedora Linux systems, the command

```
yum install ddd
```

will take care of the entire process for you. In Ubuntu Linux, a similar command, apt-get, can be used.

Eclipse

Some readers may use integrated development environments (IDEs). An *IDE* is more than just a debugging tool; it integrates an editor, build tool, debugger, and other development aids into one package. In this book, our example IDE is the highly popular Eclipse system. As with DDD, Eclipse works on top of GDB or some other debugger.

You can install Eclipse via yum or apt-get as above, or simply download the *.zip* file and unpack it in a suitable directory, say */usr/local*.

In this book, we use Eclipse version 3.3.

1.2   Programming Language Focus

Our primary view in this book is toward C/C++ programming, and most of our examples will be in that context. However, in Chapter 8 we will discuss other languages.

1.3   The Principles of Debugging

Even though debugging is an art rather than a science, there are definite principles that guide its practice. We will discuss some of them in this section.

At least one of our rules, the Fundamental Principle of Confirmation, is rather formal in nature.

1.3.1   The Essence of Debugging: The Principle of Confirmation

The following rule is the essence of debugging:

The Fundamental Principle of Confirmation

> Fixing a buggy program is a process of confirming, one by one, that the many things you *believe* to be true about the code actually *are* true. When you find that one of your assumptions is *not* true, you have found a clue to the location (if not the exact nature) of a bug.

Another way of saying this is:

> Surprises are good!

When one of the things that you think is true about the program fails to confirm, you are surprised. But it's a good surprise, because this discovery can lead you to the location of a bug.

1.3.2   Of What Value Is a Debugging Tool for the Principle of Confirmation?

The classic debugging technique is to simply add *trace code* to the program to print out values of variables as the program executes, using printf() or cout statements, for example. You might ask, "Isn't this enough? Why use a debugging tool like GDB, DDD, or Eclipse?"

First of all, this approach requires a constant cycle of strategically adding trace code, recompiling the program, running the program and analyzing the output of the trace code, removing the trace code after the bug is fixed, and repeating these steps for each new bug that is discovered. This is highly time consuming and fatigue making. Most importantly, these actions distract you from the real task and reduce your ability to focus on the reasoning process necessary to find the bug.

In contrast, with graphical debugging tools like DDD and Eclipse, all you have to do in order to examine the value of a variable is move the mouse pointer over an instance of that variable in the code display, and you are shown its current value. Why make yourself even wearier than necessary, for longer than necessary, during an all-night debugging session by doing this using printf() statements? Do yourself a favor and reduce the amount of time you have to spend and the tedium you need to endure by using a debugging tool.

You also get a lot more from a debugging tool than the ability to look at variables. In many situations, a debugger can tell you the approximate location of a bug. Suppose, for example, that your program bombs or crashes with a *segmentation fault*, that is, a memory access error. As you will see in our sample debugging session later in this chapter, GDB/DDD/Eclipse can immediately tell you the location of the seg fault, which is typically at or near the location of the bug.

Similarly, a debugger lets you set *watchpoints* that can tell you at what point during a run of the program the value of a certain variable reaches a suspect value or range. This information can be difficult to deduce by looking at the output of calls to printf().

1.3.3 Other Debugging Principles

Start small

At the beginning of the debugging process, you should run your program on easy, simple cases. This may not expose all of your bugs, but it is likely to uncover a few of them. If, for example, your code consists of a large loop, the easiest bugs to find are those that arise on the first or second iteration.

Use a top-down approach

You probably know about using a *top-down* or *modular* approach to writing code: Your main program should not be too long, and it should consist mostly of calls to functions that do substantial work. If one of those functions is lengthy, you should consider breaking it up, in turn, into smaller modules.

Not only should you *write* code in a top-down manner, you should also *debug* code from the top down.

For example, suppose your program uses a function f(). When you step through the code using a debugging tool and encounter a call to f(), the debugger will give you a choice as to where the next pause in execution will occur—either at the first line within the function about to be called or at the statement following the function call. In many cases, the latter is the better initial choice: You perform the call and then inspect the values of variables that depend on the results of the call in order to see whether or not the function worked correctly. If so, then you will have avoided the time-consuming and needless effort of stepping through the code inside the function, which was not misbehaving (in this case).

Use a debugging tool to determine the location of a segmentation fault

The very first step you take when a seg fault occurs should be to run your program within the debugger and reproduce the seg fault. The debugger will tell you the line of code at which the fault occurred. You can then get additional useful information by invoking the debugger's *backtrace* facility, which displays the sequence of function calls leading to the invocation of the function in which the fault occurred.

In some cases it may be difficult to reproduce the seg fault, but if you have a *core file*, you can still do a backtrace to determine the situation that produced the seg fault. This will be discussed in Chapter 4.

Determine the location of an infinite loop by issuing an interrupt

If you suspect your program has an infinite loop, enter the debugger and run your program again, letting it execute long enough to enter the loop. Then use the debugger's interrupt command to suspend the program, and do a backtrace to see what point of the loop body has been reached and how the program got there. (The program has not been killed; you can resume execution if you wish.)

Use binary search

You've probably seen binary search in the context of sorted lists. Say, for example, that you have an array x[] of 500 numbers, arranged in ascending order, and you wish to determine where to insert a new number, y. Start by comparing y to x[250]. If y turns out to be smaller than that element, you'd next compare it to x[125], but if y is larger than x[250], then the next comparison would instead be with x[375]. In the latter case, if y is smaller than x[375], you then compare it to x[312], which is halfway between x[250] and x[375], and so on. You'd keep cutting your search space in half at each iteration, and so find the insertion point quickly.

This principle can be applied while debugging too. Suppose you know that the value stored in a certain variable goes bad sometime during the first 1,000 iterations of a loop. One way that might help you track down the iteration where the value first goes bad is to use a *watchpoint*, an advanced technique that we will discuss in Section 1.5.3. Another approach is to use binary search, in this case in time rather than in space. You'd first check the variable's value at the 500th iteration; if it is still all right at that point, you'd next check the value at the 750th iteration, and so on.

As another example, suppose one of the source files in your program will not even compile. The line of code cited in the compiler message generated by a syntax error is sometimes far from the actual location of the error, and so you may have trouble determining that location. Binary search can help here: You remove (or comment out) one half of the code in the compilation unit, recompile the remaining code, and see if the error message persists. If it does, then the error is in that second half; if the message does not appear, then the error is in the half that you deleted. Once you determine which half of the code contains the bug, you further confine the bug to half of that portion, and keep going until you locate the problem. Of course, you should make a copy of the original code before starting this process or, better yet, use your text editor's undo feature. See Chapter 7 for tips on making good use of an editor while programming.

1.4   Text-Based vs. GUI-Based Debugging Tools, and a Compromise Between Them

The GUIs discussed in this book, DDD and Eclipse, serve as front ends to GDB for C and C++ and to other debuggers. While the GUIs have eye appeal and can be more convenient than the text-based GDB, our point of view in this book will be that text-based and GUI-based debuggers (including IDEs) are all useful, in different contexts.

1.4.1   Brief Comparison of Interfaces

To quickly get an idea of the differences between text-based and GUI debugging tools, let's consider a situation that we will use as a running example in this chapter. The program in the example is *insert_sort*. It is compiled from a source file *ins.c*, and it performs an insertion sort.

1.4.1.1 GDB: Plain Text

To initiate a debugging session on this program with GDB, you would type

```
$ gdb insert_sort
```

at the Unix command line, after which GDB would invite you to submit commands by displaying its prompt:

```
(gdb)
```

1.4.1.2 DDD: a GUI Debugging Tool

Using DDD, you would begin your debugging session by typing

```
$ ddd insert_sort
```

at the Unix command line. The DDD window would come up, after which you would submit commands through the GUI.

The typical appearance of a DDD window is shown in Figure 1-1. As you see, the DDD window lays out information in various subwindows:

*   The Source Text window displays your source code. DDD begins its display at your main() function, but you can of course move to other parts of the source file by using the scroll bar at the right edge of the window.

*   The Menu Bar presents various menu categories, including File, Edit, and View.

*   The Command Tool lists the most common DDD commands (such as Run, Interrupt, Step, and Next), so that you can access them quickly.

*   The Console: Recall that DDD is simply a GUI front end to GDB (and to other debuggers). DDD translates selections made with the mouse to the corresponding GDB commands. These commands and their output are displayed in the Console. In addition, you can submit commands to GDB directly via the Console, which is a handy feature because not all GDB commands have DDD counterparts.

*   The Data window shows the values of variables that you have requested to be continuously displayed. This subwindow will not appear until you have made such a request, so it does not appear in this figure.

Here is a quick example of how a typical debugging command is submitted to the debugger under each type of user interface. When debugging *insert_sort*, you may wish to pause execution of the program—to set a *breakpoint*—at line 16 (say) of the function get_args(). (You will see the full source code for *insert_sort* in Section 1.7.) To arrange this in GDB, you would type

```
(gdb) break 16
```

at the GDB prompt.

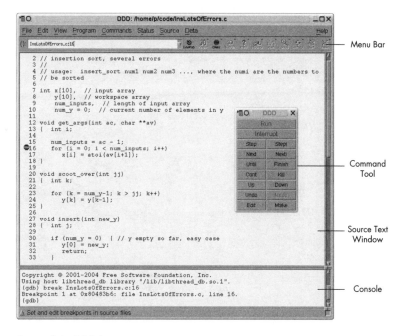

Figure 1-1: DDD layout

The full command name is break, but GDB allows abbreviations as long as there is no ambiguity, and most GDB users would type b 16 here. In order to facilitate understanding for those new to GDB, we will use full command names at first, and switch to abbreviations later in the book, after the commands have become more familiar.

Using DDD, you would look at the Source Text window, click at the beginning of line 16, and then click the Break icon at the top of the DDD screen. You could also right-click at the beginning of the line, and then select Set Breakpoint. Yet another option is to simply double-click the line of code, anywhere to the left of the start of the line. In any case, DDD would confirm the selection by displaying a little stop sign at that line, as shown in Figure 1-2. In this way you can see your breakpoints at a glance.

1.4.1.3 Eclipse: A GUI Debugger and Much More

Now, Figure 1-3 introduces the general environment in Eclipse. In Eclipse terminology, we are currently in the Debug perspective. Eclipse is a general framework for development of lots of different kinds of software. Each programming language has its own plug-in GUI—a *perspective*—within Eclipse. Indeed, there could be several competing perspectives for the same language. In our Eclipse work in this book, we will use the C/C++ perspective for C/C++ development, the Pydev perspective for writing Python programs, and so on. There is also a Debug perspective for the actual debugging (with some language-specific features), and that is what you see in the figure.

Figure 1-2: Breakpoint set

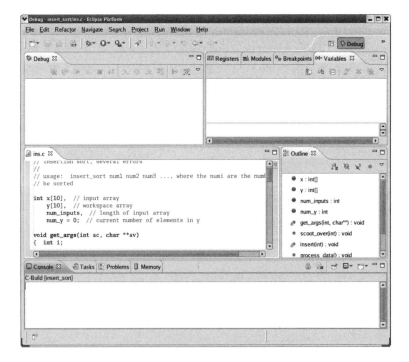

Figure 1-3: Eclipse environment

The C/C++ perspective is part of the CDT plugin. Behind the scenes CDT invokes GDB, similar to the case of DDD.

The details of that figure are generally similar to what we described for DDD above. A perspective is broken into tabbed windows called *views*. You can see a view for the source file, *ins.c*, on the left; there is the Variables view for inspecting the values of the variables (none so far in the picture); there is a Console view, whose function is quite similar to the subwindow in DDD of the same name; and so on.

You can set breakpoints and so on visually as in DDD. In Figure 1-4, for example, the line

---

```
for (i = 0; i < num_inputs; i++)
```

---

in the source file window has a blue symbol in the left margin, symbolizing that there is a breakpoint there.

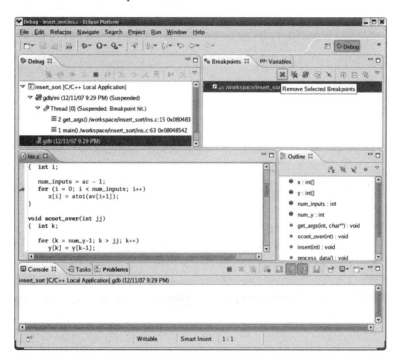

Figure 1-4: Removing a breakpoint in Eclipse

1.4.1.4 Eclipse vs. DDD

Eclipse also has some aids missing from DDD. Near the right side, for instance, note the Outline view, which lists the variables, functions and so on. If you click the entry for your function scoot_over(), for example, the cursor in the source file view will move to that function. Moreover, if you temporarily move from the Debug perspective back to the C/C++ perspective, where you are doing your editing and compiling for this project (not shown), the Outline view is at your disposal there too. This can be quite helpful in large projects.

Eclipse also better integrates the editing and compiling processes. If you have compilation errors, they are clearly marked within the editor. This can be done with the Vim editor, which both authors of this book tend to prefer over an IDE, but an IDE does it much better.

On the other hand, you can see that Eclipse, as with most IDEs, does have a major footprint on your screen (and indeed, on the pages of this book!). That Outline view is occupying precious space on the screen whether you use it much or not. Granted, you can hide the Outline by clicking the X in its right-hand corner (and if you want to get it back, select Window | Show Views | Outline), which reclaims some space, and you can also drag tabs to different locations within the Eclipse window. But in general, it may be difficult to make good use of screen space in Eclipse.

Remember that you can always execute GDB commands directly in DDD's Console. You thus have the flexibility to perform debugging commands in the most convenient way available, which is sometimes through the DDD interface and sometimes through the GDB command line. At various points in this book, you will see that there are a number of actions you can take with GDB that can make your debugging life much more convenient.

By contrast, GDB is mostly transparent to Eclipse users, and while the old saying "Ignorance is bliss" may often apply, the transparency means you lose easy access to the labor-saving actions made possible by direct usage of GDB. As of this writing, a determined user can still directly access GDB by clicking the GDB thread in Debug and then using the Console, though minus the GDB prompts. However, this "undocumented feature" may not survive in future versions.

1.4.1.5 Advantages of the GUIs

The GUI interfaces provided by DDD and Eclipse are more visually appealing than that of GDB. They also tend to be more convenient. For instance, suppose that you no longer want execution to pause at line 16 of get_args(), that is, you wish to *clear* the breakpoint. In GDB you would clear the breakpoint by typing

```
(gdb) clear 16
```

However, in order to do this, you need to remember the line number of the breakpoint—not an easy task if you have many breakpoints active at once. You could refresh your memory by using GDB's info break command to get a list of all the breakpoints, but it would still be a bit of work and would distract from the focus on finding the bug.

In DDD your task would be far simpler: To clear a breakpoint, simply click the stop sign at the desired line, then click Clear, and the stop sign would disappear, showing that the breakpoint has been cleared.

In Eclipse, you would go to the Breakpoints view, highlight the breakpoint(s) you want to remove, and then move the mouse cursor to the gray X, which symbolizes the Remove Selected Breakpoints operation (see Figure 1-4). Alternatively, you can right-click the blue breakpoint symbol in the source code window and select Toggle Breakpoint.

One task for which the GUIs are clear winners is stepping through code. It is much easier and more pleasant to do this using DDD or Eclipse rather than GDB, because you can watch your movement through the code in the GUI's source code window. The next line in your source code to be executed is indicated by an arrow, as shown for DDD in Figure 1-5. In Eclipse, your next line is highlighted in green. You can thus tell at a glance where you are relative to other program statements of interest.

1.4.1.6 Advantages of GDB

So, the GUIs have many advantages over the text-based GDB. Yet a sweeping conclusion based on this example that the GUIs are better than GDB would be unjustified.

Younger programmers who have grown up using GUIs for everything they do online naturally prefer GUIs to GDB, as do many of their older colleagues. On the other hand, GDB has some definite advantages, too:

- GDB starts up more quickly than DDD, a big advantage when you just need to quickly check something in your code. The difference in startup times is even greater in the case of Eclipse.

- In some cases, debugging is performed remotely via an SSH (or a telnet) connection, say from a public terminal. If you lack an X11 setup, the GUIs cannot be used at all, and even with X11, the screen refresh operations of the GUIs may be slow.

- When debugging several programs that work in cooperation with each other—for example, a client/server pair in a networked environment—you need a separate debugging window for each program. It is a little better in Eclipse than in DDD, as Eclipse will allow you to debug two programs simultaneously in the same window, but this does compound the space problems cited earlier. Thus the small visual footprint that GDB occupies on the screen compared to the GUI's larger footprint is a big advantage.

- If the program you are debugging has a GUI, and you use a GUI-based debugger such as DDD, they can clash. The GUI *events*—keystrokes, mouse clicks, and mouse movements—of one can interfere with those of the other, and the program may behave differently when run under the debugger than it does when run independently. This can seriously complicate finding bugs.

For those unaccustomed to the amount of typing required by GDB compared to the convenient mouse operations of the GUIs, it must be noted that GDB includes some typing-saving devices that make its text-based nature more acceptable. We mentioned earlier that most of GDB's commands have short abbreviations, and most people use these instead of the full forms. Also, the CTRL-P and CTRL-N key combinations allow you to scroll through previous commands and edit them if you wish. Simply hitting the ENTER key repeats the last command issued (which is very useful when repeatedly performing the next command to step through code one line at a time), and there is a define command that allows the user to define abbreviations and macros. Details of these features will be presented in Chapters 2 and 3.

1.4.1.7 The Bottom Line: Each Has Its Value

We consider both GDB and the GUIs to be important tools, and this book will present examples of GDB, DDD, and Eclipse. We will always begin treatment of any particular topic with GDB, as it is the commonality among these tools, then show how the material extends to the GUIs.

1.4.2 Compromises

Since version 6.1, GDB has offered a compromise between text-based and graphical user interaction in the form of a mode named TUI (Terminal User Interface). In this mode, GDB splits the terminal screen into analogs of DDD's Source Text window and Console; you can follow the progress of your program's execution in the former while issuing GDB commands in the latter. Alternatively, you can use another program, CGDB, which offers similar functionality.

1.4.2.1 GDB in TUI Mode

To run GDB in TUI mode, you can either specify the option -tui on the command line when invoking GDB or type CTRL-X-A from within GDB while in non-TUI mode. The latter command also toggles you out of TUI mode if you are currently in it.

In TUI mode, the GDB window is divided into two subwindows—one for GDB commands and one for viewing source code. Suppose you start GDB in TUI mode on *insert_sort* and then execute a couple of debugging commands. Your GDB screen may then look like this:

```
    11
    12       void get_args(int ac, char **av)
    13       {  int i;
    14
    15           num_inputs = ac - 1;
*   16           for (i = 0; i < num_inputs; i++)
 >  17               x[i] = atoi(av[i+1]);
    18       }
    19
    20       void scoot_over(int jj)
    21       {  int k;
    22
    23               for (k = num_y-1; k > jj; k++)
```

```
    File: ins.c    Procedure: get_args    Line: 17      pc: 0x80484b8
--------------------------------------------------------------------------
(gdb) break 16
Breakpoint 1 at 0x804849f: file ins.c, line 16.
(gdb) run 12 5 6
Starting program: /debug/insert_sort 12 5 6

Breakpoint 1, get_args (ac=4, av=0xbffff094) at ins.c:16
(gdb) next
(gdb)
```

The lower subwindow shows exactly what you would see if you were using GDB without TUI. Here, this subwindow shows the following things:

- We issued a break command to set a breakpoint at line 16 in the current source file.

- We executed run to run the program, passing it the command-line arguments 12, 5, and 6, after which the debugger stopped execution at the specified breakpoint. (run and the other GDB commands will be explained later.) GDB reminds us that the breakpoint is at line 16 of *ins.c* and informs us that the machine code for that source line resides at memory address 0x804849f.

- We issued a next command to step to the next line of code, line 17.

The upper subwindow offers some extra, visually helpful information. Here TUI shows us the source code surrounding the line currently being executed, just as DDD and Eclipse would. This makes it much easier to see where we are in the code. The breakpoint and the line currently being executed are indicated with an asterisk and a > sign, respectively, analogous to DDD's stop sign and green arrow icons.

We can move to other parts of the code by using the up and down arrow keys to scroll. When not in TUI mode, you can use the arrow keys to scroll through previous GDB commands, in order to modify or repeat them. In TUI mode, the arrow keys are for scrolling the source code subwindow, and you scroll through previous GDB commands by using CTRL-P and CTRL-N. Also, in TUI mode, the region of code displayed in the source code subwindow can be changed using GDB's list command. This is especially useful when working with multiple source files.

By making use of GDB's TUI mode and its typing shortcuts, we can attain a lot of the GUIs' extra functionality without incurring the GUIs' disadvantages. Note, however, that in some circumstances TUI may not behave quite as you want it to, in which case you will need to find a workaround.

1.4.2.2   CGDB

Another interface to GDB that you may wish to consider is CGDB, available at *http://cgdb.sourceforge.net/*. CGDB also offers a compromise between a text-based and a GUI approach. Like the GUIs, it serves as a front end to GDB. It's similar to the terminal-based TUI concept, but with the additional enticements that it is in color and you can browse through the source code subwindow and set breakpoints directly there. It also seems to handle screen refresh better than GDB/TUI does.

Here are a few of CGDB's basic commands and conventions:

- Hit ESC to go from the command window to the source code window; hit i to get back.

- While in the source window, move around by using the arrow keys or vi-like keys (j for down, k for up, / to search).

- The next line to be executed is marked by an arrow.

- To set a breakpoint at the line currently highlighted by the cursor, just hit the spacebar.

- Breakpoint lines have their line numbers highlighted in red.

1.5 Main Debugger Operations

Here we give an overview of the main types of operations that a debugger offers.

1.5.1 Stepping Through the Source Code

You saw earlier that to run a program in GDB, you use the run command, and that in DDD you click Run. In details to be presented later, you will see that Eclipse handles things similarly.

You can also arrange for execution of the program to pause at certain points, so that you can inspect the values of variables in order to get clues about where your bug is. Here are some of the methods you can use to do this:

Breakpoints

As mentioned earlier, a debugging tool will pause execution of your program at specified breakpoints. This is done in GDB via the break command, together with the line number; in DDD you right-click anywhere in white space in the relevant line and choose Set Breakpoint; in Eclipse you double-click in the margin to the left of the line.

Single-stepping

GDB's next command, which was also mentioned earlier, tells GDB to execute the next line and then pause. The step command is similar, except that at function calls it will enter the function, whereas next will result in the next pause in execution occurring at the line following the function call. DDD has corresponding Next and Step menu choices, while Eclipse has Step Over and Step Into icons to do the same thing.

Resume operation

In GDB, the `continue` command tells the debugger to resume execution and continue until a breakpoint is hit. There is a corresponding menu item in DDD, and Eclipse has a Resume icon for it.

Temporary breakpoints

In GDB the `tbreak` command is similar to `break`, but it sets a breakpoint that only stays in effect until the first time the specified line is reached. In DDD this is accomplished by right-clicking anywhere in the white space in the desired line in the Source Text window, and then selecting Set Temporary Breakpoint. In Eclipse, highlight the desired line in the source window, then right-click and select Run to Line.

GDB also has `until` and `finish` commands, which create special kinds of one-time breakpoints. DDD has corresponding Until and Finish menu items in its Command window, and Eclipse has Step Return. These are discussed in Chapter 2.

A typical debugging pattern for program execution is as follows (using GDB as an example): After you hit a breakpoint, you move through the code one line at a time or *single-step* for a while, via GDB's next and step commands. This allows you to carefully examine the program's state and behavior near the breakpoint. When you are done with this, you can tell the debugger to continue to execute the program without pausing until the next breakpoint is reached, by using the `continue` command.

1.5.2 Inspecting Variables

After the debugger pauses execution of our program, you can issue commands to display the values of program variables. These could be local variables, globals, elements of arrays and C structs, member variables in C++ classes, and so on. If a variable is found to have an unexpected value, that typically is a big clue to the location and nature of a bug. DDD can even graph arrays, which may reveal, at a glance, suspicious values or trends occurring within an array.

The most basic type of variable display is simply printing the current value. For example, suppose you have set a breakpoint at line 37 of the function insert() in *ins.c*. (Again, the full source code is given in Section 1.7, but the details needn't concern you for now.) When you reach that line, you can check the value of the local variable j in that function. In GDB you would use the `print` command:

```
(gdb) print j
```

In DDD it is even easier: You simply move the mouse pointer over any instance of j in the Source Text window, and then the value of j will be displayed, for a second or two, in a little yellow box—called a *value tip*—near the mouse pointer. See Figure 1-5, where the value of the variable new_y is being examined. Things work the same way with Eclipse, as seen in Figure 1-6, where we are querying the value of num_y.

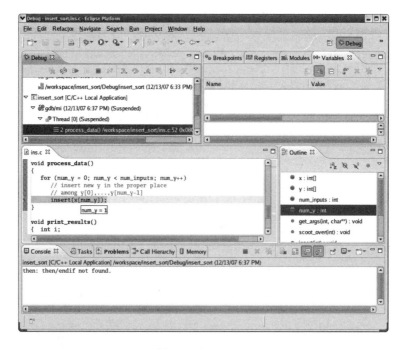

Figure 1-5: Inspecting a variable in DDD

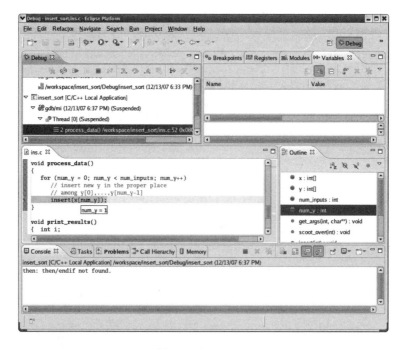

Figure 1-6: Inspecting a variable in Eclipse

As you will see in Chapter 2, in GDB or DDD you can also arrange to continuously display a variable so that you don't have to repeatedly ask to see the value. DDD has an especially nice feature for displaying linked lists, trees, and other data structures containing pointers: You can click an outgoing link of any node in such a structure to find the next node.

1.5.3   Issuing an "All Points Bulletin" for Changes to a Variable

A *watchpoint* combines the notions of breakpoint and variable inspection. The most basic form instructs the debugger to pause execution of the program whenever the value of a specified variable changes.

For example, suppose that you wish to examine a program's state during the points in the course of its execution at which the variable z changes value. In GDB, you can issue the command

```
(gdb) watch z
```

When you run the program, GDB will pause execution whenever the value of z changes. In DDD, you would set the watchpoint by clicking any instance of z in the Source Text window and then clicking the Watch icon at the top of the DDD window.

Even better, you can set watchpoints based on conditional expressions. Say, for example, that you wish to find the first point in the execution of the program at which the value of z exceeds 28. You can accomplish this by setting a watchpoint based on the expression (z > 28). In GDB, you would type

```
(gdb) watch (z > 28)
```

In DDD, you would issue this command in DDD's Console. Recall that in C the expression (z > 28) is of Boolean type and evaluates to either *true* or *false*, where *false* is represented by 0 and *true* is represented by any nonzero integer, usually 1. When z first takes on a value larger than 28, the value of the expression (z > 28) will change from 0 to 1, and GDB will pause execution of the program.

You can set a watchpoint in Eclipse by right-clicking in the source window, selecting Add a Watch Expression, and then filling in the desired expression in the dialog.

Watchpoints are usually not as useful for local variables as they are for variables with wider scope, because a watchpoint set on a local variable is canceled as soon as the variable goes out of scope, that is, when the function in which the variable is defined terminates. However, local variables in main() are an obvious exception, as such variables are not deallocated until the program finishes execution.

1.5.4   Moving Up and Down the Call Stack

During a function call, runtime information associated with the call is stored in a region of memory known as a *stack frame*. The frame contains the values of the function's local variables and its parameters and a record of the location from which the function was called. Each time a function call occurs, a new frame is created and pushed onto a stack maintained by the system; the frame at the top of the stack represents the currently executing function, and it is popped off the stack and deallocated when the function exits.

For example, suppose that you pause execution of your sample program, *insert_sort*, while in the insert() function. The data in the current stack frame will state that you got there via a function call at a specific location that turns out to be within the process_data() function (which invokes insert()). The frame will also store the current value of insert()'s only local variable, which you will see later is j.

The stack frames for the other active function invocations will contain similar information, and you can also examine these if you wish. For instance, even though execution currently resides in insert(), you may wish to take a look at the previous frame in the call stack, that is, at process_data()'s frame. You can do so in GDB with the command

```
(gdb) frame 1
```

When issuing GDB's frame command, the frame of the currently executing function is numbered 0, its parent frame (that is, the stack frame of the function's caller) is numbered 1, the parent's parent is numbered 2, and so on. GDB's up command takes you to the next parent in the call stack (for example, to frame 1 from frame 0), and down takes you in the other direction. Such operations are very useful, because the values of the local variables in some of the earlier stack frames may give you a clue as to what caused a bug.

Traversing the call stack does not change the execution path—in this example, the next line of *insert_sort* to be executed will still be the current one in insert()—but it does allow you to take a look at the ancestor frames and so examine the values of the local variables for the function invocations leading up to the current one. Again, this may give you hints about where to find a bug.

GDB's backtrace command will show you the entire stack, that is, the entire collection of frames currently in existence.

The analogous operation in DDD is invoked by clicking Status | Backtrace; a window will pop up showing all the frames, and you can then click whichever one you wish to inspect. The DDD interface also has Up and Down buttons that can be clicked to invoke GDB's up and down commands.

In Eclipse, the stack is continuously visible in the Debug perspective itself. In Figure 1-7, look at the Debug tab in the upper-left corner. You'll see that we are currently in frame 2, in the function get_args(), which we called from frame 1 in main(). Whichever frame is highlighted is the one displayed in the source window, so you can display any frame by clicking it in the call stack.

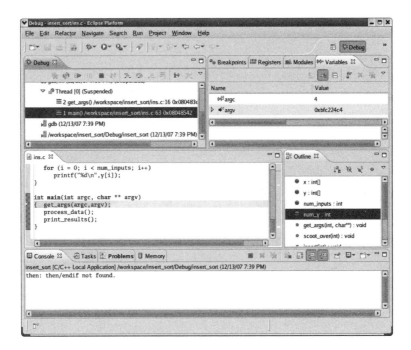

Figure 1-7: Moving within the stack in Eclipse

1.6 Online Help

In GDB, documentation can be accessed through the help command. For example,

```
(gdb) help breakpoints
```

will give you the documentation on breakpoints. The GDB command help, with no arguments, gives you a menu of command categories that can be used as arguments for help.

In DDD and Eclipse, a wealth of material is available by clicking Help.

1.7 Introductory Debugging Session

Now we will present a complete debugging session. As mentioned, the sample program is in the source file *ins.c* and does an insertion sort. This is not an efficient sorting method, of course, but the simplicity of the code makes it good for illustrating the debugging operations. Here is the code:

```
//
// insertion sort, several errors
//
// usage:  insert_sort num1 num2 num3 ..., where the numi are the numbers to
// be sorted
```

```
int x[10],  // input array
    y[10],  // workspace array
    num_inputs,  // length of input array
    num_y = 0;  // current number of elements in y

void get_args(int ac, char **av)
{   int i;

    num_inputs = ac - 1;
    for (i = 0; i < num_inputs; i++)
        x[i] = atoi(av[i+1]);
}

void scoot_over(int jj)
{   int k;

    for (k = num_y-1; k > jj; k++)
        y[k] = y[k-1];
}

void insert(int new_y)
{   int j;

    if (num_y = 0)  { // y empty so far, easy case
        y[0] = new_y;
        return;
    }
    // need to insert just before the first y
    // element that new_y is less than
    for (j = 0; j < num_y; j++)  {
        if (new_y < y[j])  {
            // shift y[j], y[j+1],... rightward
            // before inserting new_y
            scoot_over(j);
            y[j] = new_y;
            return;
        }
    }
}

void process_data()
{
    for (num_y = 0; num_y < num_inputs; num_y++)
        // insert new y in the proper place
        // among y[0],...,y[num_y-1]
        insert(x[num_y]);
```

```
}

void print_results()
{  int i;

   for (i = 0; i < num_inputs; i++)
      printf("%d\n",y[i]);
}

int main(int argc, char ** argv)
{  get_args(argc,argv);
   process_data();
   print_results();
}
```

Below is a pseudocode description of the program. The function calls are indicated by call statements, and the pseudocode for each function is shown indented under the calls:

```
call main():
   set y array to empty
   call get_args():
      get num_inputs numbers x[i] from command line
   call process_data():
      for i = 1 to num_inputs
         call insert(x[i]):
            new_y = x[i]
            find first y[j] for which new_y < y[j]
            call scoot_over(j):
               shift y[j], y[j+1], ... to right,
                  to make room for new_y
         set y[j] = new_y
```

Let's compile and run the code:

```
$ gcc -g -Wall -o insert_sort ins.c
```

Important: You can use the -g option to GCC to tell the compiler to save the *symbol table*—that is, the list of memory addresses corresponding to your program's variables and lines of code—within the generated executable file, which here is *insert_sort*. This is an absolutely essential step that allows you to refer to the variable names and line numbers in the source code during a debugging session. Without this step (and something similar would have to be done if you were to use a compiler other than GCC), you could not ask the debugger to "stop at line 30" or "print the value of x," for example.

Now let's run the program. Following the Start Small Principle from Section 1.3.3, first try sorting a list of just two numbers:

```
$ insert_sort 12 5
(execution halted by user hitting ctrl-C)
```

The program did not terminate or print any output. It apparently went into an infinite loop, and we had to kill it by hitting CTRL-C. There is no doubt about it: Something is wrong.

In the following sections, we will first present a debugging session for this buggy program using GDB, and then discuss how the same operations are done using DDD and Eclipse.

1.7.1 The GDB Approach

To track down the first bug, execute the program in GDB and let it run for a while before suspending it with CTRL-C. Then see where you are. In this manner, you can determine the location of the infinite loop.

First, start the GDB debugger on *insert_sort*:

```
$ gdb insert_sort -tui
```

Your screen will now look like this:

```
   63        {  get_args(argc,argv);
   64           process_data();
   65           print_results();
   66        }
   67
   68
   69
 File: ins.c    Procedure: ??    Line: ??      pc: ??
 -----------------------------------------------------------------------
 (gdb)
```

The top subwindow displays part of your source code, and in the bottom subwindow you see the GDB prompt, ready for your commands. There is also a GDB welcome message, which we have omitted for the sake of brevity.

If you do not request TUI mode when invoking GDB, you would receive only the welcome message and the GDB prompt, without the upper subwindow for your program's source code. You could then enter TUI mode using the GDB command CTRL-X-A. This command toggles you in and out of TUI mode and is useful if you wish, for example, to temporarily leave TUI mode so that you can read GDB's online help more conveniently, or so that you can see more of your GDB command history together on one screen.

Now run the program from within GDB by issuing the run command together with your program's command-line arguments, and then hit CTRL-C to suspend it. The screen now looks like this:

```
   46
   47 void process_data()
   48 {
   49 for (num_y = 0; num_y < num_inputs; num_y++)
   50 // insert new y in the proper place
   51 // among y[0],...,y[num_y-1]
 > 52 insert(x[num_y]);
   53 }
   54
   55 void print_results()
   56 { int i;
   57
   58 for (i = 0; i < num_inputs; i++)
   59 printf("%d\n",y[i]);
   60 } .
 File: ins.c Procedure: process_data Line: 52 pc: 0x8048483
 -----------------------------------------------------------------------
(gdb) run 12 5
Starting program: /debug/insert_sort 12 5

Program received signal SIGINT, Interrupt.
0x08048483 in process_data () at ins.c:52
(gdb)
```

This tells you that when you stopped the program, *insert_sort* was in the function process_data() and line 52 in the source file *ins.c* was about to be executed.

We hit CTRL-C at a random time and stopped at a random place in the code. Sometimes it's good to suspend and restart a program that has stopped responding two or three times by issuing continue between CTRL-Cs, in order to see where you stop each time.

Now, line 52 is part of the loop that begins on line 49. Is this loop the infinite one? The loop doesn't look like it should run indefinitely, but the Principle of Confirmation says you should verify this, not just assume it. If the loop is not terminating because somehow you haven't set the upper bound for the variable num_y correctly, then after the program has run for a while the value of num_y will be huge. Is it? (Again, it looks like it shouldn't be, but you need to confirm that.) Let's check what the current value of num_y is by asking GDB to print it out.

```
(gdb) print num_y
$1 = 1
```

The output of this query to GDB shows that the value of num_y is 1. The $1 label means that this is the first value you've asked GDB to print out. (The values designated by $1, $2, $3, and so on are collectively called the *value history* of the debugging session. They can be very useful, as you will see in later chapters.) So we seem to be on only the second iteration of the loop on line 49. If this loop were the infinite one, it would be way past its second iteration by now.

So let's take a closer look at what occurs when num_y is 1. Tell GDB to stop in insert() during the second iteration of the loop on line 49 so that you can take a look around and try to find out what's going wrong at that place and time in the program:

```
(gdb) break 30
Breakpoint 1 at 0x80483fc: file ins.c, line 30.
(gdb) condition 1 num_y==1
```

The first command places a breakpoint at line 30, that is, at the beginning of insert(). Alternatively, you could have specified this breakpoint via the command break insert, meaning to break at the first line of insert() (which here is line 30). This latter form has an advantage: If you modify the program code so that the function insert() no longer begins at line 30 of *ins.c*, your breakpoint would remain valid if specified using the function name, but not if specified using the line number.

Ordinarily a break command makes execution pause *every* time the program hits the specified line. However, the second command here, condition 1 num_y==1, makes that breakpoint *conditional*: GDB will pause execution of the program at breakpoint 1 only when the condition num_y==1 holds.

Note that unlike the break command, which accepts line numbers (or function names), condition accepts a breakpoint number. You can always use the command info break to look up the number of the desired breakpoint. (That command gives you other useful information too, such as the number of times each breakpoint has been hit so far.)

We could have combined the break and condition commands into a single step by using break if as follows:

```
(gdb) break 30 if num_y==1
```

Then run the program again, using the run command. You do not have to restate the command-line arguments if you just wish to reuse the old ones. This is the case here, and so you can simply type run. Since the program is already running, GDB asks us if you wish to restart from the beginning, and you answer "yes."

The screen will now look like this:

```
   24              y[k] = y[k-1];
   25          }
   26
   27      void insert(int new_y)
   28      {   int j;
   29
*> 30          if (num_y = 0)  { // y empty so far, easy case
   31              y[0] = new_y;
```

```
   32              return;
   33          }
   34          // need to insert just before the first y
   35          // element that new_y is less than
   36          for (j = 0; j < num_y; j++)  {
   37              if (new_y < y[j])  {
   38                  // shift y[j], y[j+1],... rightward          .
File: ins.c    Procedure: insert    Line: 30       pc: 0x80483fc
```

```
(gdb) condition 1 num_y==1
(gdb) run
The program being debugged has been started already.
Start it from the beginning? (y or n)
Starting program: /debug/insert_sort 12 5

Breakpoint 1, insert (new_y=5) at ins.c:30
(gdb)
```

We apply the Principle of Confirmation again: Since num_y is 1, line 31 should be skipped over and execution should go to line 36. But we need to *confirm* this, so we issue the next command to go on to the next line:

```
   24              y[k] = y[k-1];
   25      }
   26
   27      void insert(int new_y)
   28      {  int j;
   29
*  30      if (num_y = 0)  { // y empty so far, easy case
   31          y[0] = new_y;
   32          return;
   33      }
   34      // need to insert just before the first y
   35      // element that new_y is less than
>  36      for (j = 0; j < num_y; j++)  {
   37          if (new_y < y[j])  {
   38              // shift y[j], y[j+1],... rightward          .
File: ins.c    Procedure: insert    Line: 36       pc: 0x8048406
```

```
(gdb) run
The program being debugged has been started already.
Start it from the beginning? (y or n)
Starting program: /debug/insert_sort 12 5

Breakpoint 1, insert (new_y=5) at ins.c:30
(gdb) next
(gdb)
```

The arrow in the upper subwindow is now at line 36, so our expectation is confirmed; we did indeed skip line 31. Now let's continue to single-step through the program, confirming assumptions about the code along the way. You are now at the beginning of a loop, so issue the next command again a few times and see how the loop progresses, line by line:

```
   39                  // before inserting new_y
   40                  scoot_over(j);
   41                  y[j] = new_y;
   42                  return;
   43              }
   44          }
>  45      }
   46
   47      void process_data()
   48      {
   49          for (num_y = 0; num_y < num_inputs; num_y++)
   50              // insert new y in the proper place
   51              // among y[0],...,y[num_y-1]
   52              insert(x[num_y]);
   53      }
File: ins.c    Procedure: insert    Line: 45      pc: 0x804844d
---------------------------------------------------------------------
The program being debugged has been started already.
Start it from the beginning? (y or n)
Starting program: /debug/insert_sort 12 5

Breakpoint 1, insert (new_y=5) at ins.c:30
(gdb) next
(gdb) next
(gdb)
```

Look at where the arrow is now in the upper subwindow—we went directly from line 37 to line 45! This is quite a surprise. We did not execute even one iteration of the loop. Remember, though, that surprises are good, because they give you clues as to where bugs are.

The only way that the loop at line 36 could have executed no iterations at all is if the condition j < num_y in line 36 did not hold even when j was 0. Yet you know that num_y is 1, because you are in this function now after having imposed the condition num_y==1 on the breakpoint. Or at least you *think* you know this. Again, you haven't confirmed it. Check this now:

```
(gdb) print num_y
$2 = 0
```

Sure enough, the condition num_y==1 did hold when you entered insert(), but apparently num_y has changed since then. Somehow num_y became 0 after you entered this function. But how?

As mentioned earlier, the Principle of Confirmation doesn't tell you *what* the bug is, but it does give us clues to *where* the bug likely resides. In this case, you have now discovered that the location is somewhere between lines 30 and 36. And you can narrow down that range further, because you saw that lines 31 through 33 were skipped, and lines 34 through 35 are comments. In other words, the mysterious change of value in num_y occurred either at line 30 or at line 36.

After taking a short break—often the best debugging strategy!—we suddenly realize that the fault is a classic error, often made by beginning (and, embarrassingly, by experienced) C programmers: In line 30 we used = instead of ==, turning a test for equality into an assignment.

Do you see how the infinite loop thus arises? The error on line 30 sets up a perpetual seesaw situation, in which the num_y++ portion of line 49 repeatedly increments num_y from 0 to 1, while the error in line 30 repeatedly sets that variable's value back to 0.

So we fix that humiliating bug (which ones *aren't* humiliating?), recompile, and try running the program again:

```
$ insert_sort 12 5
5
0
```

We don't have an infinite loop anymore, but we don't have the correct output either.

Recall from the pseudocode what your program is supposed to do here: Initially the array y is empty. The first iteration of the loop at line 49 is supposed to put the 12 into y[0]. Then in the second iteration, the 12 is supposed to be shifted by one array position, to make room for insertion of the 5. Instead, the 5 appears to have replaced the 12.

The trouble arises with the second number (5), so you should again focus on the second iteration. Because we wisely chose to stay in the GDB session, rather than exiting GDB after discovering and fixing the first bug, the breakpoint and its condition, which we set earlier, are still in effect now. Thus we simply run the program again, and stop when the program begins to process the second input:

```
    24              y[k] = y[k-1];
    25      }
    26
    27      void insert(int new_y)
    28      {  int j;
    29
*>  30          if (num_y == 0)  { // y empty so far, easy case
    31              y[0] = new_y;
    32              return;
    33          }
    34          // need to insert just before the first y
    35          // element that new_y is less than
```

```
36                for (j = 0; j < num_y; j++) {
37                    if (new_y < y[j]) {
38                        // shift y[j], y[j+1],... rightward          .
File: ins.c    Procedure: insert    Line: 30      pc: 0x80483fc
------------------------------------------------------------------------
The program being debugged has been started already.
Start it from the beginning? (y or n)

`/debug/insert_sort' has changed; re-reading symbols.
Starting program: /debug/insert_sort 12 5

Breakpoint 1, insert (new_y=5) at ins.c:30
(gdb)
```

Notice the line that announces

```
`/debug/insert_sort' has changed; re-reading symbols.
```

This shows that GDB saw that we recompiled the program and automatically reloaded the new binary and the new symbol table before running the program.

Again, the fact that we did not have to exit GDB before recompiling our program is a major convenience, for a few reasons. First, you do not need to restate your command-line arguments; you just type run to re-run the program. Second, GDB retains the breakpoint that you had set, so that you don't need to type it again. Here you only have one breakpoint, but typically you would have several, and then this becomes a real issue. These conveniences save you typing, and more importantly they relieve you of practical distractions and allow you to focus better on the actual debugging.

Likewise, you should not keep exiting and restarting your text editor during your debugging session, which would also be a distraction and a waste of time. Just keep your text editor open in one window and GDB (or DDD) in another, and use a third window for trying out your program.

Now let's try stepping through the code again. As before, the program should skip line 31, but hopefully this time it will reach line 37, as opposed to the situation earlier. Let's check this by issuing the next command twice:

```
31                y[0] = new_y;
32                return;
33            }
34            // need to insert just before the first y
35            // element that new_y is less than
36            for (j = 0; j < num_y; j++) {
> 37                if (new_y < y[j]) {
38                    // shift y[j], y[j+1],... rightward
39                    // before inserting new_y
40                    scoot_over(j);
41                    y[j] = new_y;
```

```
42                  return;
43                }
44            }
45        }
File: ins.c    Procedure: insert    Line: 37    pc: 0x8048423
----------------------------------------------------------------------
`/debug/insert_sort' has changed; re-reading symbols.
Starting program: /debug/insert_sort 12 5

Breakpoint 1, insert (new_y=5) at ins.c:30
(gdb) next
(gdb) next
(gdb)
```

We have indeed reached line 37.

At this point, we believe the condition in the if in line 37 should hold, because new_y should be 5, and y[0] should be 12 from the first iteration. The GDB output confirms the former assumption. Let's check the latter:

```
(gdb) print y[0]
$3 = 12
```

Now that this assumption is also confirmed, issue the next command, which brings you to line 40. The function scoot_over() is supposed to shift the 12 to the next array position, to make room for the 5. You should check to see whether or not it does. Here you face an important choice. You could issue the next command again, which would cause GDB to stop at line 41; the function scoot_over() would be executed, *but GDB would not stop within that function.* However, if you were to issue the step command instead, GDB would stop at line 23, and this would allow you to single-step within scoot_over().

Following the Top-Down Approach to Debugging described in Section 1.3.3, we opt for the next command instead of step at line 40. When GDB stops at line 41, you can take a look at y to see if the function did its job correctly. If that hypothesis is confirmed, you will have avoided a time-consuming inspection of the detailed operation of the function scoot_over() that would have contributed nothing to fixing the current bug. If you fail to confirm that the function worked correctly, you can run the program in the debugger again and enter the function using step in order to inspect the function's detailed operation and hopefully determine where it goes awry.

So, when you reach line 40, type next, yielding

```
31              y[0] = new_y;
32              return;
33          }
34          // need to insert just before the first y
35          // element that new_y is less than
36          for (j = 0; j < num_y; j++) {
37              if (new_y < y[j]) {
```

```
38                     // shift y[j], y[j+1],... rightward
39                     // before inserting new_y
40                     scoot_over(j);
> 41                   y[j] = new_y;
42                     return;
43               }
44          }
45       }
File: ins.c    Procedure: insert    Line: 41      pc: 0x8048440
-----------------------------------------------------------------------
(gdb) next
(gdb) next
(gdb)
```

Did scoot_over() shift the 12 correctly? Let's check:

```
(gdb) print y
$4 = {12, 0, 0, 0, 0, 0, 0, 0, 0, 0}
```

Apparently not. The problem indeed lies in scoot_over(). Let's delete the breakpoint at the beginning of insert() and place one in scoot_over(), again with a condition that we stop there during the second iteration of line 49:

```
(gdb) clear 30
Deleted breakpoint 1
(gdb) break 23
Breakpoint 2 at 0x80483c3: file ins.c, line 23.
(gdb) condition 2 num_y==1
```

Now run the program again:

```
15              num_inputs = ac - 1;
16              for (i = 0; i < num_inputs; i++)
17              x[i] = atoi(av[i+1]);
18        }
19
20        void scoot_over(int jj)
21        { int k;
22
*> 23           for (k = num_y-1; k > jj; k++)
24                 y[k] = y[k-1];
25        }
26
27        void insert(int new_y)
28        { int j;
29
File: ins.c    Procedure: scoot_over    Line: 23      pc: 0x80483c3
```

```
----------------------------------------------------------------------
(gdb) condition 2 num_y==1
(gdb) run
The program being debugged has been started already.
Start it from the beginning? (y or n)
Starting program: /debug/insert_sort 12 5

Breakpoint 2, scoot_over (jj=0) at ins.c:23
(gdb)
```

Once again, follow the Principle of Confirmation: Think about what you expect to occur, and then try to confirm that it does occur. In this case, the function is supposed to shift the 12 over to the next position in the array y, which means that the loop at line 23 should go through exactly one iteration. Let's step through the program by repeatedly issuing the next command, in order to verify this expectation:

```
    15          num_inputs = ac - 1;
    16          for (i = 0; i < num_inputs; i++)
    17          x[i] = atoi(av[i+1]);
    18       }
    19
    20       void scoot_over(int jj)
    21       {  int k;
    22
  * 23          for (k = num_y-1; k > jj; k++)
    24              y[k] = y[k-1];
  > 25       }
    26
    27       void insert(int new_y)
    28       {  int j;
    29                                                          .
 File: ins.c    Procedure: scoot_over    Line: 25      pc: 0x80483f1
----------------------------------------------------------------------
The program being debugged has been started already.
Start it from the beginning? (y or n)
Starting program: /debug/insert_sort 12 5

Breakpoint 2, scoot_over (jj=0) at ins.c:23
(gdb) next
(gdb) next
(gdb)
```

Here we again get a surprise: We are now on line 25, without ever touching line 24—the loop executed no iterations, not the single iteration that we had expected it to execute. Apparently there is a bug in line 23.

As with the earlier loop that unexpectedly executed no iterations of its body, it must be that the loop condition was not satisfied at the very beginning of the loop. Is this the case here? The loop condition on line 23 is k > jj. We also know from this line that k's initial value is num_y-1, and we know from our breakpoint condition that the latter quantity is 0. Finally, the GDB screen tells us that jj is 0. So the condition k > jj was not satisfied when the the loop began.

Thus, we misspecified either the loop condition k > jj or the initialization k = num_y-1. Considering that the 12 should have moved from y[0] to y[1] in the first and only iteration of the loop—that is, line 24 should have executed with k = 1—we realize that the loop initialization is wrong. It should have been k = num_y.

Fix the error, recompile the program, and run the program again (outside GDB):

```
$ insert_sort 12 5
Segmentation fault
```

Segmentation faults, discussed in detail in Chapter 4, occur when a running program attempts to access memory that it does not have permission to access. Typically the cause is an out-of-bounds array index or an errant pointer value. Seg faults can also arise from memory references that do not explicitly involve pointer or array variables. One example of this can be seen in another classic C programmer's error, forgetting the ampersand in a function parameter that is passed using call-by-reference, for example, writing

```
scanf("%d",x);
```

instead of

```
scanf("%d",&x);
```

In general, the main value of a debugging tool such as GDB or DDD is to facilitate the process of verifying one's coding assumptions, but in the case of seg faults a debugging tool gives extra, tangible, immediate help: It tells you where in your program the fault occurred.

To take advantage of this, you need to run *insert_sort* in GDB and recreate the seg fault. First, remove your breakpoint. As seen earlier, to do this you need to give the line number of the breakpoint. You might already remember this, but it is easy to look for it: Either scroll through the TUI window (using the up and down arrow keys), looking for lines marked with asterisks, or use GDB's info break command. Then delete the breakpoint using the clear command:

```
(gdb) clear 30
```

Now run the program again, in GDB:

```
19
20        void scoot_over(int jj)
21        {  int k;
22
23           for (k = num_y; k > jj; k++)
>  24             y[k] = y[k-1];
25        }
26
27        void insert(int new_y)
28        {  int j;
29
30           if (num_y == 0)  { // y empty so far, easy case
31             y[0] = new_y;
 File: ins.c    Procedure: scoot_over    Line: 24    pc: 0x8048538
---------------------------------------------------------------------------
Start it from the beginning? (y or n)

`/debug/insert_sort' has changed; re-reading symbols.
Starting program: /debug/insert_sort 12 5

Program received signal SIGSEGV, Segmentation fault.
0x08048538 in scoot_over (jj=0) at ins.c:24
(gdb)
```

As promised, GDB tells us exactly where the seg fault occurred, at line 24, and sure enough, an array index is apparently involved, namely k. Either k was large enough to exceed the number of elements in y, or k-1 was negative. Clearly the first order of business is to determine the value of k:

```
(gdb) print k
$4 = 584
```

Whoa! The code had dimensioned y to have only 10 elements, so this value of k is indeed far out of range. We must now track down the cause.

First of all, determine the iteration of the grand loop at line 49 during which this seg fault occurred.

```
(gdb) print num_y
$5 = 1
```

So it was during the second iteration, which is the first time the function scoot_over() is executed. In other words, it is not the case that line 23 worked fine in the first few calls to scoot_over() but failed later on. There is still something fundamentally wrong with this line of code. And since the only remaining candidate is the statement

```
k++
```

(recall that you checked the other two portions of this line earlier), it must be the culprit. After taking another break to clear our heads, we realize with some embarrassment that this should have been k--.

Fix that line and once again recompile and run the program:

```
$ insert_sort 12 5
5
12
```

Now, that's progress! But does the program work for a larger data set? Let's try one:

```
$ insert_sort 12 5 19 22 6 1
1
5
6
12
0
0
```

Now you can begin to see the light at the end of the tunnel. Most of the array is being sorted correctly. The first number in the list that does not get sorted correctly is 19, so set a breakpoint at line 36, this time with the condition new_y == 19:[1]

```
(gdb) b 36
Breakpoint 3 at 0x804840d: file ins.c, line 36.
(gdb) cond 3 new_y==19
```

Then run the program in GDB (making sure to use the same arguments, 12 5 19 22 6 1). When you hit the breakpoint, you then confirm that the array y has been sorted correctly up to this point:

```
   31            y[0] = new_y;
   32            return;
   33        }
   34        // need to insert just before the first y
   35        // element that new_y is less than
*> 36        for (j = 0; j < num_y; j++) {
   37            if (new_y < y[j])  {
   38                // shift y[j], y[j+1],... rightward
   39                // before inserting new_y
   40                scoot_over(j);
   41                y[j] = new_y;
```

---

[1] It's about time to start using the common abbreviations for the commands. These include b for break, i b for info break, cond for condition, r for run, n for next, s for step, c for continue, p for print, and bt for backtrace.

```
    42              return;
    43          }
File: ins.c    Procedure: insert    Line: 36      pc: 0x8048564
------------------------------------------------------------------------
Start it from the beginning? (y or n)

Starting program: /debug/insert_sort 12 5 19 22 6 1

Breakpoint 2, insert (new_y=19) at ins.c:36
   (gdb) p y
   $1 = {5, 12, 0, 0, 0, 0, 0, 0, 0, 0}
   (gdb)
```

So far, so good. Now let's try to determine how the program swallows up the 19. We will step through the code one line at a time. Note that because 19 is not less than 5 or 12, we do not expect the condition in the if statement in line 37 to hold. After hitting n a few times, we find ourselves on line 45:

```
    35          // element that new_y is less than
*   36          for (j = 0; j < num_y; j++)  {
    37              if (new_y < y[j])  {
    38                  // shift y[j], y[j+1],... rightward
    39                  // before inserting new_y
    40                  scoot_over(j);
    41                  y[j] = new_y;
    42                  return;
    43              }
    44          }
>   45      }
    46
    47      void process_data()
File: ins.c    Procedure: insert    Line: 45      pc: 0x80485c4
------------------------------------------------------------------------
   (gdb) n
   (gdb) n
   (gdb) n
   (gdb) n
   (gdb) n
   (gdb)
```

We are on line 45, about to leave the loop, without having done anything with the 19 at all! Some inspection shows that our code was not written to cover an important case, namely that in which new_y is larger than any element we've processed so far—an oversight also revealed by the comments on lines 34 and 35:

```
// need to insert just before the first y
// element that new_y is less than
```

To handle this case, add the following code just after line 44:

```
// one more case:  new_y > all existing y elements
y[num_y] = new_y;
```

Then recompile and try it again:

```
$ insert_sort 12 5 19 22 6 1
1
5
6
12
19
22
```

This is the correct output, and subsequent testing gives correct results as well.

1.7.2   The Same Session in DDD

Let's see how the above GDB session would have been carried out in DDD. There is of course no need to repeat all the steps; simply focus on the differences from GDB.

Starting DDD is similar to starting GDB. Compile your source using GCC with the -g option, and then type

```
$ ddd insert_sort
```

to invoke DDD. In GDB, you started execution of the program via the run command, including arguments if any. In DDD, you click Program | Run, after which you will see the screen shown in Figure 1-8.

A Run window has popped up, presenting you with a history of previous sets of command-line arguments you've used. There are no previous sets yet, but if there were, you could choose one of them by clicking it, or you can type a new set of arguments, as shown here. Then click Run.

In the GDB debugging session, we ran our program for a while in the debugger and then suspended it using CTRL-C, in order to investigate an apparently infinite loop. In DDD, we suspend the program by clicking Interrupt in the Command Tool. The DDD screen now looks like the one in Figure 1-9. Because DDD acts as a front end to GDB, this mouse click is translated to a CTRL-C operation in GDB, which can be seen in the Console.

The next step in the GDB session above was to inspect the variable num_y. As shown earlier in Section 1.5, you do this in DDD by moving the mouse pointer over any instance of num_y in the Source Window.

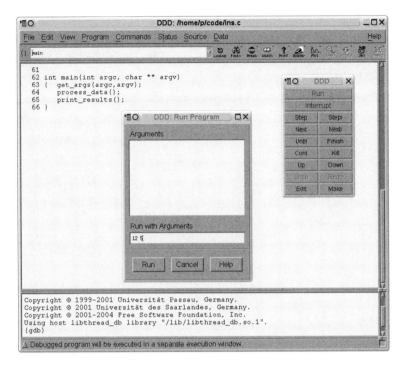

Figure 1-8: DDD Run command

You can also inspect entire arrays in the same way. For example, at one point in the GDB session, you printed out the entire array y. In DDD, you would simply move the mouse pointer to any instance of y in the Source window. If you move the cursor over the y in the expression y[j] on line 30, the screen will appear as shown in Figure 1-10. A value tip box has appeared near that line, showing the contents of y.

Your next action in the GDB session was to set a breakpoint at line 30. We have already explained how to set breakpoints in DDD, but what about putting a condition on the breakpoint, as was needed in this case? You can set a condition by right-clicking the stop sign icon in the breakpoint line and then choosing Properties. A pop-up window will appear, as seen in Figure 1-11. Then type your condition, num_y==1.

To then re-run the program, you would click Run in the Command Tool. As with GDB's run command with no arguments, this button runs the program with the last set of arguments that was provided.

DDD's analogs of GDB's n and s commands are the Next and Step buttons in the Command Tool. The analog of GDB's c is the Cont button.

This overview is enough to get you started with DDD. In later chapters we will explore some of DDD's advanced options, such as its highly useful capability of visually displaying complex data structures such as linked lists and binary trees.

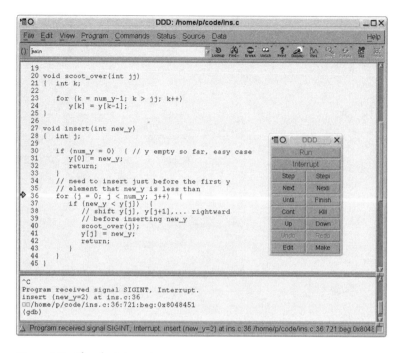

```
'■O                      DDD: /home/p/code/ins.c                        _□×

File  Edit  View  Program  Commands  Status  Source  Data                Help

()  main              ▼  Lookup Find→ Break Watch Print Display Plot Undef Rotate Set Display

   19
   20  void scoot_over(int jj)
   21  {  int k;
   22
   23      for (k = num_y-1; k > jj; k++)
   24          y[k] = y[k-1];
   25  }
   26
   27  void insert(int new_y)
   28  {  int j;                                        '■O    DDD    X
   29
   30      if (num_y = 0)  { // y empty so far, easy case    Run
   31          y[0] = new_y;                                 Interrupt
   32          return;
   33      }                                          Step      Stepi
   34      // need to insert just before the first y  Next      Nexti
   35      // element that new_y is less than         Until     Finish
⇨  36      for (j = 0; j < num_y; j++)  {             Cont      Kill
   37          if (new_y < y[jj])  {                  Up        Down
   38              // shift y[jj], y[jj+1],... rightward  Undo   Redo
   39              // before inserting new_y
   40              scoot_over(j);                     Edit      Make
   41          y[j] = new_y;
   42          return;
   43      }
   44      }
   45  }

^C
Program received signal SIGINT, Interrupt.
insert (new_y=2) at ins.c:36
□□/home/p/code/ins.c:36:721:beg:0x8048451
(gdb)

△ Program received signal SIGINT, Interrupt. insert (new_y=2) at ins.c:36 /home/p/code/ins.c:36:721:beg:0x8048
```

Figure 1-9: After the interrupt

1.7.3 The Session in Eclipse

Now let's see how the above GDB session would have been carried out in
Eclipse. As in our presentation on DDD, there is no need to repeat all the
steps; we'll simply focus on the differences from GDB.

Note that Eclipse can be rather finicky. Though it offers many ways to
accomplish a certain task, if you do not strictly follow the necessary sequence
of steps, you may find yourself in a bind with no intuitive solution other than
to restart part of your debugging process.

We assume here that you have already created your C/C++ project.[2]

The first time you run/debug your program, you will need run and debug configurations. These specify the name of your executable (and what
project it belongs to), its command-line arguments (if any), its special shell
variable environment (if any), your debugger of choice, and so on. A *run*
configuration is used to run your program outside the debugger, while a
debug configuration is used within the debugger. Make sure to create both
configurations, in that order, as follows:

1. Select **Run | Open Run Dialog**.

---

[2] Since this is a book about debugging, not project management, we will not say much here
about creating and building projects in Eclipse. A quick summary, though, would be that you
create a project as follows: Select **File | New | Project**; choose C (or C++) Project; fill in a project
name; select **Executable | Finish**. A makefile is created automatically. You build (i.e., compile
and link) your project by selecting **Project | Build Project**.

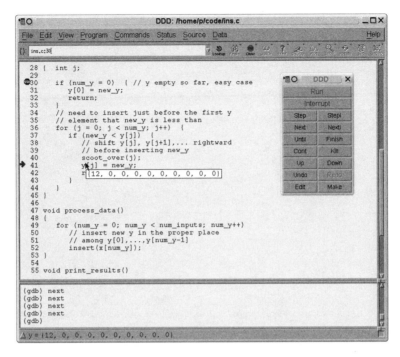

```
■O                          DDD: /home/p/code/ins.c              _□×
 File  Edit  View  Program  Commands  Status  Source  Data              Help
 (): ins.c:30
    28 {  int j;
    29
   ●30      if (num_y = 0)  { // y empty so far, easy case     ■O      DDD      ×
    31         y[0] = new_y;                                         Run
    32         return;
    33      }                                                        Interrupt
    34      // need to insert just before the first y        Step      StepI
    35      // element that new_y is less than
    36      for (j = 0; j < num_y; j++)  {                    Next      NextI
    37         if (new_y < y[j])  {
    38            // shift y[j], y[j+1],... rightward          Until     Finish
    39            // before inserting new_y
    40            scoot_over(j);                               Cont      Kill
  ➜ 41            y[j] = new_y;
    42            r[12, 0, 0, 0, 0, 0, 0, 0, 0, 0, 0]          Up        Down
    43         }
    44      }                                                  Undo      Redo
    45 }
    46                                                         Edit      Make
    47 void process_data()
    48 {
    49      for (num_y = 0; num_y < num_inputs; num_y++)
    50         // insert new y in the proper place
    51         // among y[0],...,y[num_y-1]
    52         insert(x[num_y]);
    53 }
    54
    55 void print_results()

 (gdb) next
 (gdb) next
 (gdb) next
 (gdb) next
 (gdb)
 △y = {12, 0, 0, 0, 0, 0, 0, 0, 0, 0}
```

Figure 1-10: Inspecting the array

2. Right-click **C/C++ Local Applications** and select **New**.

3. Select the **Main** tab, and fill in your run configuration, project and executable file names (Eclipse will probably suggest them for you), and check the **Connect process input and output to a terminal** box if you have terminal I/O.

4. If you have command-line arguments or special environment variables, click the **Arguments** or **Environment** tab, and fill in the desired settings.

5. Select the **Debugger** tab to see which debugger is being used. You probably will not have to touch this, but it's good to understand that there is an underlying debugger, probably GDB.

6. Hit **Apply** (if asked) and **Close** to complete creation of your run configuration.

7. Start creating your debug configuration by selecting **Run | Open Debug Dialog**. Eclipse will probably reuse the information you supplied in your run configuration, as shown in Figure 1-12, or you can change it if you wish. Again, hit **Apply** (if asked) and **Close** to complete creation of your debug configuration.

   One can create several run/debug configurations, typically with different sets of command-line arguments.

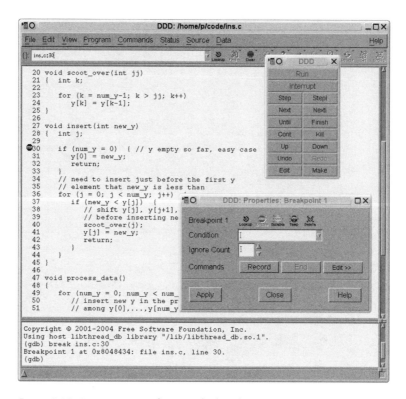

Figure 1-11: Imposing a condition on the breakpoint

To start your debugging session, you must move to the Debug perspective by selecting **Window | Open Perspective | Debug**. (There are various shortcuts, which we'll leave to you to discover.)

The first time you actually execute a run or debug action, you do so via Run | Open Run Dialog or Run | Open Debug Dialog again, as the case may be, in order to state which configuration to use. After that, though, simply select Run | Run or Run | Debug, either of which will rerun the last debug configuration.

In fact, in the debug case, there is a quicker why to launch a debug run, which is to click the Debug icon right under Navigate (see Figure 1-13). Note carefully, though, that whenever you start a new debug run, you need to kill existing ones by clicking a red Terminate square; one is in the toolbar of the Debug view, and another is in the Console view. The Debug view also has a double-X icon, Remove All Terminated Launches.

Figure 1-13 shows the screen as it appears after you have launched your debug. One can set the starting line in Eclipse debug dialogs, but they typically default to placing an automatic breakpoint at the first executable line of code. In the figure, you can see this from the breakpoint symbol in the left margin of the line

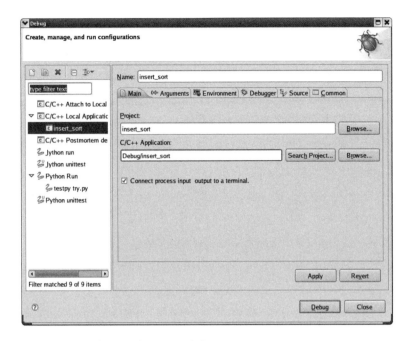

Figure 1-12: Debug configuration dialog

```
{ get_args(argc,argv);
```

That line is also highlighted, as it is the line you are about to execute. Go ahead and execute it by clicking the Resume icon in the Debug view toolbar (above a box that popped up in the window because you moved the mouse pointer to that icon).

Recall that in the sample GDB session, the first version of the program had an infinite loop, and the program was hanging. Here of course you will see the same symptom, with no output in the Console view. You need to kill the program. However, you do not want to do so by clicking one of the red Terminate squares, because this would also kill your underlying GDB session. You want to stay in GDB in order to take a look at where you were in the code—i.e., the location of the infinite loop—examine the values of variables, and so on. So, instead of a Terminate operation, choose Suspend, clicking the icon to the right of Resume in the Debug view toolbar. (In Eclipse literature, this button is sometimes called *Pause*, as its symbol is similar to that for pause operations in media players.)

After clicking Suspend, your screen looks like Figure 1-14. You'll see that just before that operation, Eclipse was about to execute the line

```
for (j = 0; j < num_y; j++)  {
```

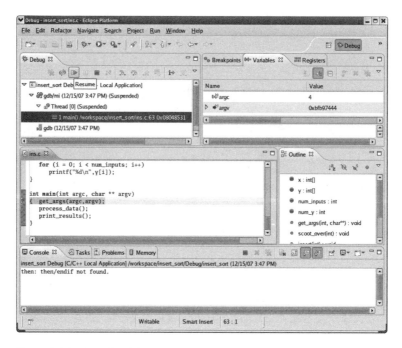

Figure 1-13: Start of a debug run

You can now examine the value of num_y by moving the mouse pointer to any instance of that variable in the source window (you find that the value is 0), and so on.

Recall again our GDB session above. After fixing a couple of bugs, your program then had a segmentation fault. Figure 1-15 shows your Eclipse screen at that point.

What had happened was that we had clicked Resume, so our program was running, but it suddenly halted, at the line

```
y[k] = y[k-1];
```

due to the seg fault. Oddly, Eclipse does not announce this in the Problems tab, but it does do so in the Debug tab, with the error message

```
(Suspended'SIGSEGV' received.  Description:  Segmentation fault.)
```

again visible in Figure 1-15.

You see in that tab that the fault occurred in the function scoot_over(), which had been called from insert(). Again you can query the values of the variables and find, for instance, that k = 544—way out of range, as in the GDB example.

In the GDB example you also set conditional breakpoints. Recall that in Eclipse you set a breakpoint by double-clicking in the left margin of the

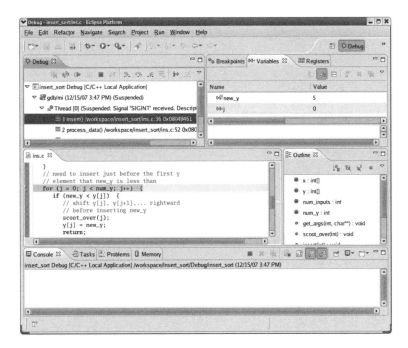

Figure 1-14: Program suspended

desired line. To make that breakpoint conditional, then right-click the breakpoint symbol for that line, and select Breakpoint Properties... | New | Common, and fill in the condition in the dialog. The dialog is depicted in Figure 1-16.

Recall too that in your GDB session you occasionally executed your program outside GDB, in a separate terminal window. You can easily do that in Eclipse too, by selecting Run | Run. The results will be in the Console view, as usual.

1.8 Use of Startup Files

As mentioned earlier, it is usually a good idea to not exit GDB while you re-compile your code. This way your breakpoints and various other actions you set up (for example, display commands, to be discussed in Chapter 3) are re-tained. If you were to exit GDB, you would have to type these all over again.

However, you may need to exit GDB before you are finished debugging. If you are quitting for a break or for the day, and you cannot stay logged in to the computer, you'll need to exit GDB. In order to not lose them, you can put your commands for breakpoints and other settings in a GDB startup file, and then they will be loaded automatically every time you start up GDB.

GDB's startup files are named *.gdbinit* by default. You can have one in your home directory for general purposes and another in the directory containing a particular project for purposes specific to that project. For in-

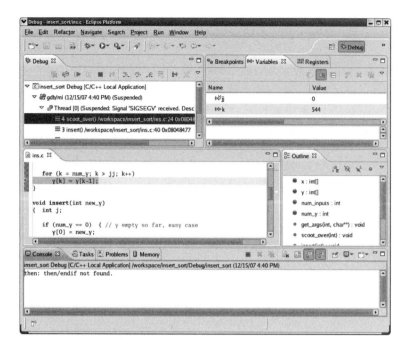

Figure 1-15: Seg fault

stance, you would put commands to set breakpoints in a startup file in the latter directory. In your *.gdbinit* file in your home directory, you may wish to store some general-purpose macros you've developed, as discussed in Chapter 2.

GDB reads the startup file in your home directory before it loads an executable. So if you were to have a command in your home directory's *.gdbinit* file such as

---

```
break g
```

---

saying to break at the function g(), then GDB would always complain at startup that it does not know that function. However, the line would be fine in your local project directory's startup file, because the local startup file is read after the executable (and its symbol table) has been loaded. Note that this feature of GDB implies that it is best to not put programming projects in your home directory, as you would not be able to put project-specific information in *.gdbinit*.

You can specify the startup file at the time you invoke GDB. For example,

---

```
$ gdb -command=z x
```

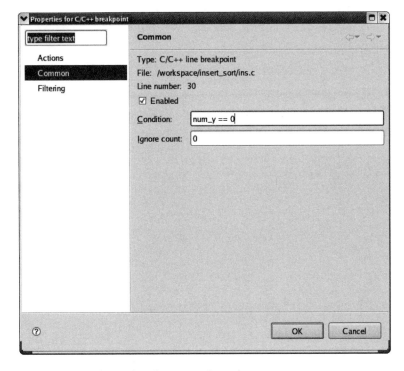

Figure 1-16: Making a breakpoint conditional

would say to run GDB on the executable file *x*, first reading in commands from the file *z*. Also, because DDD is just a front end for GDB, invoking DDD will invoke GDB's startup files as well.

Finally, you can customize DDD in various ways by selecting Edit | Preferences. For Eclipse, the sequence is Window | Preferences.

2

STOPPING TO TAKE A LOOK AROUND

A symbolic debugger such as GDB can run your program, just like you can. However, with the magic of including debugging symbols in the executable, the debugger gives the illusion of executing the program line by line of source code, instead of instruction by instruction of compiled machine code. This seemingly humble fact is precisely what makes a symbolic debugger so useful in debugging programs.

If all the debugger could do is run a program, it wouldn't be of much use to us. We could certainly do the same thing, and more efficiently, to boot. The usefulness of the debugger lies in the fact that we can instruct it to pause execution of the program. Once paused, the debugger gives us a chance to inspect variables, trace the execution path, and much more.

2.1   Mechanisms for Pause

There are three ways to instruct GDB to pause execution of your program:

- A *breakpoint* tells GDB to pause execution at a particular location within the program.

- A *watchpoint* tells GDB to pause execution when a particular memory location (or an expression involving one or more locations) changes value.

- A *catchpoint* tells GDB to pause execution when a particular event occurs.

Confusingly (at first), all three mechanisms are collectively termed *breakpoints* in the GDB documentation. This may be because they share many of the same attributes and commands. For example, you'll learn about GDB's delete command which, as the help blurb says, deletes a breakpoint:

```
(gdb) help delete
Delete some breakpoints or auto-display expressions.
Arguments are breakpoint numbers with spaces in between.
To delete all breakpoints, give no argument.
```

However, the experienced GDB user knows that the help blurb *really* means the delete command deletes breakpoints, watchpoints, and catchpoints!

2.2 Overview of Breakpoints

A breakpoint is like a tripwire within a program: You set a breakpoint at a particular "place" within your program, and when execution reaches that point, the debugger will pause the program's execution (and will, in the case of a text-based debugger such as GDB, give you a command prompt).

GDB is very flexible about the meaning of "place"; it could mean things as varied as a line of source code, an address of code, a line number within a source file, or the entry into a function.

A snippet of a debug session is shown below to illustrate what happens when GDB breaks at a line of code. In the snippet, we list part of the source code, put a breakpoint at line 35 of the program, and then run the program. GDB hits the breakpoint and pauses.

```
(gdb) list
30
31              /* Get the size of file in bytes */
32              if ((fd = open(c.filename, O_RDONLY)) == -1)
33                      (void) die(1, "Can't open file.");
34              (void) stat(c.filename, &fstat);
35              c.filesize = fstat.st_size;
36
(gdb) break 35
Breakpoint 1 at 0x8048ff3: file bed.c, line 35.
(gdb) run
Starting program: binary_editor/bed
```

```
Breakpoint 1, main (argc=1, argv=0xbfa3e1f4) at bed.c:35
35              c.filesize = fstat.st_size;
(gdb)
```

Let's be very clear about what happened here: GDB executed lines 30 through 34, but line 35 has not executed yet. This can be confusing since many people think that GDB displays the line of code that was last executed, when in fact, it shows which line of code is *about* to be executed. In this case, GDB is telling us that line 35 is the next line of source code to execute. When GDB's execution hits a breakpoint at line 35, you can think of GDB sitting and waiting between lines 34 and 35 of the source code.

However, as you may know, GDB works with machine language instructions, not lines of source code, and there may be several lines of machine language for a single line of code. GDB can work with lines of source code because of additional information included in the executable. While this fact may not seem terribly important now, it will have implications when we discuss stepping through your program throughout this chapter.

2.3 Keeping Track of Breakpoints

Each breakpoint (which includes breakpoints, watchpoints, and catchpoints) you create is assigned a unique integer identifier, starting at 1. This identifier is used to perform various operations on the breakpoint. The debugger also includes a means of listing all your breakpoints and their properties.

2.3.1 Breakpoint Lists in GDB

When you create a breakpoint, GDB tells you the number assigned to it. For instance, the breakpoint set in this example

```
(gdb) break main
Breakpoint 2 at 0x8048824: file efh.c, line 16.
```

was assigned the number 2. If you ever forget what number was assigned to which breakpoint, you can remind yourself with the info breakpoints command:

```
(gdb) info breakpoints
Num Type           Disp Enb Address    What
1   breakpoint     keep y   0x08048846 in Initialize_Game at efh.c:26
2   breakpoint     keep y   0x08048824 in main at efh.c:16
        breakpoint already hit 1 time
3   hw watchpoint  keep y              efh.level
4   catch fork     keep y
```

We'll see that these identifiers are used to perform various operations on breakpoints. To make this more concrete, a very quick example is in order.

In the previous section you saw the delete command. You could delete breakpoint 1, watchpoint 3, and catchpoint 4 by using the delete command with the identifiers for those breakpoints:

```
(gdb) delete 1 3 4
```

You'll see many other uses for breakpoint identifiers in the upcoming sections.

2.3.2 Breakpoint Lists in DDD

DDD users mainly perform breakpoint management operations with the point-and-click interface, so breakpoint identifiers are less important to DDD users than they are to GDB users. Selecting Source | Breakpoints will pop up the Breakpoints and Watchpoints window, listing all your breakpoints, as shown in Figure 2-1.

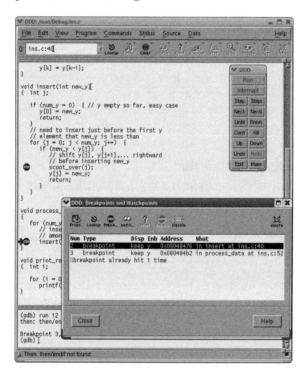

Figure 2-1: Viewing breakpoints in DDD

Recall, though, that DDD allows you to use GDB's command-based interface as well as the provided GUI. In some cases, GDB provides breakpoint operations that are not available through the DDD GUI, but the DDD user can access those special GDB operations via the DDD Console. In such cases, breakpoint identifiers can still be useful to DDD users.

Note that you can keep this Breakpoints and Watchpoints window open constantly if you wish, dragging it to a convenient part of your screen.

2.3.3   Breakpoint Lists in Eclipse

The Debug perspective includes a Breakpoints view. In Figure 2-2, for instance, you see that you currently have two breakpoints, at lines 30 and 52 of the file *ins.c*.

You can right-click the entry of any breakpoint to examine or change its properties. Also, double-clicking an entry will result in the focus of the source file window moving to that breakpoint.

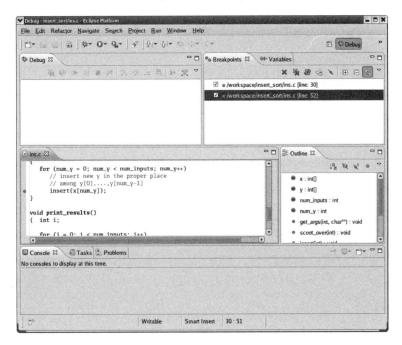

Figure 2-2: Viewing breakpoints in Eclipse

2.4   Setting Breakpoints

Debugging tools typically offer a variety of mechanisms with which to set breakpoints.

2.4.1   Setting Breakpoints in GDB

You've learned that GDB gives the illusion of running a program line by line of source code. You've also learned that in order to do anything really useful with GDB you need to instruct it where to pause execution so you can perform debugging activitites with GDB's command-line prompt. In this section, you'll learn how to set breakpoints, which tell GDB *where* to stop within your source code.

There are many different ways to specify a breakpoint in GDB; here are some of the most common methods:

break *function*

Set a breakpoint at the entry (first executable line) of the function *function*(). You saw an example of this in Section 2.3.1; the command

```
(gdb) break main
```

sets a breakpoint at the entry of main().

break *line_number*

Set a breakpoint at line *line_number* of the currently active source code file. For multi-file programs, this is either the file whose contents you last looked at using the list command or the file containing main(). You saw an example of this in Section 2.2;

```
(gdb) break 35
```

which set a breakpoint at line 35 in file *bed.c*.

break *filename:line_number*

Set a breakpoint at line *line_number* of the source code file *filename*. If *filename* isn't in your current working directory, you can give a relative or full pathname to help GDB find the file, for example:

```
(gdb) break source/bed.c:35
```

break *filename:function*

Set a breakpoint at the entry of function *function*() within the file *filename*. Using this form may be required for overloaded functions or for programs that use identically named static functions, for example:

```
(gdb) break bed.c:parseArguments
```

As we'll see, when a breakpoint is set, it stays in effect until you delete it, disable it, or quit GDB. However, a *temporary breakpoint* is a breakpoint that is automatically deleted after the first time it's reached. A temporary breakpoint is set with the tbreak command, which takes the same type of arguments that break takes. For example, tbreak foo.c:10 sets a temporary breakpoint at line 10 of file *foo.c*.

A comment needs to be made about functions with the same name. C++ allows you to overload functions (define functions with the same name). Even C allows you to do this if you use the static qualifier to declare the functions with file scope. Using break *function* will set a breakpoint at *all* functions with the same name. If you want to set a breakpoint at a particular instance of the function, you need to be unambiguous, such as by giving the line number within a source code file in your break command.

The location at which GDB actually sets a breakpoint may be different from where you requested it to be placed. This can be somewhat disconcerting for people new to GDB, so let's look at a short example that demonstrates this quirk. Consider the following short program, *test1.c*:

```
int main(void)
{
    int i;
    i = 3;

    return 0;
}
```

Compile this program *without* optimization and try setting a breakpoint at the entry of main(). You would think that the breakpoint would be placed at the top of the function—either line 1, line 2, or line 3. Those would be good guesses for the location of the breakpoint, but they're wrong. The breakpoint is actually set at line 4.

```
$ gcc -g3 -Wall -Wextra -o test1 test1.c
$ gdb test1
(gdb) break main
Breakpoint 1 at 0x6: file test1.c, line 4.
```

Line 4 is hardly the first line of main(), so what happened? As you may have guessed, one issue is that that line is *executable*. Recall that GDB actually works with machine language instructions, but with the magic of an enhanced symbol table, GDB gives the *illusion* of working with source code lines. Normally, this fact isn't terribly important, but this is a situation in which it becomes important. Actually, declaring i does generate machine code, but it is not code that GDB finds useful for our debugging purposes.[1] Therefore, when you told GDB to break at the start of main(), it set a breakpoint at line 4.

The problem may become worse when you compile the program *with* optimizations. Let's take a look. Recompile the program with optimization turned on:

```
$ gcc -O9 -g3 -Wall -Wextra -o test1 test1.c
$ gdb test1
(gdb) break main
Breakpoint 1 at 0x3: file test1.c, line 6.
```

We asked to put a breakpoint at the start of main(), but GDB placed one on the last line of main(). Now what happened? The answer is the same as before, but GCC took a more active role. With optimizations turned on, GCC noticed that although i was assigned a value, it was never used. So in an effort to generate more efficient code, GCC simply optimized lines 3 and 4 out of existence. GCC never generated machine instructions for these lines. Therefore, the first line of source code that generated machine instructions

---

[1] You can view the machine code generated by GCC via the -S option.

Catchpoints

C++ programmers will want to check out the catch command, which sets *catchpoints*. Catchpoints are similar to breakpoints, but can be triggered by different things like thrown exceptions, caught exceptions, signals, calls to fork(), loading and unloading of libraries, and many other events.

In this book, we'll go over breakpoints and watchpoints but will refer the reader to the GDB documentation for more information on catchpoints.

happens to be the last line of main(). This is one of the reasons you should never optimize code until you're finished debugging it.[2]

The upshot of all this is that if you find that setting a breakpoint doesn't produce a breakpoint exactly where you'd expect it to, you now know why. Don't be surprised.

On a related matter, we'd like to mention what happens when more than one breakpoint lives at the same line of source code. When GDB breaks at a source code line with more than one breakpoint, it will only break there *once*. In other words, after it hits that line of code, if you resume execution, the other breakpoints which happen to be on the same line will be ignored. In fact, GDB keeps track of which breakpoint "triggered" the program execution to stop. On a line of code with multiple breakpoints, the breakpoint that triggers the break will be the breakpoint with the lowest identifier.

2.4.2 Setting Breakpoints in DDD

To set breakpoints with DDD, find the line of code at which you want to set the breakpoint in the Source Window. Position the cursor over any empty space on that line and right-click to reveal a pop-up menu. Drag the mouse down until the Set Breakpoint choice is highlighted, and then release the mouse button. You should see a red stop sign next to the line of code where you set the breakpoint. If you are not doing anything special with the breakpoint, such as making it conditional (which will be discussed in Section 2.10), a shortcut is to simply double-click the given line.

If you've been experimenting with DDD, you may have noticed that when you press the right-hand button next to a line of code, the pop-up menu contains the choice Set Temporary Breakpoint. This is how you set a temporary breakpoint (a breakpoint that disappears after the first time it's reached) with DDD, which invokes GDB's tbreak command.

---

[2] Actually, some debuggers can really choke on executables compiled with optimizations turned on. GDB has the distinction of being one of the few debuggers that *can* debug optimized code, but as you saw, the results can be iffy.

Again, don't forget that DDD is really a GDB frontend. You can issue *any* GDB-style break commands in DDD using DDD's Console Window. Sometimes this is desirable; if you have a very large or a multi-file program, it could be more convenient to issue a breakpoint using GDB semantics. In fact, sometimes it's necessary because not all of GDB's breakpoint commands are invocable from the DDD interface.

2.4.3 Setting Breakpoints in Eclipse

To set a breakpoint at a given line in Eclipse, double-click on that line. A breakpoint symbol will appear, as seen, for example, in the line

```
insert(x[num_y]);
```

in Figure 2-2.

To set a temporary breakpoint, click the line, then right-click in the source window, and select Run to Line. Note, however, that the Run to Line operation only works if the target line is in the same function as your current position, and if you do not exit the function before re-entering and hitting this line.

2.5 Extended GDB Example

This has been a lot of information, so a short example of setting breakpoints that you can follow along with is warranted. Consider the following multi-file C code:

main.c:

```
#include <stdio.h>
void swap(int *a, int *b);

int main(void)
{
    int i = 3;
    int j = 5;

    printf("i: %d, j: %d\n", i, j);
    swap(&i, &j);
    printf("i: %d, j: %d\n", i, j);

    return 0;
}
```

swapper.c:

```
void swap(int *a, int *b)
{
    int c = *a;
    *a = *b;
    *b = c;
}
```

Compile this code and run GDB on the executable:

```
$ gcc -g3 -Wall -Wextra -c main.c swapper.c
$ gcc -o swap main.o swapper.o
$ gdb swap
```

NOTE   *This is the first time in this book that we've compiled a multi-file C program, so a word
is in order. The first line of the compilation process (above) produces two object files
containing unresolved object code with debugging information. The second line links
the object files into an executable containing all debugging information. There is no
need to use GCC's -g switch during the linking process.*

Setting a breakpoint at main() is very common when starting a debugging
session. This sets a breakpoint on the first line of that function.[3]

```
(gdb) break main
Breakpoint 1 at 0x80483f6: file main.c, line 6.
```

The examples below all set a breakpoint at the first line of the function
swap(). While they may not look the same, they all do the same thing: break
at the top of swap().

```
(gdb) break swapper.c:1
Breakpoint 2 at 0x8048454: file swapper.c, line 1.
(gdb) break swapper.c:swap
Breakpoint 3 at 0x804845a: file swapper.c, line 3.
(gdb) break swap
Note: breakpoint 3 also set at pc 0x804845a.
Breakpoint 4 at 0x804845a: file swapper.c, line 3.
```

At any given time, GDB has (for lack of a better word) a *focus*, which you
can think of as being the currently "active" file. This means that unless you
qualify your commands, they are performed on the file that has GDB's focus. By default, the file that has GDB's initial focus is the one containing the
main() function, but the focus is changed to a different file when any of the
following actions occurs:

- You apply the list command to a different source file.

- You step into code residing in a different source file.

- GDB hits a breakpoint while executing code in a different source file.

Let's look at an example. Although breakpoints have been set in *swap-
per.c*, we haven't actually listed code from that file. Hence, the focus is still
trained on *main.c*. You can verify this by setting a breakpoint at line 6. When

---

[3] Recall that the breakpoint may not be at *exactly* the first line of main(), but it'll be close. Unlike
our previous example of this point, though, the line here *is* executable, since it assigns a value
to i.

you set this breakpoint without a filename, GDB will set the breakpoint at line 6 of the currently active file:

```
(gdb) break 6
Breakpoint 5 at 0x8048404: file main.c, line 6.
```

Sure enough, *main.c* has the focus: When you start GDB, a breakpoint set only by line number is set within the file containing main(). You can change the focus by listing code from *swapper.c*:

```
(gdb) list swap
1    void swap(int *a, int *b)
2    {
3        int c = *a;
4        *a = *b;
5        *b = c;
6    }
```

Let's verify that *swapper.c* now has the focus by trying to set a another breakpoint at line 6:

```
(gdb) break 6
Breakpoint 6 at 0x8048474: file swapper.c, line 6.
```

Yep, the breakpoint was set at line 6 of *swapper.c*. Then you'll set a temporary breakpoint at line 4 of *swapper.c*:

```
(gdb) tbreak swapper.c:4
Breakpoint 7 at 0x8048462: file swapper.c, line 4.
```

Lastly, use the info breakpoints command that was introduced in Section 2.3.1 to marvel at all the breakpoints you've set:

```
(gdb) info breakpoints
Num Type           Disp Enb Address    What
1   breakpoint     keep y   0x080483f6 in main at main.c:6
2   breakpoint     keep y   0x08048454 in swap at swapper.c:1
3   breakpoint     keep y   0x0804845a in swap at swapper.c:3
4   breakpoint     keep y   0x0804845a in swap at swapper.c:3
5   breakpoint     keep y   0x08048404 in main at main.c:9
6   breakpoint     keep y   0x08048474 in swap at swapper.c:6
7   breakpoint     del  y   0x08048462 in swap at swapper.c:4
```

Much later on, when you are done with your GDB session, use the quit command to leave GDB:

```
(gdb) quit
$
```

2.6 Persistence of Breakpoints

We said "much later on" above to make the point that you should not exit
GDB during your debugging session. For example, when you find and fix
one bug, but other bugs remain, you should not exit and then re-enter GDB
to use the new version of your program. That would be unnecessary trouble,
and more importantly, you would have to re-enter your breakpoints.

If you do not exit GDB when you change and recompile your code, the
next time you issue GDB's run command, GDB will sense that your code has
changed and automatically reload the new version.

However, note that your breakpoints may "move." For instance, consider
the following simple program:

```
1   main()
2   {  int x,y;
3      x = 1;
4      y = 2;
5   }
```

We compile, enter GDB, and set a breakpoint at line 4:

```
(gdb) l
1       main()
2       {  int x,y;
3           x = 1;
4           y = 2;
5       }
(gdb) b 4
Breakpoint 1 at 0x804830b: file a.c, line 4.
(gdb) r
Starting program: /usr/home/matloff/Tmp/tmp1/a.out

Breakpoint 1, main () at a.c:4
4           y = 2;
```

All well and good. But suppose you now add a source line:

```
1   main()
2   {  int x,y;
3      x = 1;
4      x++;
5      y = 2;
6   }
```

Then recompile—again, keep in mind that you have not left GDB—and again issue the GDB `run` command:

```
(gdb) r
The program being debugged has been started already.
Start it from the beginning? (y or n) y
`/usr/home/matloff/Tmp/tmp1/a.out' has changed; re-reading symbols.

Starting program: /usr/home/matloff/Tmp/tmp1/a.out

Breakpoint 1, main () at a.c:4
4           x++;
```

GDB did reload the new code, but the breakpoint has seemingly shifted from the statement

```
    y = 2;
```

to

```
    x++;
```

If you take a closer look, you'll see that the breakpoint actually has not moved at all; it had been at line 4, and it is still at line 4. But that line no longer contains the statement at which you had originally set your breakpoint. Thus, you will need to move the breakpoint by deleting this one and setting a new one. (In DDD, you can do this much more easily; see Section 2.7.5.)

Eventually, your current debugging session will end, say, because it's time to eat, sleep, or relax. If you don't normally keep your computer running continuously, you will need to exit your debugger. Is there any way to save your breakpoints?

For GDB and DDD, the answer is yes, to some extent. You can place your breakpoints in a *.gdbinit* startup file in the directory where you have your source code (or the directory from which you invoke GDB).

If you are in Eclipse, you are in luck, because all of your breakpoints will be automatically saved and restored in your next Eclipse session.

2.7   Deleting and Disabling Breakpoints

During the course of a debugging session, you may find that a breakpoint has outlived its usefulness. If you're sure the breakpoint will no longer be needed, you can delete it.

It may also be the case that you think the breakpoint can be of use to you later on during the debugging session. Perhaps you'd rather not delete the breakpoint, but instead, cook things up so that for the time being the debugger will skip breaks at that point in your code. This is called *disabling* a breakpoint. You can re-enable it later if/when it becomes useful again.

This section covers deleting and disabling breakpoints. Everything mentioned applies to watchpoints as well.

2.7.1 Deleting Breakpoints in GDB

If the breakpoint in question is truly no longer needed (perhaps that particular bug was fixed!) then you can delete that breakpoint. There are two commands that are used to delete breakpoints in GDB. The delete command is used to delete breakpoints based on their identifier, and the clear command is used to delete breakpoints using the same syntax you use to create breakpoints, as discussed in Section 2.4.1.

delete *breakpoint_list*

> Deletes breakpoints using their numeric identifiers (which were explained in Section 2.3). It can be a single number, such as delete 2 which deletes the second breakpoint, or a list of numbers, like delete 2 4 which deletes the second and fourth breakpoints.

delete

> Deletes all breakpoints. GDB will ask you to confirm this operation unless you issue the set confirm off command, which can also be placed in your *.gdbinit* startup file.

clear

> Clears a breakpoint at the next instruction that GDB will execute. This method is useful when you want to delete the breakpoint that GDB has just reached.

clear *function*

clear *filename:function*

clear *line_number*

clear *filename:line_number*

> These clear a breakpoint based on its location and work analogously to the break counterparts.

> For example, suppose you set a breakpoint at the entry of foo() with:

```
(gdb) break foo
Breakpoint 2 at 0x804843a: file test.c, line 22.
```

You can delete that breakpoint either with

```
(gdb) clear foo
Deleted breakpoint 2
```

or with

```
(gdb) delete 2
Deleted breakpoint 2
```

2.7.2 Disabling Breakpoints in GDB

Each breakpoint can be enabled or disabled. GDB will pause the program's execution only when it hits an enabled breakpoint; it ignores disabled breakpoints. By default, breakpoints start life as being enabled.

Why would you want to disable breakpoints? During the course of a debugging session, you may collect a large number of breakpoints. For loop structures or functions that repeat often, it can be extremely inconvenient for GDB to break so often. If you want to keep the breakpoints for later use but don't want GDB to stop execution for the time being, you can disable them and enable them later.

You disable a breakpoint with the `disable` *breakpoint-list* command and enable a breakpoint with the `enable` *breakpoint-list* command, where *breakpoint-list* is a space-separated list of one or more breakpoint identifiers. For example,

```
(gdb) disable 3
```

will disable the third breakpoint. Similarly,

```
(gdb) enable 1 5
```

will enable the first and fifth breakpoints.

Issuing the `disable` command without any arguments will disable all existing breakpoints. Similarly, the `enable` command with no arguments will enable all existing breakpoints.

There's also an `enable once` command that will cause a breakpoint to become disabled after the next time it causes GDB to pause execution. The syntax is:

```
enable once breakpoint-list
```

For example, `enable once 3` will cause breakpoint 3 to become disabled the next time it causes GDB to stop execution of your program. It's very similar to the `tbreak` command, but it disables rather than deletes when the breakpoint is encountered.

2.7.3 Deleting and Disabling Breakpoints in DDD

Deleting breakpoints in DDD is just as easy as setting them. Position the cursor over the red stop sign and right-click the mouse, as you would to set a breakpoint. One of the options in the pop-up menu will be Delete Breakpoint. Hold down the right mouse button and drag the mouse down until this option is highlighted. Then release the button and you'll see the red stop sign disappear, indicating that the breakpoint was deleted.

Disabling breakpoints with DDD is very similar to deleting them. Right-click and hold the red stop sign, and select Disable Breakpoint. The red stop sign will turn gray, indicating that the breakpoint is still there but is disabled for now.

Your other option is to use DDD's Breakpoints and Watchpoints window, shown in Figure 2-1. You can click a breakpoint entry there to highlight it, and then select Delete, Disable, or Enable.

In fact, you can highlight several entries in that window by dragging the mouse over them, as seen in Figure 2-3. You thus can delete, disable, or enable multiple breakpoints at once.

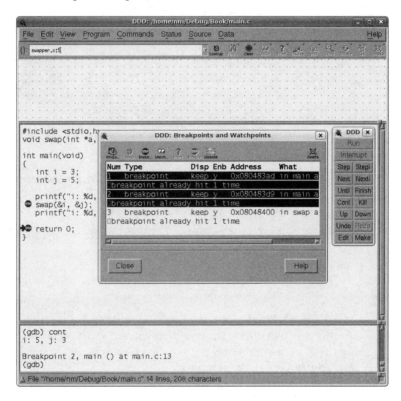

Figure 2-3: Deleting/disabling/enabling multiple breakpoints in DDD

After clicking Delete in the breakpoints window, the screen looks like Figure 2-4. Sure enough, two of the old breakpoints are gone now.

2.7.4   Deleting and Disabling Breakpoints in Eclipse

As with DDD, you can delete or disable a breakpoint in Eclipse by right-clicking the breakpoint symbol in the line in question. A menu will pop up, shown in Figure 2-5. Note that the Toggle option means to delete the breakpoint, while Disable/Enable means the obvious.

Similar to DDD's breakpoints window, Eclipse has its Breakpoints view, which you can see in the upper-right portion of Figure 2-5. Unlike the DDD case, in which we needed to request the Breakpoints and Watchpoints win-

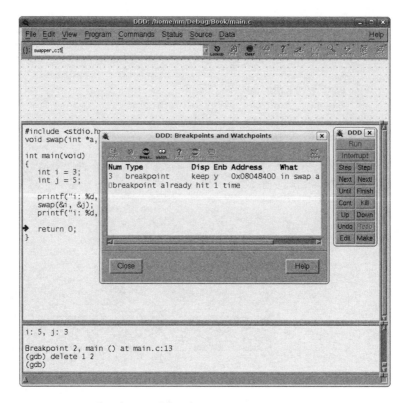

Figure 2-4: Two breakpoints deleted

dow, Eclipse's Breakpoints view is automatically displayed in the Debug perspective. (You can hide it, though, if you are short on screen space, by clicking the X in its right-hand corner. If you want to get it back later, select **Window** | **Show Views** | **Breakpoints**.)

One nice aspect of the Eclipse Breakpoints view is that you can click the double X (Remove All Breakpoints) icon. The need for this occurs more often than you might guess. At some points in a long debugging session, you may find that none of the breakpoints you set earlier is now useful, and thus want to delete them all.

2.7.5 "Moving" Breakpoints in DDD

DDD has another really nice feature: drag-and-drop breakpoints. Left-click and hold a breakpoint stop sign in the Source Window. As long as you keep the left button pressed, you can drag the breakpoint to another location within your source code. What happens "behind the scenes" is that DDD deletes the original breakpoint and sets a new breakpoint with the same attributes. As a result, you'll find that the new breakpoint is entirely equivalent to the old breakpoint, except for its numeric identifier. Of course you can do this with GDB as well, but DDD expedites the process.

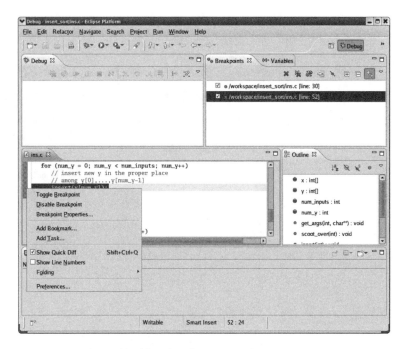

Figure 2-5: Deleting/disabling breakpoints in Eclipse

Figure 2-6 illustrates this—it is a snapshot taken in the midst of the breakpoint-move operation. There had been a breakpoint at the line

```
if (new_y < y[i]) {
```

which we wished to move to the line

```
scoot_over(j);
```

We clicked on the stop sign at that old line and dragged it to the new line. In the picture, we had not yet released the mouse button, so the original stop sign was still there, and a "hollow" stop sign appeared on the new line. Upon our release of the mouse button, the stop sign at the old line disappeared and the one at the new line filled out.

Why is this so useful? First of all, if you are in a situation in which you want to delete one breakpoint and add another, this does both operations in one fell swoop. But more importantly, as noted earlier in Section 2.6, when you add or delete source code lines, the line numbers of some remaining lines change, thus "shifting" existing breakpoints to lines at which you did not intend to have one. In GDB, this necessitates your doing a delete-breakpoint and new-breakpoint action at each of the affected breakpoints. This is tedious, especially if some of them had conditions attached to them.

But in DDD, you can simply drag the stop sign icon to the new locations—
very nice and convenient.

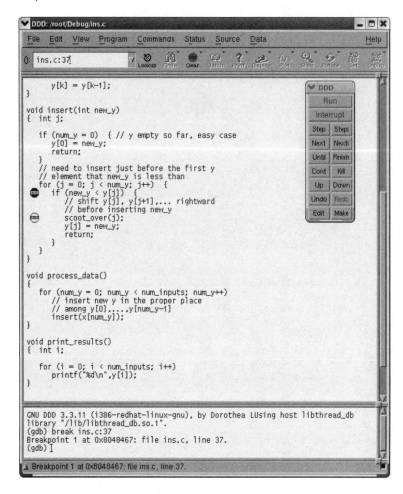

Figure 2-6: "Moving" a breakpoint in DDD

2.7.6   Undoing/Redoing Breakpoint Actions in DDD

One of DDD's really nice features is Undo/Redo, accessed by clicking Edit.
As an example, consider the situation in Figures 2-3 and 2-4. Suppose you
suddenly realize that you did not want to delete those two breakpoints—
maybe you just wished to disable them. You can select Edit | Undo Delete,
shown in Figure 2-7. (You could also click Undo in the Command Tool, but
going through Edit has the advantage that DDD will remind us *what* will be
undone.)

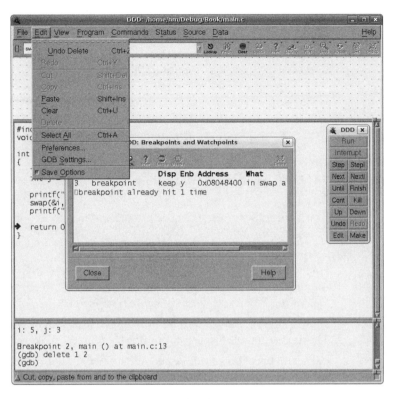

Figure 2-7: A chance to restore two breakpoints in DDD

2.8 More on Viewing Breakpoint Attributes

Each breakpoint has various attributes—its line number, the condition imposed on it (if any), its current enabled/disabled status, and so on. We showed in Section 2.3 a bit about keeping track of these attributes, and now we'll go into more detail.

2.8.1 GDB

As you saw in Section 2.3.1, each breakpoint you create is assigned a unique integer identifier. The first breakpoint you set is assigned to '1', and each new breakpoint thereafter is assigned an integer one greater than the previously assigned identifier. Each breakpoint also has a number of attributes that control and fine-tune its behavior. Using the unique identifiers, you can adjust the attributes of each breakpoint individually.

You can use the info breakpoints command (abbreviated as i b) to obtain a listing of all the breakpoints you've set, along with their attributes. The output of info breakpoints will look more or less like this:

```
(gdb) info breakpoints
Num Type           Disp Enb Address    What
```

```
1    breakpoint      keep y    0x08048404 in main at int_swap.c:9
        breakpoint already hit 1 time
2    breakpoint      keep n    0x08048447 in main at int_swap.c:14
3    breakpoint      keep y    0x08048460 in swap at int_swap.c:20
        breakpoint already hit 1 time
4    hw watchpoint   keep y                    counter
```

Let's look at this output from `info breakpoints` in detail:

Identifier (`Num`):
The breakpoint's unique identifier.

Type (`Type`):
This field tells you whether the breakpoint is a breakpoint, watchpoint, or catchpoint.

Disposition (`Disp`):
Each breakpoint has a disposition, which indicates what will happen to the breakpoint after the next time it causes GDB to pause the program's execution. There are three possible dispositions:

keep   The breakpoint will be unchanged after the next time it's reached. This is the default disposition of newly created breakpoints.

del   The breakpoint will be deleted after the next time it's reached. This disposition is assigned to any breakpoint you create with the `tbreak` command (see Section 2.4.1).

dis   The breakpoint will be disabled the next time it's reached. This is set using the `enable once` command (see Section 2.7.2).

Enable Status (`Enb`):
This field tells you whether the breakpoint is currently enabled or disabled.

Address (`Address`):
This is the location in memory where the breakpoint is set. This would mainly be of use to assembly language programmers or people trying to debug an executable that wasn't compiled with an augmented symbol table.

Location (`What`):
As discussed, each breakpoint lives at a particular line within your source code. The `What` field shows the line number and filename of the location of the breakpoint.

For watchpoints, this field shows which variable is being watched. This makes sense because a variable is actually a memory address with a name, and a memory address is a location.

As you can see, in addition to listing all the breakpoints and their attributes, the `i b` command also tells you how many times a particular breakpoint has caused GDB to halt execution of the program so far. If, for instance, you have a breakpoint within a loop, it will tell you at a glance how many iterations of the loop have been executed so far, which can be very useful.

2.8.2 DDD

As you saw in Figure 2-1, DDD's Breakpoints and Watchpoints window provides the same information as GDB's info breakpoints command. However, it is more convenient than GDB, in that you can display this window constantly (i.e., off to the side of your screen), thus avoiding issuing a command each time you want to view your breakpoints.

2.8.3 Eclipse

Again, as seen earlier (Figure 2-2), Eclipse's Breakpoints view constantly displays your breakpoints and their properties. Eclipse is a little less informative than DDD here, in that it does not tell you how many times a breakpoint has been hit so far (this information is not even in the Properties window).

2.9 Resuming Execution

Knowing how to instruct the debugger where or when to pause execution of your program is important, but knowing how to instruct it to resume execution is just as important. After all, inspecting your variables may not be enough. Sometimes you need to know how the variables' values interact with the rest of the code.

Recall the Principle of Confirmation in Chapter 1: You continue to confirm that certain variables have the values you think they do, until you encounter one that fails to match your expectation. That failure will then be a clue as to the likely location of your bug. But typically the failure will not occur until you have paused and resumed execution at a number of breakpoints (or multiple times at the same breakpoint). Thus, resuming execution at a breakpoint is just as important as setting the breakpoint itself, which is why a debugging tool will typically have a fairly rich set of methods for resuming execution.

There are three classes of methods for resuming execution. The first involves "single stepping" through your program with step and next, executing only the next line of code and then pausing again. The second consists of using continue, which makes GDB unconditionally resume execution of the program until it hits another breakpoint or the program finishes. The last class of methods involves conditions: resuming with the finish or until commands. In this case, GDB will resume execution and the program will run until either some predetermined condition is met (e.g., the end of a function is reached), another breakpoint is reached, or the program finishes.

We'll consider each method of resuming execution in turn for GDB, and then show how to perform such operations in DDD and Eclipse.

2.9.1 In GDB

We'll start this section by discussing the various ways you can resume execution once GDB is paused at a breakpoint.

2.9.1.1 Single-stepping with step and next

Once GDB stops at a breakpoint, the next (abbreviated as n) and step (abbreviated as s) commands are used to single-step through your code. After a breakpoint is triggered and GDB pauses, you can use next and step to execute just the very next line of code. After the line is executed, GDB will again pause and give a command prompt. Let's take a look at this in action. Consider the program *swapflaw.c*:

```
1   /* swapflaw.c: A flawed function that swaps two integers. */
2   #include <stdio.h>
3   void swap(int a, int b);
4
5   int main(void)
6   {
7     int i = 4;
8     int j = 6;
9
10    printf("i: %d, j: %d\n", i, j);
11    swap(i, j);
12    printf("i: %d, j: %d\n", i, j);
13
14    return 0;
15  }
16
17  void swap(int a, int b)
18  {
19    int c = a;
20    a = b;
21    b = c;
22  }
```

Listing 2-1: swapflaw.c

We'll set a breakpoint at the entry to main() and run the program in GDB.

```
$ gcc -g3 -Wall -Wextra -o swapflaw swapflaw.c
$ gdb swapflaw
(gdb) break main
Breakpoint 1 at 0x80483f6: file swapflaw.c, line 7.
(gdb) run
Starting program: swapflaw
```

```
Breakpoint 1, main () at swapflaw.c:7
7                    int i = 4;
```

GDB is now at line 7 of the program, meaning that line 7 has not been executed yet. We can use the next command to execute just this line of code, leaving us just before line 8:

```
(gdb) next
8                    int j = 6;
```

We'll use step to execute the next line of code, line 8, which moves us to line 10.

```
(gdb) step
10                   printf("i: %d, j: %d\n", i, j);
```

We see that both next and step execute the next line of code. So the big question is: "How are these commands different?" They both appear to execute the next line of code. The difference between these two commands is how they handle function calls: next will execute the function, *without pausing within it*, and then pause at the first statement following the call. step, on the other hand, will pause at the first statement within the function.

A call to swap() is coming up at line 11. Let's look at the effect of next and step side by side.

Using step:

```
(gdb) step
i: 4, j: 6
11        swap(i, j);
(gdb) step
swap (a=4, b=6) at swapflaw.c:19
19        int c = a;
(gdb) step
20        a = b;
(gdb) step
21        b = c;
(gdb) step
22        }
(gdb) step
main () at swapflaw.c:12
12        printf("i: %d, j: %d\n", i, j);
(gdb) step
i: 4, j: 6
14        return 0;
```

Using next:

```
(gdb) next
i: 4, j: 6
11        swap(i, j);
(gdb) next
12        printf("i: %d, j: %d\n", i, j);
(gdb) next
i: 4, j: 6
14        return 0;
```

The step command works the way you might expect it to. It executed the printf() on line 10, then the the call to swap() on line 11,[4] and then it began executing lines of code within swap(). This is called stepping *into* a function. Once we step through all the lines of swap(), step brings us back to main().

In contrast, it appears that next never left main(). This is the main difference between the two commands. next considers the function call to be a single line of code, and executes the entire function in one operation, which is called stepping *over* the function.

However, don't be fooled; it may *look* like next skipped over the body of swap(), but it didn't really step "over" anything. GDB silently executed each line of swap() without showing us the details (although it shows any screen output that swap() may print) and without prompting us to execute individual lines from the function.

The difference between stepping *into* a function (what step does) and stepping *over* a function (what next does) is such an important concept that, at the risk of belaboring the point, we'll demonstrate the difference between next and step with a diagram that shows the program execution using arrows.

Figure 2-8 illustrates the behavior of the step command. Imagine that the program is paused at the first printf() statement. The figure shows where each step statement will take us:

```
int main(void)
{
    int i = 4;
    int j = 6;

    printf("i: %d, j: %d\n", i, j);                step
    swap(i, j);
    printf("i: %d, j: %d\n", i, j);
                                                    step
    return 0;
}

void swap(int a, int b)
{                                                   step
    int c = a;
    a = b;                          step
    b = c;                          step
}
```

Figure 2-8: step *steps into the function.*

Figure 2-9 illustrates the same thing, but using next instead.

---

[4] You may wonder why step did not take you to the first line of the function printf(). The reason is that GDB does not stop within code for which it does not have debugging information (i.e., the symbol table). The function printf(), being linked in from the C library, is an example of such code.

```
int main(void)
{
    int i = 4;
    int j = 6;

    printf("i: %d, j: %d\n", i, j);              next
    swap(i, j);
    printf("i: %d, j: %d\n", i, j);              next

    return 0;
}

void swap(int a, int b)
{
    int c = a;
    a = b;
    b = c;
}
```

Figure 2-9: next *steps over the function.*

Whether you use next or step is really a matter of what you are trying to do. If you're in a part of the code with no function calls, it doesn't matter which one you use. In this case, the two commands are completely equivalent.

However, if you're debugging a program and find yourself about to step into a function that you know is free of bugs (or irrelevent to the bug you're trying to track down), clearly you'd want to use next to save yourself from stepping through each line of a function you're not interested in.

One of the general debugging principles laid out in Chapter 1 was to take a top-down approach to debugging. If you're stepping through source code and encounter a function call, it is typically better to use next instead of step. Immediately after using next in this situation, you would check if the result of the call was correct. If so, the bug is likely not in the function, meaning the use of next instead of step saved you the time and effort of stepping through every line of the function. On the other hand, if the result of the function is incorrect, you can re-run the program with a temporary breakpoint set at the function call, and then use step to enter the function.

Both the next and step commands take an optional numerical argument which indicates the number of extra lines to next or step through. In other words, next 3 is the same as typing next three times in a row (or typing next once followed by hitting the ENTER key twice).[5] Figure 2-10 shows an illustration of what next 3 does:

---

[5] Vim users should feel right at home with the concept of specifying a count for a given command.

```
void swapper(int *a, int *b)
{
    int c = *a;
    *a = *b;
    *b = c;                              next 3
    printf("swapped!\n");
}
```

Figure 2-10: next *with a count*

2.9.1.2   Resuming Program Execution with continue

The second method of resuming execution is with the continue command,
abbreviated as c. In contrast to step and next, which execute only one line of
code, this command causes GDB to resume execution of your program until
a breakpoint is triggered or the program terminates.

The continue command can take an optional integer argument, n. This
number tells GDB to ignore the next n breakpoints. For instance, continue 3
tells GDB to resume program execution and ignore the next 3 breakpoints.

2.9.1.3   Resuming Program Execution with finish

Once a breakpoint is triggered, the next and step commands are used to execute the program line by line. Sometimes this can be a painful endeavor.
For example, suppose GDB reached a breakpoint within a function. You've
inspected a few variables and have gathered all the information you had intended to get. At this point, you're not interested in single-stepping through
the remainder of the function. You'd like to return back to the calling function where GDB was before you stepped into the called function. However,
setting an extraneous breakpoint and using continue seems wasteful if all
you want to do is skip the remainder of the function. That's where finish
comes in.

The finish command (abbreviated fin) instructs GDB to resume execution until just after the current stack frame finishes. In English, this means
that if you're in a function other than main(), the finish command will cause
GDB to resume execution until just after the function returns. Figure 2-11
illustrates the use of finish.

Although you could type next 3 instead of finish, it is easier to type the
latter, which involves counting lines (anything more than a half dozen would
be a needless nuisance).

It may not look like finish executes each line of code as it takes you to
the bottom of the function, but it does. GDB executes each line without
pausing[6] except to show the program's output.

Another common use of finish is when you've accidentally stepped into
a function that you meant to step over (in other words, you used step when

---

[6] If there are any intervening breakpoints, finish *will* pause at them.

```
void swapper(int *a, int *b)
{
    int c = *a;
    *a = *b;
    *b = c;
    printf("swapped!\n");                    finish
}
```

Figure 2-11: `finish` *resumes execution until the current function returns.*

you meant to use `next`). In this case, using `finish` places you right back where you would've been had you used `next`.

If you're within a recursive function, `finish` will only take you one level up in the recursion. This is because each call is considered a function call in its own right, since each one has its own stack frame. If you want to get completely out of a recursive function when the recursive level is high, a temporary breakpoint along with `continue`, or using the `until` command, is more appropriate. We will discuss `until` next.

2.9.1.4   Resuming Program Execution with until

Recall that the `finish` command completes execution of the current function without further pauses within the function (except at any intervening breakpoints). Similarly, the `until` command (abbreviated simply as `u`) is typically used to complete an executing loop, without further pauses within the loop, except at any intervening breakpoints within the loop. Consider the following code snippet.

...previous code...

```
int i = 9999;
while (i--) {
    printf("i is %d\n", i);
    ... lots of code ...
}
```

...future code...

Suppose GDB is stopped at a breakpoint at the `while` statement, you've inspected a few variables, and now you'd like to leave the loop to debug "future code."

The problem is that `i` is so large, it would take forever to use `next` to complete the loop. You can't use `finish` because that command will pass right over "future code" and take us out of the function. You *could* set a temporary breakpoint at the future code and use `continue`; however, this is exactly the situation that `until` was meant to address.

Using until will execute the rest of the loop, leaving GDB paused at the first line of code following the loop. Figure 2-12 shows an illustration of what using until will do:

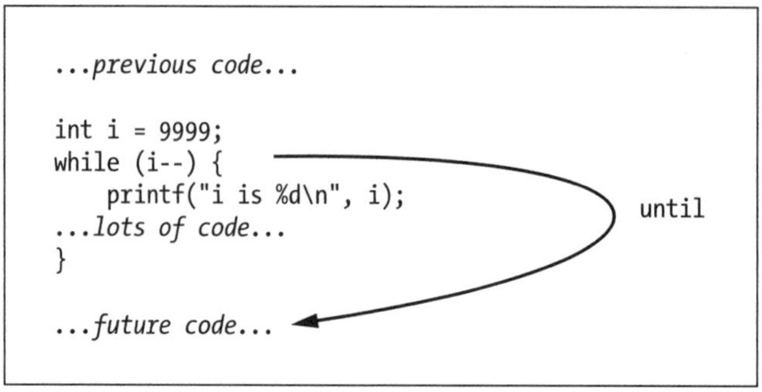

Figure 2-12: until *gets us to the next highest line of source code.*

Of course if GDB encounters a breakpoint before leaving the loop, it will still pause there: If there were a breakpoint at the printf() statement in Figure 2-12, you'd certainly want to disable it.

The GDB User's Guide gives the official definition of until as:

> Execute until the program reaches a source line greater than the current [one].

However, the documentation also warns that this can be a little counter-intuitive. To demonstrate why, consider the following program:

```
#include <stdio.h>

int main(void)
{
    int i;

    for (i=0; i<10; ++i)
        printf("hello world!");

    return 0;
}
```

Listing 2-2: until-anomaly.c

We'll set a breakpoint at the entry of main(), run the program, and use until to reach the return statement.

```
$ gdb until-anomaly
Using host libthread_db library "/lib/tls/libthread_db.so.1".
(gdb) break main
```

```
Breakpoint 1 at 0x80483b4: file until-anomaly.c, line 7.
(gdb) run
Starting program: until-anomaly

Breakpoint 1, main () at until-anomaly.c:7
7           for (i=0; i<10; ++i)
(gdb) until
8               printf("hello world!");
(gdb) until
7           for (i=0; i<10; ++i)
(gdb) until
10          return 0;
(gdb)
```

Whoa! Using until, GDB went from line 7 to line 8 and then back to line 7. Surely this doesn't mean that source line 7 is greater than source line 8? Actually, it does. Perhaps you can guess the answer by now, since it seems to be a common theme. GDB ultimately works with machine instructions. Although the for construct is written with the loop test at the top of the body, GCC compiled the program with the conditional at the *bottom* of the loop body. Since the conditional is associated with line 7 of the source code, it appears that GDB went backwards in the source code. In fact, what until really does is execute until it reaches a machine instruction that has a higher memory address than the current one, rather than until it reaches a larger line number in the source code.

In practice, this sort of thing may not arise too often, but it's nice to understand it when it does occur. Additionally, by looking at some of GDB's odd behavior, you can glean information about how compilers turn source code into machine instructions—not a bad bit of knowledge to have.

If you are curious and you know the assembly language of your machine, you can take a quick look at the machine code, using GDB's disassemble command, followed by p/x $pc to print out the current location.[7] This will show you what until will do. But it's just a quirk, and in practical terms, it is not an issue. If you are at the end of a loop and issuing the until command causes a jump back to the top of the loop, simply issue until a second time, and you will leave the loop as desired.

The until command can also take an argument of a location within your source code. In fact, it takes the same arguments as the break command that was discussed in Section 2.4.1. Returning to Listing 2-1, if GDB triggered a breakpoint on the entry of main(), these are all equivalent ways of conveniently executing the program until the the entry to swap():

- until 17

- until swap

---

[7] You can also view the machine code by using the -S option of GCC. This will produce an assembly language file with suffix *.s*, showing the code that was produced by the compiler. Note that this produces the assembly language file only, not an executable.

- until `swapflaw.c:17`

- until `swapflaw.c:swap`

2.9.2   In DDD

We'll start this section by discussing the various ways you can resume execution once DDD is paused at a breakpoint.

2.9.2.1   Standard Operations

DDD has buttons for both next and step in the Command Tool. In addition, you can perform a step and next with the F5 and F6 function keys, respectively.

If you want to use next or step with an argument in DDD, that is, accomplish what you would do in GDB via

```
(gdb) next 3
```

you'll need to use GDB itself in DDD's Console Window.

DDD has a button for continue in the Command Tool, but again, if you want to execute continue with an argument, use the GDB Console. You can left-click the Source Window to bring up a "continue until here" option, which really sets a temporary breakpoint (see Section 2.4.1) at that line of source code. More accurately, "continue until here" means "continue until this point, but also stop at any intervening breakpoints."

In GDB, one might achieve the same effect as finish via next with a numerical argument, so that finish would be only marginally more convenient. But in DDD, using finish is a clear win, requiring a single mouse click in the Command Tool.

If you're using DDD, you can perform an until by using the button labeled Until on the Command Tool, or left-click the Program | Until menu bar, or use the keyboard shortcut F7. Of all those options, you're bound to find one of them convenient! As with many other GDB commands, if you want to use until with an argument, you'll need to give them directly to GDB in the DDD Console Window.

2.9.2.2   Undo/Redo

As noted in Section 2.7.6, DDD has an invaluable Undo/Redo feature. In that section, we showed how to undo an accidental breakpoint deletion. It can also be used on actions such as Run, Next, Step, and so on.

Consider, for example, the situation depicted in Figure 2-13. We had reached the breakpoint at the call to swap() and had intended to do a Step operation, but accidentally clicked Next. But by clicking Undo, you can roll back time, as shown in Figure 2-14. DDD reminds you that you have undone something by displaying its current-line cursor as an outline, instead of the solid green it normally uses.

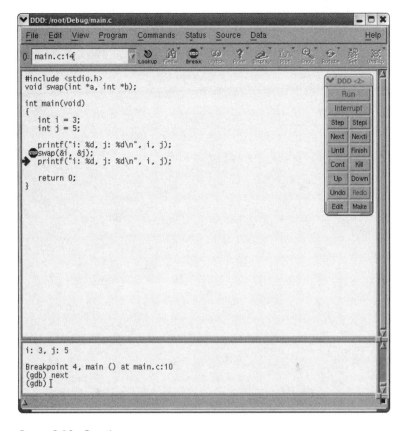

Figure 2-13: Oops!

2.9.3   In Eclipse

Eclipse's analogs of step and next are the Step Into and Step Over icons. The
Step Into icon is visible in the Debug view (upper left) in Figure 2-15; the
mouse pointer has temporarily caused the icon label to appear. The Step
Over icon is just to the right of it. Note that the next statement you will execute will be the call to get_args(), so clicking Step Into would result in the
next pause of execution occurring at the first statement within that function,
while selecting Step Over would mean the next pause would be at the call to
process_data().

Eclipse has a Step Return icon (next to Step Over) that performs finish.
It has nothing exactly corresponding to until. Its Run to Line (invoked by
clicking the target line and then right-clicking in the source code window)
will typically accomplish what you would want with until.

2.10   Conditional Breakpoints

As long as a breakpoint is enabled, the debugger always stops at that breakpoint. However, sometimes it's useful to tell the debugger to stop at a break-

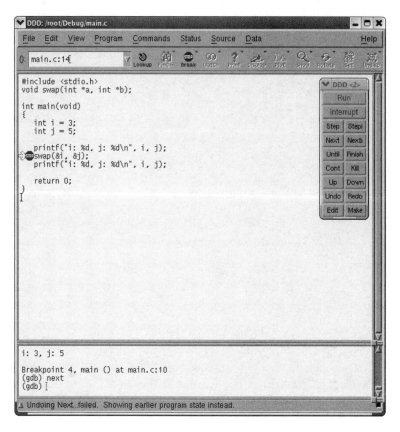

Figure 2-14: Putting the toothpaste back into the tube

point only if some condition is met, like the when a variable has a particularly interesting value.

This is similar to how watchpoints work, but with an important distinction. If you have a suspicion about where a variable is getting a bogus value, a conditional breakpoint is preferable to a watchpoint. The watchpoint will break whenever that variable changes value. The conditional breakpoint will only break at the suspected problem code, and then, only when the variable takes on the bogus value. In this sense, watchpoints are good when you haven't a clue where the variable is receiving its bogus value. This is particularly useful for global variables or local variables that are continually passed between functions. But in most other cases, a well placed conditional breakpoint is more useful and convenient.

2.10.1 GDB

The syntax for setting a conditional breakpoint is:

```
break break-args if (condition)
```

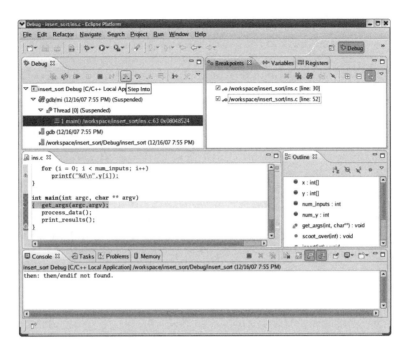

Figure 2-15: Step Into icon in Eclipse

where *break-args* is any of the arguments you can pass to break to specify a location for a breakpoint, as discussed in Section 2.4.1, and *condition* is a Boolean expression as defined in Section 2.12.2. The parentheses around *condition* are optional. They may make some C programmers feel more at home, but on the other hand, you might prefer the uncluttered look.

For example, here's how you would break at main() if the user had typed some command line arguments to the program:[8]

```
break main if argc > 1
```

Conditional breaking is *extremely* useful, particularly in loop constructs in which something bad happens at a particular value of the index variable. Consider the following code snippet:

```
for (i=0; i<=75000; ++i) {
    retval = process(i);
    do_something(retval);
}
```

---

[8] Providing you had declared argc and argv as arguments to main(). (Of course, if you declared them with different names, say ac and av, use those.) By the way, note that a program always receives at least one argument—the name of the program itself, which is pointed to by argv[0], which we are not counting as a "user argument" here.

Suppose you know your program goes haywire when i is 70,000. You want to break at the top of the loop, but you don't want to do next through 69,999 iterations. This is where conditional breaking really shines. You can set a breakpoint at the top of the loop, but only when i equals 70,000 with the following:

```
break if (i == 70000)
```

Of course, you could achieve the same effect by typing, say, continue 69999, but that would be less convenient.

Conditional breaking is also *extremely* flexible. You can do much more than just test a variable for equality or inequality. What kinds of things can you use in a *condition*? Pretty much any expression you can use in a valid C conditional statement. Whatever you use needs to have a Boolean value, that is, true (nonzero) or false (zero). This includes:

- Equality, logical, and inequality operators (<, <=, ==, !=, >, >=, &&, ||, etc.); e.g.:

```
break 180 if string==NULL && i < 0
```

- Bitwise and shift operators (&, |, ^, >>, <<, etc.); e.g.:

```
break test.c:34 if (x & y) == 1
```

- Arithmetic operators (+, -, x, /, %); e.g.:

```
break myfunc if i % (j + 3) != 0
```

- Your own functions, as long as they're linked into the program; .e.g:

```
break test.c:myfunc if ! check_variable_sanity(i)
```

- Library functions, as long as the library is linked into your code; e.g.:

```
break 44 if strlen(mystring) == 0
```

Order of precedence rules are in effect, so you may need to use parentheses around constructs like (x & y) == 0.

Also, if you use a library function in a GDB expression, and the library was not compiled with debugging symbols (which is almost certainly the case), the only return values you can use in your breakpoint conditions are those of type int. In other words, without debugging information, GDB assumes the return value of a function is an int. When this assumption isn't correct, the function's return value will be misinterpreted.

```
(gdb) print cos(0.0)
$1 = 14368
```

Unfortunately, typecasting doesn't help, either:

```
(gdb) print (double) cos(0.0)
$2 = 14336
```

In case your trigonometry is rusty, the cosine of 0 is 1.

Using Non-int Returning Functions

Actually, there is a way to use functions that don't return an int in GDB expressions, but it's fairly arcane. The trick is to define a GDB convenience variable with the proper datatype that points to the function.

```
(gdb) set $p = (double (*) (double)) cos
(gdb) ptype $p
type = double (*)()
(gdb) p cos(3.14159265)
$2 = 14368
(gdb) p $p(3.14159265)
$4 = -1
```

In case your trigonometry is *still* rusty, 3.14159265 is approximately π and the cosine of π is -1.

It is possible to set conditions on normal breakpoints to turn them into conditional breakpoints. For example, if you have set breakpoint 3 as unconditional but now wish to add the condition i == 3, simply type

```
(gdb) cond 3 i == 3
```

If you later want to remove the condition but keep the breakpoint, simply type

```
(gdb) cond 3
```

2.10.2 DDD

You can set conditional breakpoints with DDD using GDB semantics with the Console Window. Or, use DDD as follows. Set a normal (i.e., unconditional) breakpoint at the location in your code where you want the conditional breakpoint to be. Right click and hold the red stop sign to bring up a menu and choose **Properties**. A pop-up window will appear with a text entry box labelled Condition. Type the *condition* in that box, click Apply, and then click Close. The breakpoint is now a conditional breakpoint.

This is illustrated in Figure 2-16. We see the condition j == 0 on break-point 4. By the way, the stop sign on that line will now contain a question mark, to remind us that it is a conditional break.

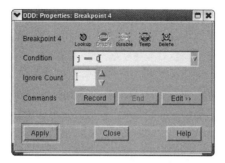

Figure 2-16: Imposing a condition on a breakpoint in DDD

2.10.3 Eclipse

To make a breakpoint conditional, right-click the breakpoint symbol for that line, select **Breakpoint Properties...** | **Common**, and fill in the condition in the dialog box. The dialog box is depicted in Figure 2-17.

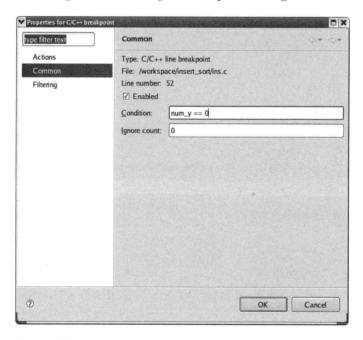

Figure 2-17: Imposing a condition on a breakpoint in Eclipse

2.11 Breakpoint Command Lists

After GDB hits a breakpoint, you'll almost always inspect a variable. If the same breakpoint gets hit repeatedly (as with a breakpoint inside a loop), you'll inspect the same variable repeatedly. Wouldn't it be nice to automate the procedure by telling GDB to automatically perform a set of commands each time it reaches a breakpoint?

In fact, you can do just this with "breakpoint command lists." We'll use GDB's printf command to illustrate command lists. You haven't been formally introduced to it yet, but printf basically works the same way in GDB as it does in C, but the parentheses are optional.

You set command lists using the commands command:

```
commands breakpoint-number
...
commands
...
end
```

where *breakpoint-number* is the identifier for the breakpoint you want to add the commands to, and *commands* is a newline-separated list of any valid GDB commands. You enter the commands one by one, and then type end to signify that you're done entering commands. Thereafter, whenever GDB breaks at this breakpoint, it'll execute whatever commands you gave it. Let's take a look at an example. Consider the following program:

```c
#include <stdio.h>
int fibonacci(int n);

int main(void)
{
        printf("Fibonacci(3) is %d.\n", fibonacci(3));

        return 0;
}

int fibonacci(int n)
{
        if ( n <= 0 || n == 1 )
                return 1;
        else
                return fibonacci(n-1) + fibonacci(n-2);
}
```

Listing 2-3: fibonacci.c

We'd like to see what values are passed to fibonacci() and in what order. However, you don't want to stick printf() statements in and recompile the code. First of all, that would be gauche in a book on debugging, wouldn't it? But more importantly, it would take time to insert code and recompile/link, and to later remove that code and recompile/link after you fix this particular bug, especially if your program is large. Moreover, it would clutter up your code with statements not related to the code, thus making it harder to read during the debugging process.

You could step through the code and print n with each invocation of fibonacci(), but command lists are better, because they alleviate the need to repeatedly type the print command. Let's see.

First, set a breakpoint at the top of fibonacci(). This breakpoint will be assigned identifier 1, since it's the first breakpoint you've set. Then set a command on breakpoint 1 to print the variable n.

```
$ gdb fibonacci
(gdb) break fibonacci
Breakpoint 1 at 0x80483e0: file fibonacci.c, line 13.
(gdb) commands 1
Type commands for when breakpoint 1 is hit, one per line.
End with a line saying just "end".
>printf "fibonacci was passed %d.\n", n
>end
(gdb)
```

Now run the program and see what happens.

```
(gdb) run
Starting program: fibonacci

Breakpoint 1, fibonacci (n=3) at fibonacci.c:13
13              if ( n <= 0  ||  n == 1 )
fibonacci was passed 3.
(gdb) continue
Continuing.

Breakpoint 1, fibonacci (n=2) at fibonacci.c:13
13              if ( n <= 0  ||  n == 1 )
fibonacci was passed 2.
(gdb) continue
Continuing.

Breakpoint 1, fibonacci (n=1) at fibonacci.c:13
13              if ( n <= 0  ||  n == 1 )
fibonacci was passed 1.
(gdb) continue
Continuing.

Breakpoint 1, fibonacci (n=0) at fibonacci.c:13
13              if ( n <= 0  ||  n == 1 )
```

```
fibonacci was passed 0.
(gdb) continue
Continuing.

Breakpoint 1, fibonacci (n=1) at fibonacci.c:13
13              if ( n <= 0  ||  n == 1 )
fibonacci was passed 1.
(gdb) continue
Continuing.
Fibonacci(3) is 3.

Program exited normally.
(gdb)
```

Well, that's pretty much what we expected, but the output is too verbose. After all, we already know where the breakpoint is. Fortunately, you can make GDB more quiet about triggering breakpoints using the silent command, which needs to be the first item in the command list. Let's take a look at silent in action. Note how we're redefining the command list by placing a new command list "over" the one we previously set:

```
(gdb) commands 1
Type commands for when breakpoint 1 is hit, one per line.
End with a line saying just "end".
>silent
>printf "fibonacci was passed %d.\n", n
>end
(gdb)
```

And here's the output:

```
(gdb) run
Starting program: fibonacci
fibonacci was passed 3.
(gdb) continue
Continuing.
fibonacci was passed 2.
(gdb) continue
Continuing.
fibonacci was passed 1.
(gdb) continue
Continuing.
fibonacci was passed 0.
(gdb) continue
Continuing.
fibonacci was passed 1.
(gdb) continue
Continuing.
```

```
Fibonacci(3) is 3.

Program exited normally.
(gdb)
```

Nice. One last feature to demonstrate: If the last command in a commands list is continue, GDB will automatically continue executing the program after it completes the commands in the commands list:

```
(gdb) command 1
Type commands for when breakpoint 1 is hit, one per line.
End with a line saying just "end".
>silent
>printf "fibonacci was passed %d.\n", n
>continue
>end
(gdb) run
Starting program: fibonacci
fibonacci was passed 3.
fibonacci was passed 2.
fibonacci was passed 1.
fibonacci was passed 0.
fibonacci was passed 1.
Fibonacci(3) is 3.

Program exited normally.
(gdb)
```

You might want to do this type of thing in other programs, or at other
lines of this program, so let's make a macro out of it, using GDB's define
command.

First, let's define the macro, which we'll name print_and_go:

```
(gdb) define print_and_go
Redefine command "print_and_go"? (y or n) y
Type commands for definition of "print_and_go".
End with a line saying just "end".
>printf $arg0, $arg1
>continue
>end
```

To use it as above, you would type:

```
(gdb) commands 1
Type commands for when breakpoint 1 is hit, one per line.
End with a line saying just "end".
>silent
```

```
>print_and_go "fibonacci() was passed %d\n" n
>end
```

Note that there is no comma between arguments of print_and_go. You would then get the same output as before when you run the program, but the point is that now you can use it generally, anywhere in the code. Moreover, you can put it in your *.gdbinit* file for use in other programs. By the way, up to ten arguments are allowed, though there are just two in the example here.

You can get a list of all the macros by typing show user.

Command lists are very useful, but you can also combine them with conditional breaking, and that's *powerful*. With this kind of conditional input/output, you might even be tempted to throw C away and simply use GDB as your programming language of choice. Just kidding, of course.

Commands and Expressions

Actually, any valid GDB expression as outlined in Section 2.12.2 can go into a commands list. You can use library functions or even your own functions, as long as they're linked into the executable, and you can use their return value as long as they return an int. For instance:

```
(gdb) command 2
Type commands for when breakpoint 2 is hit, one per line.
End with a line saying just "end".
>silent
>printf "string has a length of %d\n", strlen(string)
>end
```

Command lists in DDD are similar to conditional breakpoints in DDD. First, set a breakpoint. Right-click the red stop sign and choose **Properties**. A pop-up window will appear. A large subwindow will be on the right (if you don't see the large subwindow, left-click the Edit button, which toggles the visibility of the commands window). You can type your commands right into this window. There's also a Record button. If you right-click this button, you can enter your commands into the GDB Console.

Eclipse does not appear to have a command-list feature.

2.12   Watchpoints

A *watchpoint* is a special kind of breakpoint which, like a normal breakpoint, is an instruction that tells GDB to pause execution of your program. The difference is that watchpoints don't "live" at a line of source code. Instead, a watchpoint is an instruction that tells GDB to pause execution whenever an expression changes value.[9] That expression can be quite simple, like the name of a variable:

```
(gdb) watch i
```

which will make GDB pause whenever i changes value. The expression can also be quite complex:

```
(gdb) watch (i | j > 12) && i > 24 && strlen(name) > 6
```

You can think of a watchpoint as being "attached" to an expression; when the value of that expression changes, GDB will pause the program's execution.

Although watchpoints and breakpoints are managed the same way, there is an important difference between them. A breakpoint is associated with a location within your source code. Since your code doesn't change, there is no risk of a line of code "going out of scope." Because C has rigid scoping rules, you can only watch a variable that exists and is in scope. Once the variable no longer exists in any frame of the call stack (when the function containing a local variable returns), GDB automatically deletes the watchpoint.

For example, in Section 2.5, we looked at a program named swap. In this program, a local variable c was used for temporary storage. You would not be able to set a watch on c until GDB reached line 3 of *swapper.c*, where c is defined. Additionally, if you did set a watch on c, the watch would be automatically deleted once GDB returned from swapper() since c would no longer be in existence.

Having GDB break any time a variable changes can be something of a nuisance in tightly wrapped loops or repetitive code. Although watchpoints sound great, well-placed breakpoints may be far more useful. However, watchpoints are invaluable if one of your variables changes, especially a global variable, and you have no idea where or how it changed. If you're dealing with threaded code, watchpoints have limited usefulness; GDB is only capable of watching a variable within a single thread. You can read more about this in Chapter 5.

2.12.1 Setting Watchpoints

When the variable *var* exists and is within scope, you can set a watchpoint on it by using the command

```
watch   var
```

which will cause GDB to break whenever the value for the variable *var* changes. This is how many people think of watchpoints, because it's simple and convenient; however, there's a bit more to the story. What GDB really does is break if the *memory location* for *var* changes value. Normally, it doesn't matter

---

[9] Expressions will be discussed more fully in Section 2.12.2.

Hardware Watchpoints?

You may see a message about a "hardware" watchpoint when you set a watchpoint:

```
(gdb) watch i
Hardware watchpoint 2: i
```

or list your breakpoints:

```
(gdb) info breakpoints
Num Type           Disp Enb Address    What
2   hw watchpoint  keep y              i
```

Clearly, 2 refers to the watchpoint identifier, and i is the variable being watched, but what is this "hardware" stuff about?

Many platforms have dedicated hardware that can be used to implement a watchpoint. GDB will try to use the hardware, if it's available, because implementing *anything* with hardware is fast.

It's possible that GDB cannot set hardware watchpoints (the platform may not have the necessary hardware, or the hardware may be busy with something else). If so, GDB will try to implement the watchpoint using VM techniques, which is also fast.

If neither technique is available, GDB will implement the watchpoint itself, via software, which can be very, very slow.

Your CPU can implement only a limited number of hardware-assisted breaks, which includes watchpoints and hardware-assisted breakpoints. This number is architecture dependent, but if you exceed this limit, GDB will print the message:

```
Stopped; cannot insert breakpoints.
You may have requested too many hardware breakpoints and watchpoints.
```

If you see this message, you should delete or disable some of your watchpoints or hardware-assisted breakpoints.

whether you think of a watchpoint as watching the variable or the address of the variable, but it may be important in special cases, like when dealing with pointers to pointers.

Let's look at one example scenario in which watchpoints would be very useful. Suppose you have two int variables, x and y, and somewhere in the code you perform p = &y when you meant to do p = &x. This could result in y mysteriously changing value somewhere in the code. The actual location of the resulting bug may be well hidden, so a breakpoint may not be very useful. However, by setting a watchpoint, you could instantly know when and where y changes value.

There's even more to the story. You aren't limited to watching a variable. In fact, you can watch an *expression* involving variables. Whenever the expression changes value, GDB will break. As an example, consider the following code:

```
1   #include <stdio.h>
2   int i = 0;
3
4   int main(void)
5   {
6       i = 3;
7       printf("i is %d.\n", i);
8
9       i = 5;
10      printf("i is %d.\n", i);
11
12      return 0;
13  }
```

We'd like to know whenever i becomes greater than 4. So let's put a breakpoint at the entry of main() in order get i in scope, and set a watchpoint to tell you when i becomes larger than 4. You can't set a watchpoint on i because, before the program runs, i doesn't exist. So you have to set a breakpoint at main() first, and *then* set a watchpoint on i:

```
(gdb) break main
Breakpoint 1 at 0x80483b4: file test2.c, line 6.
(gdb) run
Starting program: test2

Breakpoint 1, main () at test2.c:6
```

Now that i is in scope, set the watchpoint and tell GDB to continue executing the program. We fully expect that i > 4 becomes true at line 9.

```
1  (gdb) watch i > 4
2  Hardware watchpoint 2: i > 4
3  (gdb) continue
4  Continuing.
5  Hardware watchpoint 2: i > 4
6
7  Old value = 0
8  New value = 1
9  main () at test2.c:10
```

Sure enough, GDB is paused between lines 9 and 10, where the expression i > 4 changed value from 0 (not true) to 1 (true).

You can use this method to set watchpoints with DDD in the Console Window; however, you might find it more convenient to use the GUI interface. In the Source Window, locate the variable you want to set a watchpoint on. It doesn't need to be the first instance of the variable; you can use any mention of the variable within the source code. Left-click the variable to highlight it, then left-click the watchpoint symbol in the icon Menu Bar. There won't be an indication that a watchpoint is set like the red stop sign for breakpoints. To see which watchpoints you've set, you'll have to actually list all your breakpoints, which we covered in Section 2.3.2.

In Eclipse, you can set a watchpoint by right-clicking in the source window, selecting Add a Watch Expression, and then filling in the desired expression in the dialog box.

2.12.2 Expressions

We saw an example of using an *expression* with GDB's watch command. It turns out that there are quite a few GDB commands, like print, that also accept *expression* arguments. Therefore, we should probably mention a bit more about them.

An expression in GDB can contain many things:

- GDB convenience variables

- Any in-scope variable from your program, like i from the previous example

- Any kind of string, numerical, or character constant

- Pre-processor macros, if the program was compiled to include pre-preprocessor debugging information[10]

- The conditionals, function calls, casts, and operators defined by the language you're using

---

[10] As of this writing, the official GNU GDB User's Manual states that pre-processor macros cannot be used in expressions; however, this is not true. If you compile the program with GCC's -g3 option, pre-processor macros can be used in expressions.

So, if you were debugging a Fortran-77 program and wanted to know when the variable i became larger than 4, instead of using watch i > 4 as you did in the last section, you would use watch i .GT. 4.

You often see tutorials and documentation that use C syntax for GDB expressions, but that's due to the ubiquitous nature of C and C++; if you use a language other than C, GDB expressions are built from elements of that language.

3

INSPECTING AND SETTING VARIABLES

You found in Chapter 1 that in GDB you can print the value of a variable using the print command and that this can be done in DDD and Eclipse by moving the mouse pointer to an instance of the variable anywhere in the source code. But both GDB and the GUIs also offer much more powerful ways to inspect variables and data structures, as we will see in this chapter.

3.1 Our Main Example Code

Following is a straightforward (though not necessarily efficient, modular, etc.) implementation of a binary tree:

```
// bintree.c:  routines to do insert and sorted print of a binary tree

#include <stdio.h>
#include <stdlib.h>
```

```
struct node {
    int val;            // stored value
    struct node *left;   // ptr to smaller child
    struct node *right;  // ptr to larger child
};

typedef struct node *nsp;

nsp root;

nsp makenode(int x)
{
    nsp tmp;

    tmp = (nsp) malloc(sizeof(struct node));
    tmp->val = x;
    tmp->left = tmp->right = 0;
    return tmp;
}

void insert(nsp *btp, int x)
{
    nsp tmp = *btp;

    if (*btp == 0) {
        *btp = makenode(x);
        return;
    }

    while (1)
    {
        if (x < tmp->val) {

            if (tmp->left != 0) {
                tmp = tmp->left;
            } else {
                tmp->left = makenode(x);
                break;
            }

        } else {

            if (tmp->right != 0) {
                tmp = tmp->right;
            } else {
                tmp->right = makenode(x);
                break;
```

```
            }

        }
      }
}

void printtree(nsp bt)
{
    if (bt == 0) return;
    printtree(bt->left);
    printf("%d\n",bt->val);
    printtree(bt->right);
}


int main(int argc, char *argv[])
{   int i;

    root = 0;
    for (i = 1; i < argc; i++)
        insert(&root, atoi(argv[i]));
    printtree(root);
}
```

At each node, all elements of the left subtree are less than the value in the given node, and all elements of the right subtree are greater than or equal to the one in the given node. The function insert() creates a new node and places it in the proper position in the tree. The function printtree() displays the elements of any subtree in ascending numerical order, while main() runs a test, printing out the entire sorted array.[1]

For the debugging examples here, suppose that you had accidentally coded the second call to makenode() in insert() as

```
tmp->left = makenode(x);
```

instead of

```
tmp->right = makenode(x);
```

If you run this buggy code, something immediately goes wrong:

```
$ bintree 12 8 5 19 16
16
12
```

---

[1] By the way, note the typedef in line 12, nsp. This stands for *node struct pointer*, but our publisher thinks it's *No Starch Press*.

Let's explore how the various inspection commands in the debugging tools can help expedite finding the bug.

3.2 Advanced Inspection and Setting of Variables

Our tree example here has greater complexity, and thus, more sophisticated methods are needed. We'll take a look at some here.

3.2.1 Inspection in GDB

In earlier chapters you have used GDB's basic print command. How might you use it here? Well, the main work is obviously done in insert(), so that would be a good place to start. While running GDB within the while loop in that function, you could issue a set of three GDB commands each time you hit a breakpoint:

```
(gdb) p tmp->val
$1 = 12
(gdb) p tmp->left
$2 = (struct node *) 0x8049698
(gdb) p tmp->right
$3 = (struct node *) 0x0
```

(Recall from Chapter 1 that the output from GDB is labeled $1, $2, and so on, with these quantities collectively called the *value history*. We will discuss them further in Section 3.4.1.)

Here you would find that the node currently pointed to by tmp contains 12, with a nonzero left pointer but a zero right pointer. Of course, the actual value of the left pointer, that is, the actual memory address, is probably not of direct interest here, but the fact that a pointer is nonzero or zero is important. The point is that you see that there currently is a left subtree below 12 but no right subtree.

First improvement: Print the struct in its entirety
It would be quite laborious to keep typing those three print commands each time we reached a breakpoint. Here is how we could do the same thing with just one print command:

```
(gdb) p *tmp
$4 = {val = 12, left = 0x8049698, right = 0x0}
```

Since tmp points to the struct, *tmp then is the struct itself, and thus GDB shows us the entire contents.

Second improvement: Use the GDB display command
Typing p *tmp above saves time and effort. Each time you hit a breakpoint, you would need to type only one GDB command, not three. But if you know you will type this each time you hit a breakpoint, you can save even more time and effort using GDB's display command, abbrevi-

ated disp. This command tells GDB to automatically print the specified item each time there is a pause in execution (due to a breakpoint, the next or step commands, and so on):

```
(gdb) disp *tmp
1: *tmp = {val = 12, left = 0x8049698, right = 0x0}
(gdb) c
Continuing.

Breakpoint 1, insert (btp=0x804967c, x=5) at bintree.c:37
37              if (x < tmp->val)  {
1: *tmp = {val = 8, left = 0x0, right = 0x0}
```

As seen here, GDB automatically printed *tmp after hitting the break-point, since you had issued the display command.

Of course, a variable in the display list will only be displayed during times in which it is in scope.

Third improvement: Use the GDB commands command

Suppose you wish to look at the values in the child nodes when you are at a given node. Recalling GDB's commands command from Chapter 1, you could do something like this:

```
(gdb) b 37
Breakpoint 1 at 0x8048403: file bintree.c, line 37.
(gdb) commands 1
Type commands for when breakpoint 1 is hit, one per line.
End with a line saying just "end".
>p tmp->val
>if (tmp->left != 0)
 >p tmp->left->val
 >else
 >printf "%s\n", "none"
 >end
>if (tmp->right != 0)
 >p tmp->right->val
 >else
 >printf "%s\n", "none"
 >end
>end
```

Note in this example that GDB's print command has a more powerful cousin, printf(), with formatting similar to that of its C-language namesake.

Here is a sampling of the resulting GDB session:

```
Breakpoint 1, insert (btp=0x804967c, x=8) at bintree.c:37
37              if (x < tmp->val)
$7 = 12
```

```
none
none
(gdb) c
Continuing.

Breakpoint 1, insert (btp=0x804967c, x=5) at bintree.c:37
37              if (x < tmp->val)
$6 = 12
$7 = 8
none
(gdb) c
Continuing.

Breakpoint 1, insert (btp=0x804967c, x=5) at bintree.c:37
37              if (x < tmp->val)
$8 = 8
none
none
```

Of course, you could make the output fancier with labels, and so on.

Fourth improvement: Use the GDB call command

A common approach in debugging is to isolate the first data item at which trouble appears. In the context here, that could be accomplished by printing out the entire tree each time you finish a call to insert(). Since you have a function in your source file to do this anyway—printtree()— you could simply add a call to this function right after your call to insert() in the source code:

```
for (i = 1; i < argc; i++)  {
   insert(&root,atoi(argv[i]));
   printtree(root);
}
```

However, this would be undesirable from various points of view. It would mean, for instance, that you would have to take time to edit your source file and recompile it. The former would be distracting and the latter could take some time if you had a large program. This, after all, is what you are trying to get away from by using a debugger.

Instead, it would be nice to do the same thing from within GDB. You can do this via GDB's call command. For example, you could set a breakpoint at line 57, the end of insert(), and then do the following:

```
(gdb) commands 2
Type commands for when breakpoint 1 is hit, one per line.
End with a line saying just "end".
>printf "*********** current tree ***********"
>call printtree(root)
>end
```

A sampling of the resulting GDB session is:

```
Breakpoint 2, insert (btp=0x8049688, x=12) at bintree.c:57
57 }
******** current tree ********
12
(gdb) c
Continuing.

Breakpoint 2, insert (btp=0x8049688, x=8) at bintree.c:57
57 }
********** current tree **********
8
12
(gdb) c
Continuing.

Breakpoint 2, insert (btp=0x8049688, x=5) at bintree.c:57
57 }
********** current tree **********
5
8
12
(gdb) c
Continuing.

Breakpoint 2, insert (btp=0x8049688, x=19) at bintree.c:57
57 }
********** current tree **********
19
12
```

Note that this shows that the first data item to cause trouble was the number 19. This information will allow you to zero in on the bug very quickly. You would re-run the program with the same data, setting a breakpoint at the beginning of insert() but with the condition x == 19, and then investigate what happens there.

The command set for a given breakpoint can be modified dynamically, or simply canceled by redefining an empty set:

```
(gdb) commands 1
Type commands for when breakpoint 1 is hit, one per line.
End with a line saying just "end".
>end
```

3.2.2 Inspection in DDD

As you know by now, you can invoke any GDB command from within DDD in the DDD Console Window. But one of the real advantages of DDD is that many of the GDB commands can be run more conveniently in DDD, and in some cases, DDD is capable of powerful operations not offered by GDB, such as the displaying of linked data structures described below.

As mentioned in earlier chapters, checking the value of a variable in DDD is highly convenient: Simply move the mouse pointer to any instance of the variable in the Source Code Window. But there are other goodies well worth using as well, especially for programs using linked data structures. We will illustrate that by using the same binary tree example from earlier in this chapter.

Recall the illustration of GDB's `display` command:

```
(gdb) disp *tmp
```

Here the contents of the struct pointed to by `tmp` are printed automatically each time you hit a breakpoint or otherwise cause the execution of your program to pause. Since `tmp` was a pointer to the current node in the tree, this automatic printing was helpful to monitoring your progress in traversing the tree.

Somewhat analogous is the Display command in DDD. If you right-click any instance of a variable, say `root` in the example here, in the Source Code Window, a menu pops up, as seen in Figure 3-1. As you can see, you have a number of choices here with regard to viewing `root`. The choices `Print root` and `Print *root` work exactly like their GDB counterparts, and in fact their output appears in DDD's Console (where GDB commands are echoed/entered). But for the case at hand here, the most interesting choice is `Display *root`. The result of selecting that choice, after hitting the breakpoint at line 48 of the source code, is shown in Figure 3-2.

A new DDD window has appeared—the Data Window, with the node corresponding to `root`. So far, this is nothing more than just a graphical analog to GDB's `display` command. But what is really nice here is that you can follow the tree links! To follow the left branch of the tree, for instance, right-click the `left` field of the displayed root node. (You wouldn't do so on the `right` node at this time, since the link is 0.) Then select the `Display *()` choice in the pop-up menu, and now DDD is as seen in Figure 3-3. So, DDD is presenting you with a drawing of the tree (or this portion of it) just as you would write yourself on a blackboard—very cool!

The display of the contents of an existing node will automatically update whenever the node contents change. Each time a link changes from zero to nonzero, you can right-click it to display the new node.

Clearly, the Data Window can become cluttered quite quickly. You can expand the window by clicking and dragging the little square at the lower right of that window, but a better approach would be to anticipate this situation before you even start DDD. If you invoke DDD with the `separate` command-line option

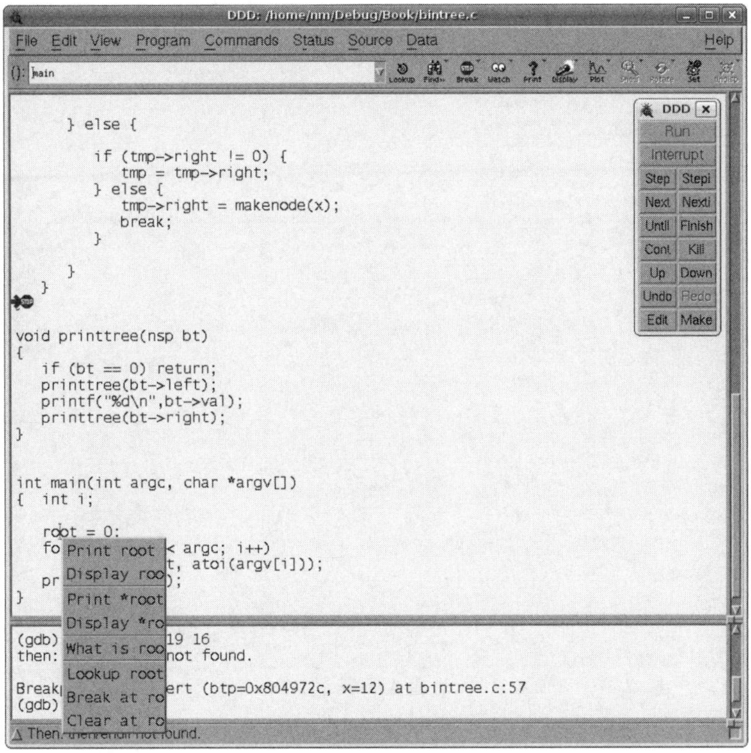

```
} else {

    if (tmp->right != 0) {
        tmp = tmp->right;
    } else {
        tmp->right = makenode(x);
        break;
    }

  }
}

void printtree(nsp bt)
{
  if (bt == 0) return;
  printtree(bt->left);
  printf("%d\n",bt->val);
  printtree(bt->right);
}


int main(int argc, char *argv[])
{ int i;

  root = 0;
  fo  Print root  < argc; i++)
      Display roo t, atoi(argv[i]));
  pr            );
}           Print *root
            Display *ro
(gdb)       What is roo 19 16
then:       Lookup root not found.
Break       Break at ro ert (btp=0x804972c, x=12) at bintree.c:57
(gdb)       Clear at ro
Then.       ound.
```

Figure 3-1: Popup window for viewing a variable

```
$ ddd --separate bintree
```

---

then separate windows—Source Code, Console, and Data—will come up, which you can resize at will.

If you want to remove part or all of the contents of the Data Window during your DDD session, there are many ways to do it. You can, for instance, right-click an item, and then choose the Undisplay option.

3.2.3   Inspection in Eclipse

As with DDD, to inspect a scalar variable in Eclipse, just move the mouse pointer to any instance of the variable in the source code window. Note that this must be an independent scalar, not one within a struct, for example. This is illustrated in Figure 3-4. We have successfully queried the value of x here, but if we were to move the mouse pointer to the val portion of tmp->val in the same line, it would not tell us what's there.

At this point, you would make use of Eclipse's Variables view, which you can see in the upper-right portion of Figure 3-5. Click the triangle next to

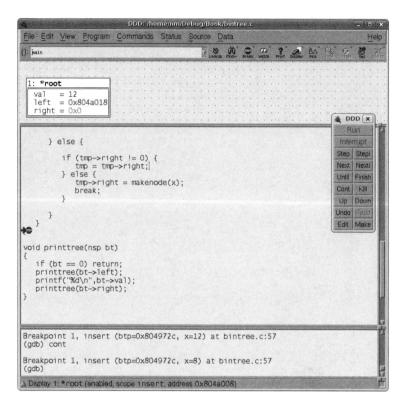

Figure 3-2: Display of a node

tmp to point it downward, then scroll down a line and find that tmp->val is displayed. (It turns out to contain 12.)

And you can continue this process. After clicking the triangle next to left, you'll find the screen shown in Figure 3-6, where you'll see that tmp->left->val is 8.

By default, the Variables view does not show global variables. In the program here, there is one, root. You can add that to the Variables view by right-clicking within that view, selecting Add Global Variables, checking the box for root in the resulting pop-up window, and then clicking OK.

3.2.4 Inspecting Dynamic Arrays

As discussed in Chapter 1, in GDB you can print an entire array, say declared as

```
int x[25];
```

by typing

```
(gdb) p x
```

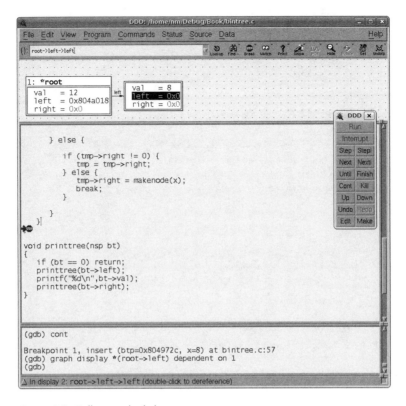

Figure 3-3: Following the links

But what if the array had been created dynamically, say as

```
int *x;
...
x = (int *) malloc(25*sizeof(int));
```

If you wanted to print out the array in GDB, you could not type

```
(gdb) p x
```

This would simply print the address of the array. Nor could you type

```
(gdb) p *x
```

That would print out only one element of the array, x[0]. You could still print out individual elements, as in the command p x[5], but you could not print the entire array simply using the print command on x.

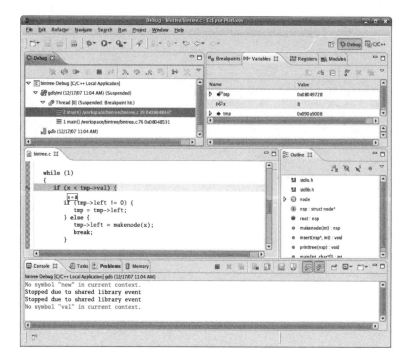

Figure 3-4: Inspecting a scalar variable in Eclipse

3.2.4.1 Solutions in GDB

In GDB you can solve this problem by creating an *artificial array*. Consider the code

```
1   int *x;
2
3   main()
4   {
5       x = (int *) malloc(25*sizeof(int));
6       x[3] = 12;
7   }
```

Then you could do something like this:

```
Breakpoint 1, main () at artif.c:6
6           x = (int *) malloc(25*sizeof(int));
(gdb) n
7           x[3] = 12;
(gdb) n
8       }
(gdb) p *x@25
$1 = {0, 0, 0, 12, 0 <repeats 21 times>}
```

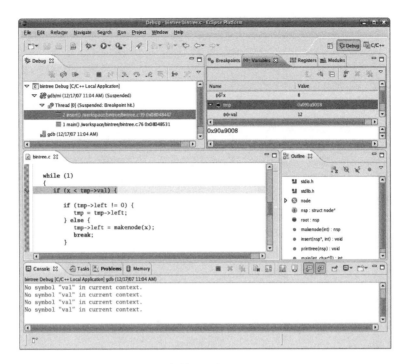

Figure 3-5: Inspecting a struct field in Eclipse

As you can see, the general form is

```
*pointer@number_of_elements
```

GDB also allows casts to be used when appropriate, for example,

```
(gdb) p (int [25]) *x
$2 = {0, 0, 0, 12, 0 <repeats 21 times>}
```

3.2.4.2   Solutions in DDD

As always, you could utilize the GDB method, in this case artificial arrays, through the DDD Console.

Another option would be to print or display a range of memory (see Section 3.2.7 below).

3.2.4.3   Solutions in Eclipse

Here you can use Eclipse's Display as Array command.

For instance, let's extend our earlier example a bit:

```
1   int *x;
2
3   main()
```

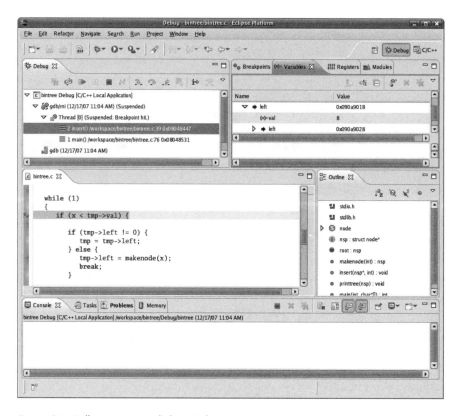

Figure 3-6: Following pointer links in Eclipse

```
 4  {
 5      int y;
 6      x = (int *) malloc(25*sizeof(int));
 7      scanf("%d%d",&x[3],&x[8]);
 8      y = x[3] + x[8];
 9      printf("%d\n",y);
10  }
```

Say you are currently at the assignment to y. You would first get x into the Variables view by right-clicking in that view and choosing x. You would then right-click x in the Variables view again, and select Display As Array. In the resulting pop-up box, you would fill in the Start Index and Length fields, say with 0 and 25 to display the entire array. The screen would now be as in Figure 3-7. You can see the array there in the Variables view, shown as

```
(0,0,0,1,0,0,0,0,2,0,<repeats 16 times>)
```

The values 1 and 2 came from our input to the program, seen in the Console view.

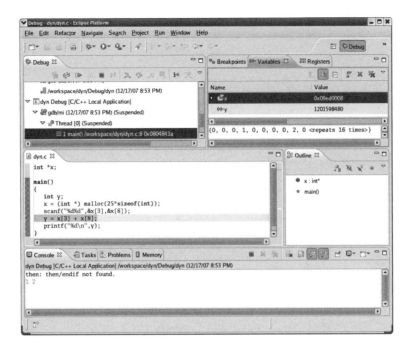

Figure 3-7: Displaying a dynamic array in Eclipse

3.2.5 What About C++?

To illustrate the situation for C++ code, here is a C++ version of the binary tree example used earlier:

```
// bintree.cc: routines to do insert and sorted print of a binary tree in C++

#include <iostream.h>

class node {
   public:
      static class node *root;  // root of the entire tree
      int val;  // stored value
      class node *left;  // ptr to smaller child
      class node *right;  // ptr to larger child
      node(int x);  // constructor, setting val = x
      static void insert(int x);  // insert x into the tree
      static void printtree(class node *nptr);  // print subtree rooted at *nptr
};

class node *node::root = 0;


node::node(int x)
```

```
{
   val = x;
   left = right = 0;
}


void node::insert(int x)
{
   if (node::root == 0)  {
      node::root = new node(x);
      return;
   }
   class node *tmp=root;
   while (1)
   {
      if (x < tmp->val)
      {

         if (tmp->left != 0) {
            tmp = tmp->left;
         } else {
            tmp->left = new node(x);
            break;
         }

      } else {

         if (tmp->right != 0) {
            tmp = tmp->right;
         } else {
            tmp->right = new node(x);
            break;
         }

      }
   }
}


void node::printtree(class node *np)
{
   if (np == 0) return;
   node::printtree(np->left);
   cout << np->val << endl;
   node::printtree(np->right);
}
```

```
int main(int argc, char *argv[])
{
    for (int i = 1; i < argc; i++)
        node::insert(atoi(argv[i]));
    node::printtree(node::root);
}
```

You still compile as usual, making sure to tell the compiler to retain the symbol table in the executable file.[2]

The same GDB commands work, but with somewhat different output. For example, again printing out the contents of the object pointed to by `tmp` within `insert()`, you get the following output:

```
(gdb) p *tmp
$6 = {static root = 0x8049d08, val = 19, left = 0x0, right = 0x0}
```

This is similar to the case of the C program, except that now the value of the static variable `node::root` is printed as well (which it should be, since it is part of the class).

Of course, you do have to keep in mind that GDB needs you to specify variables according to the same scope rules that C++ uses. For example:

```
(gdb) p *root
Cannot access memory at address 0x0
(gdb) p *node::root
$8 = {static root = 0x8049d08, val = 12, left = 0x8049d18, right = 0x8049d28}
```

We needed to specify `root` via its full name, `node::root`.

GDB and DDD do not have built-in class browsers, but the GDB's `ptype` command is handy to get a quick review of the structure of a class or struct, for example,

```
(gdb) ptype node
type = class node {
  public:
    static node *root;
    int val;
    node *left;
    node *right;

    node(int);
    static void insert(int);
```

---

[2] There are various issues which may arise in this regard, though. See the GDB manual concerning executable file formats. The examples here use the G++ compiler (a C++ wrapper for GCC), with the -g option for specifying that the symbol table should be retained. We also tried the -gstabs option, which worked but with somewhat less-desirable results.

```
        static void printtree(node*);
}
```

In DDD, one can right-click the class or variable name, and then choose What Is in the pop-up menu to get the same information.

Eclipse has its Outline view, so you can easily get class information in that manner.

3.2.6 Monitoring Local Variables

In GDB, you can get a list of values of all the local variables in the current stack frame by invoking the info locals command.

In DDD, you can even *display* the local variables by clicking Data | Display Local Variables. This will result in a section of the DDD Data Window being devoted to displaying the locals (updated as you step through the program). There appears to be no direct way of doing this within GDB, though you could do it on a per-breakpoint basis by including an info locals command within a commands routine for each breakpoint at which you wish to have the locals automatically printed out.

Eclipse displays the local variables in the Variables view, as you've seen.

3.2.7 Examining Memory Directly

In some cases, you might wish to examine memory at a given address, rather than via the name of a variable. GDB provides the x ("examine") command for this purpose. In DDD one selects Data | Memory, specifies the starting point and number of bytes, and chooses between Print and Display. Eclipse has a Memory view, in which you can create Memory Monitors.

This is normally useful mainly in assembly language contexts and is discussed in detail in Chapter 8.

3.2.8 Advanced Options for Print and Display

The print and display commands allow you to specify alternative formats. For example,

```
(gdb) p/x y
```

will display the variable y in hex format instead of decimal. Other commonly used formats are c for character, s for string, and f for floating-point.

You can temporarily disable a display item. For instance,

```
(gdb) dis disp 1
```

temporarily disables item 1 in the display list. If you do not know the item numbers, you can check via the info disp command. To re-enable an item, use enable, for example,

```
(gdb) enable disp 1
```

To delete a display item entirely, use undisplay, for example,

```
(gdb) undisp 1
```

3.3 Setting Variables from Within GDB/DDD/Eclipse

In some cases, it is useful to set the value of a variable using the debugger, in the midst of stepping through a program. This way you can quickly answer "what if" questions that arise when you are hypothesizing various sources for a bug.

In GDB, you can set values very easily, for example,

```
(gdb) set x = 12
```

will change the current value of x to 12.

There appears to be no mouse-based way to do this in DDD, but again you can issue any GDB command from within DDD in the DDD Console Window.

In Eclipse, go to the Variables view, right-click the variable whose value you want to set, and select Change Value. A pop-up window will then allow you to fill in the new value.

You can set the command-line arguments for your program via GDB's set args command. However, there is no advantage to this over the method described in Chapter 1, which simply uses the new arguments when you invoke GDB's run command. These two methods are completely equivalent. It is not the case, for instance, that

```
(gdb) set args 1 52 19 11
```

would immediately change argv[1] to 1, argv[2] to 52, and so on. Those changes would not occur until the next time you issue the run command.

GDB has the info args command, which you can use to check the arguments of the current function. DDD provides this when you click Data | Display Arguments.

3.4 GDB's Own Variables

In addition to the variables you declare in your program, GDB also provides mechanisms for others.

3.4.1 Making Use of the Value History

Output values from GDB's print command are labeled $1, $2, and so on, with these quantities collectively being called the *value history*. They can be used to produce shortcuts in future print commands that you issue.

For instance, consider the bintree example from Section 3.1. Part of a GDB session might look like this:

```
(gdb) p tmp->left
$1 = (struct node *) 0x80496a8
(gdb) p *(tmp->left)
$2 = {val = 5, left = 0x0, right = 0x0}
(gdb) p *$1
$3 = {val = 5, left = 0x0, right = 0x0}
```

What happened here is that after we printed out the value of the pointer tmp->left and found it to be nonzero, we decided to print out what this pointer pointed to. We did so twice, first the conventional way, and then via the value history.

In that third printing, we referred to $1 in the value history. If we had not done the conventional printing, we could have made use of the special value history variable $:

```
(gdb) p tmp->left
$1 = (struct node *) 0x80496a8
(gdb) p *$
$2 = {val = 5, left = 0x0, right = 0x0}
```

3.4.2 Convenience Variables

Say you have a pointer variable p which at different times points to different nodes in a linked list. During your debugging session, you may wish to record the address of a particular node, say because you wish to recheck the value in the node at various times during the debugging process. The first time p gets to that node, you could do something like

```
(gdb) set $q = p
```

and from then on do things like

```
(gdb) p *$q
```

The variable $q here is called a *convenience variable*.

Convenience variables can change values according to C rules. For example, consider the code

```
int w[4] = {12,5,8,29};

main()

{
   w[2] = 88;
}
```

In GDB you might do something like

```
Breakpoint 1, main () at cv.c:7
7          w[2] = 88;
(gdb) n
8       }
(gdb) set $i = 0
(gdb) p w[$i++]
$1 = 12
(gdb)
$2 = 5
(gdb)
$3 = 88
(gdb)
$4 = 29
```

To understand what happened here, recall that if we simply hit the ENTER key in GDB without issuing a command, GDB takes this as a request to repeat the last command. In the GDB session above, you kept hitting the ENTER key, which meant you were asking GDB to repeat the command

```
(gdb) p w[$i++]
```

That meant not only that a value would be printed, but also that the convenience variable $i would increment.

NOTE *You can choose almost any name for a convenience variable, with some natural exceptions. You cannot, for instance, have a convenience variable named $3, since that is reserved for items in the value history. Also, you should not use register names if you are working in assembly language. For Intel x86–based machines, for instance, one of the register names is EAX, and within GDB it is referred to as $eax; you would not want to choose this name for a convenience variable if you were working at the assembly-language level.*

4

WHEN A PROGRAM CRASHES

It's said that C is a low-level language. Part of what is meant by this is that much of the memory management for an application program is left to the programmer to implement. Although this approach can be quite powerful, it also places a great responsibility on the programmer.

It's also said that C is a relatively small language and an easy one to learn. However, C is only small if you don't consider a typical implementation of the standard C library, which is huge—and many programmers find C to be an easy language to use only up until they encounter pointers.

In general, a program bug can cause one of two things to happen:

- It can cause the program to do something that the programmer doesn't intend. Such bugs are often due to flaws in logic, as in the number-sorting program in Chapter 3, where we put a node into the wrong branch of a tree. We've concentrated on this type of bug up until now.

- It can cause the program to "bomb" or "crash." These bugs are often associated with the mishandling or misuse of pointers. This is the type of bug we'll deal with in this chapter.

4.1 Background Material: Memory Management

What really happens when a program crashes? We'll explain it here and show how it relates to finding the bug that produces the crash.

4.1.1 Why Does a Program Crash?

In the vernacular of the programming world, a program *crashes* when an error causes it to cease to execute, abruptly and abnormally. By far the most common cause of a crash is for a program to attempt to access a memory location without having the permission to do so. The hardware will sense this and execute a jump to the operating system (OS). On Unix-family platforms, which are our focus here and in most of this book, the OS will normally announce that the program has caused a segmentation fault, commonly referred to as a *seg fault*, and discontinue execution of the program. On Microsoft Windows systems, the corresponding term is *general protection fault*. Whatever the name, the hardware must support virtual memory and the OS must make use of it in order for this error to occur. Although this is standard for today's general-purpose computers, the reader should keep in mind that it is often not the case for small, special-purpose computers, such as the embedded computers used to control machines.

In order to effectively use GDB/DDD to deal with seg faults, it is important to understand exactly *how* memory access errors occur. In the next few pages, we will present a brief tutorial on the role played by virtual memory (VM) during the execution of programs. Our specific focus will be on how VM issues relate to seg faults. Thus, even if you have studied VM in computing courses, the focus here may give you some new insights that will help you deal with seg faults in your debugging work.

4.1.2 Program Layout in Memory

As mentioned earlier, a seg fault occurs when your program has a memory access problem. To discuss this, it is important to first understand how a program is laid out in memory.

On Unix platforms, a program's set of allocated virtual addresses typically is laid out something like the diagram in Figure 4-1.

Here virtual address 0 is at the bottom, and the arrows show the direction of growth of two of the components, the heap and the stack, eating up the free area as they grow. The roles of the various pieces are as follows:

- The *text section* consists of the machine instructions produced by the compiler from your program's source code. Each line of C code, for instance, will typically translate into two or three machine instructions, and the collection of all the resulting instructions makes up the text section of the executable. The formal name for this section is *.text*.

  This component includes statically linked code, including */usr/lib/crt0.o*, system code that does some initialization and then calls your main().

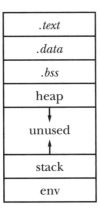

.text
.data
.bss
heap
↓
unused
↑
stack
env

Figure 4-1: Program memory layout

- The *data section* contains all the program variables that are allocated at compile time—that is, your global variables.

  Actually, this section consists of various subsections. The first is called *.data* and consists of your initialized variables, that is, those given in declarations like

```
int x = 5;
```

  There is also a *.bss* section for uninitialized data, given in declarations like

```
int y;
```

- When your program requests additional memory from the operating system at run time—for example, when you call malloc() in C, or invoke the new construct in C++—the requested memory is allocated in an area called the *heap*. If you run out of heap space, a call to brk() can be used to expand the heap (which is precisely what malloc() and friends do).

- The *stack section* is space for dynamically allocated data. The data for function calls—including arguments, local variables, and return addresses—are stored on the stack. The stack grows each time a function call is made and shrinks each time a function returns to its caller.

- Your program's dynamically linked code is not shown in the picture above due to the platform dependence of its location, but it is somewhere in there.

  Let's explore this a bit. Consider the following code:

```
int q[200];

int main( void )
{
```

```
    int i, n, *p;
    p = malloc(sizeof(int));
    scanf("%d", &n);
    for (i = 0; i < 200; i++)
        q[i] = i;

    printf("%x  %x  %x  %x  %x\n", main, q, p, &i, scanf);

        return 0;
}
```

The program itself doesn't do much, but we've written it as a tool to informally explore the layout of virtual address space. To that end, let's run it:

```
% a.out
5
80483f4   80496a0   9835008   bfb3abec   8048304
```

You can see that the approximate locations of the text section, data section, heap, stack, and dynamically linked functions are 0x080483f4, 0x080496a0, 0x09835008, 0xbfb3abec, and 0x08048304, respectively.

You can get a precise account of the program's memory layout on Linux by looking at the process's *maps* file. The process number happens to be 21111, so we'll look at the corresponding file, */proc/21111/maps*:

```
$ cat /proc/21111/maps
009f1000-009f2000 r-xp 009f1000 00:00 0          [vdso]
009f2000-00a0b000 r-xp 00000000 08:01 4116750    /lib/ld-2.4.so
00a0b000-00a0c000 r-xp 00018000 08:01 4116750    /lib/ld-2.4.so
00a0c000-00a0d000 rwxp 00019000 08:01 4116750    /lib/ld-2.4.so
00a0f000-00b3c000 r-xp 00000000 08:01 4116819    /lib/libc-2.4.so
00b3c000-00b3e000 r-xp 0012d000 08:01 4116819    /lib/libc-2.4.so
00b3e000-00b3f000 rwxp 0012f000 08:01 4116819    /lib/libc-2.4.so
00b3f000-00b42000 rwxp 00b3f000 00:00 0
08048000-08049000 r-xp 00000000 00:16 18815309   /home/matloff/a.out
08049000-0804a000 rw-p 00000000 00:16 18815309   /home/matloff/a.out
09835000-09856000 rw-p 09835000 00:00 0          [heap]
b7ef8000-b7ef9000 rw-p b7ef8000 00:00 0
b7f14000-b7f16000 rw-p b7f14000 00:00 0
bfb27000-bfb3c000 rw-p bfb27000 00:00 0          [stack]
```

You needn't understand all of this. The point is that in this display, you can see your text and data sections (from the file *a.out*), as well as the heap and stack. You can also see where the C library (for calls to scanf(), malloc(), and printf()) has been placed (from the file */lib/libc-2.4.so*). You should also recognize a permissions field whose format is similar to the familiar file permissions displayed by *ls*, indicating privileges such as rw-p, for example. The latter will be explained shortly.

4.1.3   The Notion of Pages

The virtual address space shown in Figure 4-1 conceptually extends from 0 to $2^w - 1$, where w is the word size of your machine in bits. Of course, your program will typically use only a tiny fraction of that space, and the OS may reserve part of the space for its own work. But your code, through pointers, could generate an address anywhere in that range. Often such addresses will be incorrect be due to "entomological conditions"—that is, because of bugs in your program!

This virtual address space is viewed as organized into chunks called *pages*. On Pentium hardware, the default page size is 4,096 bytes. Physical memory (both RAM and ROM) is also viewed as divided into pages. When a program is loaded into memory for execution, the OS arranges for some of the pages of the program to be stored in pages of physical memory. These pages are said to be *resident*, and the rest are stored on disk.

At various times during execution, some program page that is not currently resident will be needed. When this occurs, it will be sensed by the hardware, which transfers control to the OS. The latter brings the required page into memory, possibly replacing another program page that is currently resident (if there are no free pages of memory available), and then returns control to our program. The evicted program page, if any, becomes nonresident and will be stored on disk.

To manage all of this, the OS maintains a *page table* for each process. (The Pentium's page tables have a hierarchical structure, but here we assume just one level for simplicity, and most of this discussion will not be Pentium-specific.) Each of the process's virtual pages has an entry in the table, which includes the following information:

- The current physical location of this page in memory or on disk. In the latter case, the entry will indicate that the page is nonresident and may consist of a pointer to a list which ultimately leads to a physical location on disk. It may show, for instance, that virtual page 12 of the program is resident and is located in physical page 200 of memory.

- Permissions—read, write, execute—for this page.

Note that the OS will not allocate partial pages to a program. For example, if the program to be run has a total size of about 10,000 bytes, it would occupy three pages of memory if fully loaded. It would not merely occupy about 2.5 pages, as pages are the smallest unit of memory manipulated by the VM system. This is an important point to understand when debugging, because it implies that some erroneous memory accesses by the program will *not* trigger seg faults, as you will see below. In other words, during your debugging session, you cannot say something like, "This line of source code must be okay, since it didn't cause a seg fault."

4.1.4 Details on the Role of the Page Table

Keep the virtual address space in Table 4-1 in mind, and continue to assume that the page size is 4,096 bytes. Then virtual page 0 comprises bytes 0 though 4,095 of the virtual address space, page 1 comprises bytes 4,096 through 8,191, and so on.

As mentioned, when we run a program, the OS creates a *page table* that it uses to manage the virtual memory of the process that executes the program code. (A review of OS processes is presented in the material on threads in Chapter 5.) Whenever that process runs, the hardware's page table register will point to that table.

Conceptually speaking, each page of the virtual address space of the process has an entry in the page table (in practice, various tricks can be used to compress the table). This page table entry stores various pieces of information related to the page. The data of interest in relation to seg faults are the *access permissions* for the page, which are similar to file access permissions: read, write, and execute. For example, the page table entry for page 3 will indicate whether your process has the right to read data from that page, the right to write data to it, and the right to execute instructions on it (if the page contains machine code).

As the program executes, it will continually access its various sections, described above, which causes the page table to be consulted by the hardware as follows:

- Each time the program uses one of its global variables, read/write access to the data section is required.

- Each time the program accesses a local variable, the program accesses the stack, requiring read/write access to the stack section.

- Each time the program enters or leaves a function, it makes one or more accesses to the stack, requiring read/write access to the stack section.

- Each time the program accesses storage that had been created by a call to malloc() or new, a heap access occurs, again requiring read/write access.

- Each machine instruction that the program executes will be fetched from the text section (or from the area for dynamically linked code), thus requiring read and execute permission.

During the execution of the program, the addresses it generates will be virtual. When the program attempts to access memory at a certain virtual address, say y, the hardware will convert that to a virtual page number v, which equals y divided by 4,096 (where the division uses integer arithmetic, discarding the remainder). The hardware will then check entry v in the page table to see whether the permissions for the page match the operation to be performed. If they do match, the hardware will get the desired location's actual physical page number from this table entry and then carry out the requested memory operation. But if the table entry shows that the requested operation does not have the proper permission, the hardware will execute an internal interrupt. This will cause a jump to the OS's error-handling routine. The OS will normally then announce a memory access violation and discontinue execution of the program (i.e., remove it from the process table and from memory).

A bug in your program could result in a permissions mismatch and generate a seg fault during any of the types of memory access listed above. For instance, suppose your program contains a global declaration

```
int x[100];
```

and suppose your code contains a statement

```
x[i] = 3;
```

Recall that in C/C++, the expression x[i] is equivalent to (and really means) *(x+i), that is, the contents of the memory location pointed to by the address x+i. If the offset i is, say, 200000, then this will likely produce a virtual memory address y that is outside the set of pages that the OS has assigned for the program's data section, where the compiler and linker arranged for the array x[] to be stored. A seg fault will then occur when the write operation is attempted.

If x were instead a local variable, then the same problem would occur in your stack section.

Violations related to execute permission can occur in more subtle ways. In an assembly language program, for instance, you might have a data item named sink and a function named sunk(). When calling the function, you may accidentally write

```
call sink
```

instead of

```
call sunk
```

This would cause a seg fault because the program would attempt to execute an instruction at the address of sink, which lies in the data section, and the pages of the data section do not have execute permission enabled.

The exact analog of this coding error would not lead to a seg fault in C, since the compiler would object to a line like

```
z = sink(5);
```

when sink has been declared as a variable. But this bug could easily occur when pointers to functions are used. Consider code like this:

```
int f(int x)
{
   return x*x;
}
```

```
int (*p)(int);

int main( void )
{
    p = f;
    u = (*p)(5);
    printf("%d\n", u);

        return 0;
}
```

If you were to forget the statement p = f; then p would be 0, and you would attempt to execute instructions lying in page 0, a page for which you would not have execute (or other) permission for (recall Figure 4-1).

4.1.5   A Slight Memory-Access Bug Might *Not* Cause a Seg Fault

In order to deepen your understanding of how seg faults occur, consider the following code, whose behavior when executed shows that seg faults do *not* always occur in situations where you might expect them to:

```
int q[200];

main()
{
    int i;
    for (i = 0; i < 2000; i++) {
        q[i] = i;
    }
}
```

Notice that the programmer has apparently made a typographical error in the loop, setting up 2,000 iterations instead of 200. The C compiler will not catch this at compile time, nor will the machine code generated by the compiler check at execution time, whether the array index is out of bounds. (This is GCC's default, although it also offers a -fmudflap option that does provide such run-time index checking.)

At execution time, a seg fault is quite likely to occur. However, the timing of the error may surprise you. The error is not likely to appear at the "natural" time, that is, when i = 200; rather, it is likely to happen much later than that.

To illustrate this, we ran this program on a Linux PC under GDB, in order to conveniently query addresses of variables. It turned out that the seg fault occurred not at i = 200, but at i = 728. (Your system may give different results, but the principles will be the same.) Let's see why.

From queries to GDB we found that the array q[] ended at address 0x80497bf; that is, the last byte of q[199] was at that memory location. Taking into account the Intel page size of 4,096 bytes and the 32-bit word size of this machine, a virtual address breaks down into a 20-bit page number and a 12-bit offset. In our case, q[] ended in virtual page number 0x8049 = 32841, offset 0x7bf = 1983. So there were still 4,096 − 1,984 = 2,112 bytes on the page of memory on which q was allocated. That space can hold 2112 / 4 = 528 integer variables (since each is 4 bytes wide on the machine used here), and our code treated it as if it contained elements of q at "positions" 200 through 727.

Those elements of q[] don't exist, of course, but the compiler did not complain. Neither did the hardware, since the writes were still being performed to a page for which we certainly had write permission (because some of the actual elements of q[] lay on it, and q[] is allocated in the data segment). Only when i became 728 did q[i] refer to an address on a different page. In this case, it was a page for which we didn't have write (or any other) permission; the virtual memory hardware detected this and triggered a seg fault.

Since each integer variable is stored in 4 bytes, this page then contains 528 (2,112 / 4) additional "phantom" elements that the code treats as belonging to the array q[]. So, although we didn't intend that it should be done, it is still legal to access q[200], q[201], and so on, all the way up to element 199 + 528 = 727, that is, q[727]—without triggering a seg fault! Only when you try to access q[728] do you encounter a new page, for which you may or may not have the required access permissions. Here, we did not, and so the program seg faulted. However, the next page might, by sheer luck, actually have had the proper privileges assigned to it, and then there would have been even more phantom array elements.

The moral: As stated earlier, we can't conclude from the absence of a seg fault that a memory operation is correct.

4.1.6 Seg Faults and Unix Signals

In the discussion above, we said that a seg fault normally results in the termination of the program. That is correct, but for serious debugging, there is a bit more you should be aware of, in connection with Unix signals.

Signals indicate exceptional conditions and are reported during program execution to allow the OS (or your own code) to react to a variety of events. A signal can be raised on a process by the underlying hardware of the system (as with SIGSEGV or SIGFPE), by the operating system (as with SIGTERM or SIGABRT), or by another process (as with SIGUSR1 or SIGUSR2), or it can even be self-sent by the process itself (via the raise() library call).

The simplest example of a signal results from hitting CTRL-C on your keyboard while a program is running. Pressing (or releasing) any key on your keyboard generates a hardware interrupt that causes an OS routine to run. When you hit CTRL-C, the OS recognizes this key combination as a special pattern and raises a signal called SIGINT for the process on the controlling terminal. In common parlance, it's said that the OS "sends a signal to the process." We will use that phrase, but it's important to realize that nothing is actually "sent" to the process. All that happens is that the OS records the signal in its process table, so that the next time the process receiving the signal gets a timeslice on the CPU, the appropriate signal handler function will be executed, as explained below. (However, given the presumed urgency of signals, the OS may also decide to give the receiving process its next timeslice sooner than it would have otherwise.)

There are many different types of signals that can be raised on a process. In Linux, you can view the entire list of signals by typing

```
man 7 signal
```

at the shell prompt. Signals have been defined under various standards, such as POSIX.1, and these signals will be present on all operating systems that are compliant. There are also signals that are unique to individual operating systems.

Each signal has its own *signal handler*, which is a function that is called when that particular signal is raised on a process. Going back to our CTRL-C example, when SIGINT is raised, the OS sets the current instruction of the process to the beginning of the signal handler for that particular signal. Thus, when the process resumes, it will execute the handler.

There is a default signal handler for each type of signal, which conveniently frees you from having to write them yourself unless you need to. Most harmless signals are ignored by default. More serious types of signals, like ones arising from violations of memory-access permissions, indicate conditions that make it inadvisable or even impossible for the program to continue to execute. In such cases, the default signal handler simply terminates the program.

Some signal handlers cannot be overriden, but in many cases you can write your own handler to replace the default handler provided by the OS. This is done in Unix by using either the signal() or sigaction() system calls.[1] Your custom handler function may, for instance, ignore the signal or even ask the user to choose a course of action.

Just for fun, we wrote a program that illustrates how you can write your own signal handler and, using signal(), invoke or override the default OS handler, or ignore the signal. We picked SIGINT, but you can do the same thing for any signal that can be caught. The program also demonstrates how raise() is used.

```
#include <signal.h>
#include <stdio.h>

void my_sigint_handler( int signum )
{
    printf("I received signal %d (that's 'SIGINT' to you).\n", signum);
    puts("Tee Hee!  That tickles!\n");
```

---

[1] There are two functions that are used to override default signal handlers because Linux, as with other Unixes, conforms to multiple standards. The signal() function, which is eaiser to use than sigaction(), conforms to the ANSI standard, whereas the sigaction() function is more complicated, but also more versatile, and conforms to the POSIX standard.

```c
}


int main(void)
{
   char choicestr[20];
   int  choice;

   while ( 1 )
   {
      puts("1. Ignore control-C");
      puts("2. Custom handle control-C");
      puts("3. Use the default handler control-C");
      puts("4. Raise a SIGSEGV on myself.");
      printf("Enter your choice: ");

      fgets(choicestr, 20, stdin);
      sscanf(choicestr, "%d", &choice);

      if ( choice == 1 )
         signal(SIGINT, SIG_IGN);   // Ignore control-C
      else if ( choice == 2 )
         signal(SIGINT, my_sigint_handler);
      else if ( choice == 3 )
         signal(SIGINT, SIG_DFL);
      else if ( choice == 4 )
         raise(SIGSEGV);
      else
         puts("Whatever you say, guv'nor.\n\n");
   }

   return 0;
}
```

When a program commits a memory-access violation, a SIGSEGV signal is raised on the process. The default seg fault handler terminates the process and writes a "core file" to disk, which we will explain shortly.

If you wish to keep the program alive, instead of allowing it to be terminated, you can write a custom handler for SIGSEGV. Indeed, you may want to deliberately cause seg faults in order to get some kind of work done. For example, some parallel-processing software packages use artificial seg faults, to which a special handler responds, to maintain consistency between the various nodes of the system, as you will see in Section 5. Another use for specialized handlers for SIGSEGV, to be discussed in Chapter 7, involves tools for detecting and gracefully reacting to seg faults.

However, custom signal handlers may cause complications when using GDB/DDD/Eclipse. Whether it is used on its own or through the DDD GUI,

GDB stops a process whenever any signal occurs. In the case of applications that operate like the parallel-processing software just mentioned, this means that GDB will halt very frequently for reasons not related to your debugging work. In order to deal with this, you will need to tell GDB not to stop when certain signals occur, using the handle command.

4.1.7 Other Types of Exceptions

There are other sources of crashes besides segmentation faults. *Floating-point exceptions (FPEs)* cause a SIGFPE signal to be raised. Although it's called a "floating-point" exception, this signal covers integer arithmetic exceptions as well, like overflow and divide-by-zero conditions. On GNU and BSD systems, FPE handlers are passed a second argument that gives the reason for the FPE. The default handler will ignore a SIGFPE under some circumstances, such as floating point overflow, and terminate the process in other circumstances, such as integer divide-by-zero.

A *bus error* occurs when the CPU detects an anomalous condition on its bus while executing machine instructions. Different architectures have different requirements for what should be happening on the bus, and the exact cause of the anomaly is architecture dependent. Some examples of situations that might cause a bus error include the following:

- Accessing a physical address that does not exist. This is distinct from a seg fault, in that a seg fault involves access to memory for which there is insufficient privilege. Seg faults are a matter of permissions; bus errors are a matter of an invalid address being presented to the processor.

- On many architectures, machine instructions that access 32-bit quantities are required to be *word aligned*, meaning that the memory address of the quantity must be a multiple of 4. A pointer error that results in trying to access a 4-byte number at an odd-numbered address might cause a bus error:

```
int main(void)
{
    char *char_ptr;
    int  *int_ptr;
    int   int_array[2];

    // char_ptr points to first array element
    char_ptr = (char *) int_array;

    // Causes int_ptr to point one byte past the start of an existing int.
    // Since an int can't be only one byte, int_ptr is no longer aligned.
    int_ptr = (int *) (char_ptr+1);

    *int_ptr = 1;                    // And this might cause a bus error.
```

```
    return 0;
}
```

This program will not cause a bus error under Linux running on the x86 architecture, because on these processors nonaligned memory accesses are legal; they just execute more slowly than aligned accesses do.

In any event, a bus error is a processor-level exception that causes a SIGBUS signal to be raised on a Unix system. By default, SIGBUS will cause a process to dump core and terminate.

4.2 Core Files

As mentioned earlier, some signals indicate that it's inadvisable or even impossible for a process to continue. In these cases, the default action is to prematurely terminate the process and write a file called a *core file*, colloquially known as *dumping core*. The writing of core files may be suppressed by your shell (see Section 4.2.2 for details).

If a core file is created during a run of your program, you can open your debugger, say GDB, on that file and then proceed with your usual GDB operations.

4.2.1 How Core Files Are Created

A core file contains a detailed description of the program's state when it died: the contents of the stack (or, if the program is threaded, the stacks for each thread), the contents of the CPU's registers (again with one set of register values per thread if the program is multithreaded), the values of the program's statically-allocated variables (global and static variables), and so on.

It's very easy to create a core file. Here's code that generates one:

```
int main(void)
{
   abort();

   return 0;
}
```

Listing 4-1: abort.c

The abort() function causes the current process to receive a SIGABRT signal, and the default signal handler for SIGABRT terminates the program and dumps core. Here's another short program that dumps core. In this program, we intentionally dereference a NULL pointer:

```
int main(void)
{
```

```
    char *c = 0;
    printf("%s\n", *c);

    return 0;
}
```

Listing 4-2: sigsegv.c

Let's generate a core file. Compile and run *sigsegv.c*:

```
$ gcc -g -W -Wall sigsegv.c -o sigsegv
$ ./sigsegv
Segmentation fault (core dumped)
```

If you list your current directory, you'll notice a new file named *core* (or some variant thereof). When you see a core file somewhere in your filesystem, it may not be obvious which program generated it. The Unix command file helpfully tells us the name of the executable that dumped this particular core file:

```
$ file core
core: ELF 32-bit LSB core file Intel 80386, version 1 (SYSV), SVR4-style,
SVR4-style, from 'sigsegv'
```

Core Filenaming Conventions

The naming convention for core files used to be simple: They were all called *core*.

Then, under GNU/Linux, multithreaded programs started to dump core using filenames like *core.3928*, where the numeric portion of the filename indicates the process ID of the process that dumped the core.

Starting with the Linux 2.5 kernel, you have control over the names assigned to core files using the */proc/sys/kernel/* interface. The mechanism is quite simple and is well documented in *Documentation/sysctl/kernel.txt* under the Linux kernel source tree.

4.2.2   Your Shell May Suppress the Creation of a Core File

In many, if not most cases, the debugging process does not involve core files. If a program seg faults, the programmer simply opens a debugger, such as GDB, and runs the program again to recreate the fault. For that reason, and because core files tend to be large, most modern shells have mechanisms to prevent core files from being written in the first place.

In bash, you can control the creation of core files with the `ulimit` command:

```
ulimit -c n
```

where *n* is the maximum size for a core file, in kilobytes. Any core file larger than *n*KB will not be written. If you don't specify *n*, the shell will display the current limitation on core files. If you want to allow a core file of any size, you can use

```
ulimit -c unlimited
```

For `tcsh` and `csh` users, the `limit` command controls core file sizes. For example,

```
limit coredumpsize 1000000
```

will tell the shell you do not want a core file created if it will be more than a million bytes in size.

If you didn't get a core file after running sigsegv, check the current core file restrictions using `ulimit -c` for bash or `limit -c` for tcsh or csh.

Why would you ever need a core file in the first place? Since you can simply re-run a program that has seg faulted from within GDB and recreate the seg fault, why bother with core files at all? The answer is that in some situations, such as the following ones, this assumption is not justified:

- The seg fault only occurs after the program has run for a long period of time, so that it is infeasible to recreate the fault in the debugger.

- The program's behavior depends on random, environmental events, so that running the program again may not reproduce the seg fault.

- The seg fault occurs when the program is run by a naive user. Here the user, who would typically not be a programmer (or not have access to the source code), would not do the debugging. However, such a user could still send the core file (if it were available) to the programmer for inspection and debugging purposes.

Note, though, that if the program's source code isn't available or if the executable wasn't compiled with an enhanced symbol table, or even when we don't plan to debug the executable, core files are simply not very useful.

4.3 Extended Example

In this section we present a detailed example of debugging seg faults.

Below is some C code that might be part of an implementation of a managed string type similar to C++ strings. The code, contained in the source file *cstring.c*, implements a type called CString; however, it's riddled with bugs, obvious and subtle. Our goal is to find all these bugs and correct them.

CString is a typedefed alias for a structure containing a pointer to storage for a char string together with a variable that stores the string's length. Some utility functions useful for string handling have been implemented:

Init_CString()   Takes an old-style C string as an argument and uses it to initialize a new CString.

Delete_CString()   CStrings are allocated on the heap, and their memory must be freed when it is not needed anymore. This function takes care of the garbage collection.

Chomp()   Removes and returns the last character of a CString.

Append_Chars_To_CString()   Appends a C-style string to a CString.

Lastly, main() is our driver function to test the CString implementation.

Our code makes use of an extremely useful library function, snprintf(). In case you haven't encountered this function yet, it's almost like printf(), except that it writes its output into a character array instead of to stdout. To help prevent buffer overflows (which may occur with any function that copies null-terminated strings, if the null character is left out of the source string), snprintf() also lets you specify the maximum number of bytes to write, including the trailing null character:

```c
#include <stdio.h>
#define STRSIZE 22

int main(void)
{
    char s1[] = "brake";
    char *s2 = "breakpoints";
    char logo[STRSIZE];

    snprintf(logo, STRSIZE, "%c %s %d %s.", 'I', s1, 2+2, s2);

    puts(logo);
    return 0;
}
```

This program will write the string "I brake 4 breakpoints." into the character array logo, ready for printing onto a bumper sticker.

Now here's the implementation of our CString:

```c
#include <stdio.h>
#include <stdlib.h>
#include <string.h>

typedef struct {
    char *str;
    int   len;
} CString;
```

```
CString *Init_CString(char *str)
{
   CString *p = malloc(sizeof(CString));
   p->len = strlen(str);
   strncpy(p->str, str, strlen(str) + 1);
   return p;
}


void Delete_CString(CString *p)
{
   free(p);
   free(p->str);
}


// Removes the last character of a CString and returns it.
//
char Chomp(CString *cstring)
{
   char lastchar = *( cstring->str + cstring->len);
   // Shorten the string by one
   *( cstring->str + cstring->len) = '0';
   cstring->len = strlen( cstring->str );

   return lastchar;
}


// Appends a char * to a CString
//
CString *Append_Chars_To_CString(CString *p, char *str)
{
   char *newstr = malloc(p->len + 1);
   p->len = p->len + strlen(str);

   // Create the new string to replace p->str
   snprintf(newstr, p->len, "%s%s", p->str, str);
   // Free old string and make CString point to the new string
   free(p->str);
   p->str = newstr;

   return p;
}
```

```
int main(void)
{
    CString *mystr;
    char c;

    mystr = Init_CString("Hello!");
    printf("Init:\n  str: `%s' len: %d\n", mystr->str, mystr->len);
    c = Chomp(mystr);
    printf("Chomp '%c':\n  str:`%s' len: %d\n", c, mystr->str, mystr->len);
    mystr = Append_Chars_To_CString(mystr, " world!");
    printf("Append:\n  str: `%s' len: %d\n", mystr->str, mystr->len);

    Delete_CString(mystr);

    return 0;
}
```

Study the code and try to guess what the output should be. Then compile and run it.

```
$ gcc -g -W -Wall cstring.c -o cstring
$ ./cstring
Segmentation fault (core dumped)
```

Oops! The first thing we need to do is find out where the seg fault happened. Then we can try to figure out why it happened.

Before continuing, we'd like to mention that our office colleague in the next cubicle, Milton, is also trying to fix the bugs in this program. Unlike us, Milton doesn't know how to use GDB, so he's about to open up Wordpad, insert calls to printf() all over the code, and recompile the program in an attempt to figure out where the seg fault happened. Let's see if we can debug the program faster than Milton.

While Milton opens up Wordpad, we'll use GDB to examine the core file:

```
$ gdb cstring core
Core was generated by `cstring'.
Program terminated with signal 11, Segmentation fault.
#0  0x400a9295 in strncpy () from /lib/tls/libc.so.6

(gdb) backtrace
#0  0x400a9295 in strncpy () from /lib/tls/libc.so.6
#1  0x080484df in Init_CString (str=0x80487c5 "Hello!") at cstring.c:15
#2  0x080485e4 in main () at cstring.c:62
```

According to the backtrace output, the seg fault happened at line 15, in Init_CString(), during the call to strncpy(). Without even looking at the code, we already know that the chances are pretty good that we passed a NULL pointer to strncpy() on line 15.

At this point, Milton is still trying to decide where to insert the first of many calls to printf().

4.3.1 First Bug

GDB told us that the seg fault occured at line 15 in Init_CString(), so we'll change the current frame to the one for the invocation of Init_CString().

```
(gdb) frame 1
#1  0x080484df in Init_CString (str=0x80487c5 "Hello!") at cstring.c:15
15              strncpy(p->str, str, strlen(str) + 1);
```

We'll apply the Principle of Confirmation by looking at each of the pointer arguments passed to strncpy()—namely, str, p, and p->str—and verifying that their values are what we think they should be. We first print the value of str:

```
(gdb) print str
$1 = 0x80487c5 "Hello!"
```

Since str is a pointer, GDB gives us its value as the hex address 0x80487c5. And since str is a pointer to char, and thus the address of a character string, GDB helpfully tells us the value of the string as well: "Hello!" This was also clear in the backtrace output we saw above, but we should check anyway. So, str is not NULL and points to a valid string, and everything is okay so far.

Now let's turn our attention to the other pointer arguments, p and p->str:

```
(gdb) print *p
$2 = {
  str = 0x0,
  len = 6
}
```

The problem is now clear: p->str, which is also a pointer to a string, is NULL. That explains the seg fault: We had tried to write to location 0 in memory, which is off limits to us.

But what could cause p->str (the string pointer in the CString under construction) to be NULL? Well, taking a look at the code,

```
(gdb) list Init_CString
5       typedef struct {
6               char *str;
7               int   len;
8       } CString;
```

```
9
10
11      CString *Init_CString(char *str)
12      {
13              CString *p = malloc(sizeof(CString));
14              p->len = strlen(str);
15              strncpy(p->str, str, strlen(str) + 1);
16              return p;
17      }
18
```

we see that there are only two lines of code before the line in which the seg fault occurred, and between them, line 13 is much more likely to be the culprit.

We'll re-run the program from within GDB, set a temporary breakpoint at the entry into Init_CString(), and step through this function line by line, looking at the value of p->str.

```
(gdb) tbreak Init_CString
Breakpoint 1 at 0x804849b: file cstring.c, line 13.
(gdb) run

Breakpoint 1, Init_CString (str=0x80487c5 "Hello!") at cstring.c:13
13              CString *p = malloc(sizeof(CString));
(gdb) step
14              p->len = strlen(str);
(gdb) print p->str
$4 = 0x0
(gdb) step
15              strncpy(p->str, str, strlen(str) + 1);
```

Here's the trouble: We're about to commit a seg fault because the next line of code dereferences p->str, and p->str is still NULL. Now we use the little gray cells to figure out what happened.

When we allocated memory for p we got enough memory for our struct: a pointer to hold the address of the string and an int to hold the string length, but we did *not* allocate memory to hold the string itself. We made the common error of declaring a pointer and not making it point to anything! What we need to do is first allocate enough memory to hold str, and then make p->str point to that newly allocated memory. Here's how we can do that (we need to add one to the length of the string because strlen() doesn't count the terminating '\0'):

```
CString *Init_CString(char *str)
{
   // Allocate for the struct
   CString *p = malloc(sizeof(CString));
   p->len = strlen(str);
```

```
// Allocate for the string
p->str = malloc(p->len + 1);
strncpy(p->str, str, strlen(str) + 1);
return p;
}
```

By the way, Milton has just finished putting `printf()` calls into his code and is about to recompile. If he's lucky, he'll find out where the seg fault happened. If not, he'll have to add even more `printf()` calls.

4.3.2   Don't Leave GDB During a Debugging Session

During the debugging session, we don't ever exit GDB while we make changes to our code. As discussed earlier, this way we avoid the time-consuming startups, we retain our breakpoints, and so on.

Similarly, we keep the text editor open. By staying in the same editor session between compilations while debugging, we can make good use of our editor's "undo" capability. For example, a common strategy in the debugging process is to temporarily remove parts of the code, so as to focus on the remaining sections, where you think a bug lies. After you finish that inspection, you can simply use the undo capability of the editor to restore the deleted lines.

So, on the screen we'll typically have one window for GDB (or DDD) and one window for the editor. We'd also either have a third window open for issuing compiler commands or, better yet, execute them through the editor. For instance, if you use the Vim editor, you can issue the following command, which will save your editing changes *and* recompile the program in one step:

```
: make
```

(We're assuming you've set Vim's `autowrite` variable, using `set autowrite`, in your Vim startup file. This feature of Vim will also move your cursor to the first reported compilation warning or error, if there are any, and you can go back and forth within the compilation error list via Vim's `:cnext` and `:cprev` commands. Of course, all of this is made easier if you put short aliases for these commands in your Vim startup file.)

4.3.3   Second and Third Bugs

After fixing the the first bug, we run the program again from within GDB (remember that when GDB notices you've recompiled the program, it will automatically load the new executable, so that again there's no need to quit and restart GDB):

```
(gdb) run
    The program being debugged has been started already.
    Start it from the beginning? (y or n) y
```

```
`cstring' has changed; re-reading symbols.

Starting program: cstring

Init:
  str: `Hello!' len: 6
Chomp '':
  str:`Hello!0' len: 7
Append:
  str: `Hello!0 world' len: 14

Program exited normally.
(gdb)
```

There appear to be two problems with Chomp(). First, it should have chomped a '!', but it looks like it chomped a nonprinting character. Second, a zero character appears at the end of our string. Since Chomp() is an obvious place to look for these bugs, we'll start the program and place a temporary breakpoint at the entry of Chomp().

```
(gdb) tbreak Chomp
Breakpoint 2 at 0x8048523: file cstring.c, line 32.
(gdb) run
Starting program: cstring

Init:
  str: `Hello!' len: 6

Breakpoint 1, Chomp (cstring=0x804a008) at cstring.c:32
32              char lastchar = *( cstring->str + cstring->len);
(gdb)
```

The last character of the string ought to be '!'. Let's confirm this.

```
(gdb) print lastchar
$1 = 0 '\0'
```

We were expecting lastchar to be '!', but instead it's the null character. This looks like it's probably an "off by one" error. Let's figure it out. We can visualize the string like so:

```
pointer offset: 0 1 2 3 4 5 6
cstring->str:   H e l l o ! \0
string length:  1 2 3 4 5 6
```

The last character of the string is stored at the address cstring->str + 5, but because the string length is a character count, rather than an index, the address `cstring->str + cstring->len` points to one array location past the last character, where the terminating `NULL` is, instead of where we wanted it to point. We can fix this problem by changing line 31 from

```
char lastchar = *( cstring->str + cstring->len);
```

to

```
char lastchar = *( cstring->str + cstring->len - 1);
```

There is a third bug hiding in this part of the code. After the call to `Chomp()`, the string "Hello!" became "Hello!0" (instead of "Hello"). The next line to execute in GDB, line 33, is where we wanted to shorten the string by replacing its last character with a terminating null character:

```
*( cstring->str + cstring->len) = '0';
```

Immediately we see that this line contains the same problem that we just fixed in line 31: We're referencing the last character of the string incorrectly. Furthermore, now that our eyes are trained on this line of code, it appears that we're storing the character `'0'` at that location, which is not the null character. We meant to place `'\0'` at the end of the string. After making these two corrections, line 33 reads

```
*( cstring->str + cstring->len - 1) = '\0';
```

At this point, Milton, our `printf()`-using colleague, has found the first seg fault and is just now correcting the memory allocation issue in `Init_CString()`. Instead of moving on to the bugs we just fixed in `Chomp()`, he'll have to remove all the calls to `printf()` and recompile the program. How inconvenient!

4.3.4 Fourth Bug

Let's make the corrections discussed in the previous section, recompile the code, and run the program again:

```
(gdb) run
`cstring' has changed; re-reading symbols.
Starting program: cstring

Init:
  str: `Hello!' len: 6
Chomp '!':
  str:`Hello' len: 5
Append:
  str: `Hello world' len: 12
```

```
Program received signal SIGSEGV, Segmentation fault.
0xb7f08da1 in free () from /lib/tls/libc.so.6
(gdb)
```

Another seg fault. Judging by the missing exclamation point after the append operation, it appears that the next bug might be hiding in `Append_Chars_To_CString()`. A simple backtrace should confirm or refute this hypothesis:

```
1  (gdb) backtrace
2  #0  0xb7f08da1 in free () from /lib/tls/libc.so.6
3  #1  0x0804851a in Delete_CString (p=0x804a008) at cstring3.c:24
4  #2  0x08048691 in main () at cstring3.c:70
5  (gdb)
```

According to line 3 of the backtrace output, our assumption is wrong: The program actually crashed in `Delete_CString()`. That doesn't mean that we don't also have a bug in `Append_Chars_To_CString()`, but our immediate bug, the one that caused the seg fault, is in `Delete_CString()`. This is exactly why we use GDB here to check our expectations—it completely removes any guesswork in finding where a seg fault occured. Once our `printf()`-using friend catches up to this point in his debugging, he'll be putting trace code in the wrong function!

Luckily, `Delete_CString()` is short, so we should be able to find what's wrong quickly.

```
(gdb) list Delete_CString
20
21   void Delete_CString(CString *p)
22   {
23       free(p);
24       free(p->str);
25   }
26
```

We first free `p`, then we free `p->str`. This counts as a not-so-subtle bug. After `p` is freed, there's no guarantee that `p->str` points to the correct location in memory anymore; it can point anywhere. In this case, that "anywhere" was memory we couldn't access, causing the seg fault. The fix is to reverse the order of the calls to `free()`:

```
void Delete_CString(CString *p)
{
    free(p->str);
    free(p);
}
```

By the way, Milton got too frustrated trying to track down the off-by-one error in Chomp() that we so easily fixed. That's him calling us on the phone now for help.

4.3.5   Fifth and Sixth Bugs

We correct, recompile, and re-run the code once more.

```
(gdb) run
`cstring' has changed; re-reading symbols.
Starting program: cstring

Init:
  str: `Hello!' len: 6
Chomp '!':
  str:`Hello' len: 5
Append:
  str: `Hello world' len: 12

Program exited normally.
(gdb)
```

After the append operation, we're missing the exclamation point in the string, which should be "Hello world!" Curiously, the reported string length of 12 is correct even though the string is incorrect. The most logical place to look for this bug is in Append_Chars_To_CString(), so we'll place a breakpoint there:

```
(gdb) tbreak Append_Chars_To_CString
Breakpoint 3 at 0x8048569: file cstring.c, line 45.
(gdb) run
Starting program: cstring

Init:
  str: `Hello!' len: 6
Chomp '!':
  str:`Hello' len: 5

Breakpoint 1, Append_Chars_To_CString (p=0x804a008, str=0x8048840 " world!")
    at cstring.c:45
45              char *newstr = malloc(p->len + 1);
```

The C string newstr needs to be big enough to hold both p->str and str. We see that the call to malloc() on line 45 doesn't allocate enough memory; it only allocates enough space for p->str and a terminating null. Line 45 should be changed to

```
        char *newstr = malloc(p->len + strlen(str) + 1);
```

After making this correction and recompiling, we get the following output:

```
(gdb) run
`cstring' has changed; re-reading symbols.
Starting program: cstring

Init:
  str: `Hello!' len: 6
Chomp '!':
  str:`Hello' len: 5
Append:
  str: `Hello world' len: 12
```

Our correction didn't fix the bug we had in mind. What we found and fixed was a "silent bug." Make no mistake: It *was* a bug, and the fact that it didn't manifest itself as a seg fault was purely a matter of luck. It's highly probable that the remaining bug is still in Append_Chars_To_CString(), so we'll set another breakpoint there:

```
(gdb) tbreak Append_Chars_To_CString
Breakpoint 4 at 0x8048569: file cstring.c, line 45.
(gdb) run
Starting program: cstring

(gdb) run
Init:
  str: `Hello!' len: 6
Chomp '!':
  str:`Hello' len: 5

Breakpoint 1, Append_Chars_To_CString (p=0x804a008, str=0x8048840 " world!")
    at cstring.c:45
45              char *newstr = malloc(p->len + strlen(str) + 1);
(gdb) step
46              p->len = p->len + strlen(str);
```

Line 46 shows why the string length is correct even though the string itself is incorrect: The addition correctly calculates the length of p->str concatenated with str. No problem here, so we'll step forward.

```
(gdb) step
49              snprintf(newstr, p->len, "%s%s", p->str, str);
```

The next line of code, line 49, is where we form the new string. We expect that newstr will contain "Hello world!" after this step. Let's apply the Principle of Confirmation and verify this.

```
(gdb) step
51                  free(p->str);
(gdb) print newstr
$2 = 0x804a028 "Hello world"
```

The exclamation point is missing from the string constructed on line 51 of the code, so the bug probably occurs at line 49, but what can it be? In the call to snprintf(), we requested that at most p->len bytes be copied into newstr. The value of p->len was confirmed to be 12, and the text "Hello world!" has 12 characters. We didn't tell snprintf() to copy the terminating null character in the source string. But then shouldn't we have gotten a malformed string, with an exclamation point in the last position and no null?

This is one of the great things about snprintf(). It *always* copies a terminating null character into the target. If you goof and specify a maximum number of characters to copy that is less than the actual number of characters in the source (as we did here), snprintf() will copy however many characters it can, but the last character written to the target is guaranteed to be a null character. To fix our mistake we need to tell snprintf() to copy enough bytes to hold the source string's text *and* the terminating null.

So line 45 needs to be changed. Here's the complete, fixed function:

```
CString *Append_Chars_To_CString(CString *p, char *str)
{
   char *newstr = malloc(p->len + strlen(str) + 1);
   p->len = p->len + strlen(str);

   // Create the new string to replace p->str
   snprintf(newstr, p->len + 1, "%s%s", p->str, str);
   // Free old string and make CString point to the new string
   free(p->str);
   p->str = newstr;

   return p;
}
```

Let's recompile the fixed code and run the program:

```
(gdb) run
`cstring' has changed; re-reading symbols.
Starting program: cstring

Init:
  str: `Hello!' len: 6
Chomp '!':
```

```
  str:`Hello' len: 5
Append:
  str: `Hello world!' len: 12

Program exited normally.
(gdb)
```

Looks good!

We've covered quite a bit of territory and encountered some difficult concepts, but it was well worth it. Even if our buggy `CString` implementation was a little contrived, our debugging session was fairly realistic and encompasses the many aspects of debugging:

- The Principle of Confirmation

- Using core files for post-mortem analysis of a process that crashed

- Correcting, compiling, and re-running a program without ever leaving GDB

- The inadequacy of `printf()`-style debugging

- Using good old fashioned brain power—there's no substitute for that

If you come from a `printf()`-style debugging background, you may want to think about how much more difficult it would have been to track down some of these bugs using `printf()`. Diagnostic code using `printf()` has its place in debugging, but as a general-purpose "tool," it is woefully inadequate and inefficient for tracking down most of the bugs that occur in real code.

5

DEBUGGING IN A
MULTIPLE-ACTIVITIES CONTEXT

Debugging is a difficult task, and it becomes even more challenging when the misbehaving application is trying to coordinate multiple, simultaneous activities; client/server network programming, programming with threads, and parallel processing are examples of this paradigm. This chapter presents an overview of the most commonly used multiprogramming techniques and offers some tips on how to deal with bugs in these kinds of programs, focusing on the use of GDB/DDD/Eclipse in the debugging process.

5.1 Debugging Client/Server Network Programs

Computer networks are extremely complex systems, and rigorous debugging of networked software applications can sometimes require the use of hardware monitors to collect detailed information about the network traffic. An entire book could be written on this debugging topic alone. Our goal here is to simply introduce the subject.

Our example consists of the following *client/server pair*. The client application allows a user to check the load on the machine on which the server application runs, even if the user does not have an account on the latter machine. The client sends a request for information to the server—here, a query about the load on the server's system, via the Unix w command—over a network connection. The server then processes the request and returns the results, capturing the output of w and sending it back over the connection. In general, a server can accept requests from multiple remote clients; to keep things simple in our example, let's assume there is only one instance of the client.

The code for the server is shown below:

```
1   // srvr.c
2
3   //  a server to remotely run the w command
4   //  user can check load on machine without login privileges
5   //  usage:  svr
6
7   #include <stdio.h>
8   #include <sys/types.h>
9   #include <sys/socket.h>
10  #include <netinet/in.h>
11  #include <netdb.h>
12  #include <fcntl.h>
13  #include <string.h>
14  #include <unistd.h>
15  #include <stdlib.h>
16
17  #define WPORT 2000
18  #define BUFSIZE 1000  // assumed sufficient here
19
20  int clntdesc,  // socket descriptor for individual client
21      svrdesc;  // general socket descriptor for server
22
23  char outbuf[BUFSIZE];  // messages to client
24
25  void respond()
26  { int fd,nb;
27
28      memset(outbuf,0,sizeof(outbuf));  // clear buffer
29      system("w > tmp.client");  // run 'w' and save results
30      fd = open("tmp.client",O_RDONLY);
31      nb = read(fd,outbuf,BUFSIZE);  // read the entire file
32      write(clntdesc,outbuf,nb);  // write it to the client
33      unlink("tmp.client");  // remove the file
34      close(clntdesc);
```

```
35    }
36
37    int main()
38    {   struct sockaddr_in bindinfo;
39
40        // create socket to be used to accept connections
41        svrdesc = socket(AF_INET,SOCK_STREAM,0);
42        bindinfo.sin_family = AF_INET;
43        bindinfo.sin_port = WPORT;
44        bindinfo.sin_addr.s_addr = INADDR_ANY;
45        bind(svrdesc,(struct sockaddr *) &bindinfo,sizeof(bindinfo));
46
47        // OK, listen in loop for client calls
48        listen(svrdesc,5);
49
50        while (1)  {
51            // wait for a call
52            clntdesc = accept(svrdesc,0,0);
53            // process the command
54            respond();
55        }
56    }
```

Here is the code for the client:

```
1     // clnt.c
2
3     // usage:  clnt server_machine
4
5     #include <stdio.h>
6     #include <sys/types.h>
7     #include <sys/socket.h>
8     #include <netinet/in.h>
9     #include <netdb.h>
10    #include <string.h>
11    #include <unistd.h>
12
13    #define WPORT 2000  // server port number
14    #define BUFSIZE 1000
15
16    int main(int argc, char **argv)
17    {   int sd,msgsize;
18
19        struct sockaddr_in addr;
20        struct hostent *hostptr;
21        char buf[BUFSIZE];
22
23        // create socket
```

```
24    sd = socket(AF_INET,SOCK_STREAM,0);
25    addr.sin_family = AF_INET;
26    addr.sin_port = WPORT;
27    hostptr = gethostbyname(argv[1]);
28    memcpy(&addr.sin_addr.s_addr,hostptr->h_addr_list[0],hostptr->h_length);
29
30    // OK, now connect
31    connect(sd,(struct sockaddr *) &addr,sizeof(addr));
32
33    // read and display response
34    msgsize = read(sd,buf,BUFSIZE);
35    if (msgsize > 0)
36       write(1,buf,msgsize);
37    printf("\n");
38    return 0;
39 }
```

For those unfamiliar with client/server programming, here is an overview of how the programs work:

On line 41 of the server code, you create a *socket*, which is an abstraction similar to a file descriptor; just as one uses a file descriptor to perform I/O operations on a filesystem object, one reads from and writes to a network connection via a socket. On line 45, the socket is bound to a specific *port number*, arbitrarily chosen to be 2000. (User-level applications such as this one are restricted to port numbers of 1024 and higher.) This number identifies a "mailbox" on the server's system to which clients send requests to be processed for this particular application.

The server "opens for business" by calling listen() on line 48. It then waits for a client request to come in by calling accept() on line 52. That call blocks until a request arrives. It then returns a new socket for communicating with the client. (When there are multiple clients, the original socket continues to accept new requests even while an existing request is being serviced, hence the need for separate sockets. This would require the server to be implemented in a threaded fashion.) The server processes the client request with the respond() function and sends the machine load information to the client by locally invoking the w command and writing the results to the socket in line 32.

The client creates a socket on line 24 and then uses it on line 31 to connect to the server's port 2000. On line 34, it reads the load information sent by the server and then prints it out.

Here is what the output of the client should look like:

```
$ clnt laura.cs.ucdavis.edu
 13:00:15 up 13 days, 39 min,  7 users,  load average: 0.25, 0.13, 0.09
USER     TTY     FROM            LOGIN@   IDLE   JCPU   PCPU WHAT
matloff  :0      -               14Jun07 ?xdm?  25:38  0.15s -/bin/tcsh -c /
matloff  pts/1   :0.0            14Jun07 17:34  0.46s  0.46s -csh
matloff  pts/2   :0.0            14Jun07 18:12  0.39s  0.39s -csh
```

```
matloff  pts/3    :0.0              14Jun07 58.00s  2.18s  2.01s /usr/bin/mutt
matloff  pts/4    :0.0              14Jun07  0.00s  1.85s  0.00s clnt laura.cs.u
matloff  pts/5    :0.0              14Jun07 20.00s  1.88s  0.02s script
matloff  pts/7    :0.0              19Jun07 4days 22:17    0.16s -csh
```

Now suppose the programmer had forgotten line 26 in the client code, which specifies the port on the server's system to connect to:

```
addr.sin_port = WPORT;
```

Let's pretend we don't know what the bug is and see how we might track it down.

The client's output would now be

```
$ clnt laura.cs.ucdavis.edu

$
```

It appears that the client received nothing at all back from the server. This of course could be due to a variety of causes in either the server or the client, or both.

Let's take a look around, using GDB. First, check to see that the client actually did succeed in connecting to the server. Set a breakpoint at the call to connect(), and run the program:

```
(gdb) b 31
Breakpoint 1 at 0x8048502: file clnt.c, line 31.
(gdb) r laura.cs.ucdavis.edu
Starting program: /fandrhome/matloff/public_html/matloff/public_html/Debug
/Book/DDD/clnt laura.cs.ucdavis.edu

Breakpoint 1, main (argc=2, argv=0xbf81a344) at clnt.c:31
31              connect(sd,(struct sockaddr *) &addr,sizeof(addr));
```

Use GDB to execute the connect() and check the return value for an error condition:

```
(gdb) p connect(sd,&addr,sizeof(addr))
$1 = -1
```

It is indeed -1, the code for failure. That is a big hint. (Of course, as a matter of defensive programming, when we wrote the client code, we would have checked the return value of connect() and handled the case of failure to connect.)

By the way, note that in manually executing the call to connect(), you have to remove the cast. With the cast retained, you'd get an error:

```
(gdb) p connect(sd,(struct sockaddr *) &addr,sizeof(addr))
No struct type named sockaddr.
```

This is due to a quirk in GDB, and it arises because we haven't used the struct elsewhere in the program.

Also note that if the connect() attempt had succeeded in the GDB session, you could *not* have then gone ahead and executed line 31. Attempting to open an already-open socket is an error.

You would have had to skip over line 31 and go directly to line 34. You could do this using GDB's jump command, issuing jump 34, but in general you should use this command with caution, as it might result in skipping some machine instructions that are needed further down in the code. So, if the connection attempt had succeeded, you would probably want to rerun the program.

Let's try to track down the cause of the failure by checking the argument addr in the call to connect():

```
(gdb) p addr
...
connect(3, {sa_family=AF_INET, sin_port=htons(1032),
sin_addr=inet_addr("127.0.0.1")}, 16) = -1 ECONNREFUSED (Connection refused)
...
```

Aha! The value htons(1032) indicates port 2052 (see below), not the 2000 we expect. This suggests that you either misspecified the port or forgot to specify it altogether. If you check, you'll quickly discover that the latter was the case.

Again, it would have been prudent to include a bit of machinery in the source code to help the debugging process, such as checking the return values of system calls. Another helpful step is inclusion of the line

```
#include <errno.h>
```

which, on our system, creates a global variable errno, whose value can be printed out from within the code or from within GDB:

```
(gdb) p errno
$1 = 111
```

From the file */usr/include/linux/errno.h*, you find that this error number codes a *connection refused* error.

However, the implementation of the errno library may differ from platform to platform. For example, the header file may have a different name, or errno may be implemented as a macro call instead of a variable.

Another approach would be to use strace, which traces all system calls made by a program:

```
$ strace clnt laura.cs
...
connect(3, {sa_family=AF_INET, sin_port=htons(1032),
sin_addr=inet_addr("127.0.0.1")}, 16) = -1 ECONNREFUSED (Connection refused)
...
```

This gives you two important pieces of information for the price of one. First, you see right away that there was an ECONNREFUSED error. Second, you also see that the port was htons(1032), which has the value 2052. You can check this latter value by issuing a command like

```
(gdb) p htons(1032)
```

from within GDB, which shows the value to be 2052, which obviously is not 2000, as expected.

You will find strace to be a handy tool in many contexts (networked and otherwise) for checking the results of system calls.

As another example, suppose that you accidentally omit the write to the client in the server code (line 32):

```
write(clntdesc,outbuf,nb);  // write it to the client
```

In this case, the client program would hang, waiting for a reply that is not forthcoming. Of course, in this simpleminded example you'd immediately suspect a problem with the call to write() in the server and quickly find that we had forgotten it. But in more complex programs the cause may not be so obvious. In such cases, you would probably set up *two* simultaneous GDB sessions, one for the client and one for the server, stepping through *both* of the programs in tandem. You would find that at some point in their joint operation that the client hangs, waiting to hear from the server, and thus obtain a clue to the likely location of the bug within the server. You'd then focus your attention on the server GDB session, trying to figure out why it did not send to the client at that point.

In really complex network debugging cases, the open source ethereal program can be used to track individual TCP/IP packets.

5.2 Debugging Threaded Code

Threaded programming has become quite popular. For Unix, the most widespread threads package is the POSIX standard Pthreads, so we will use it for our example in this section. The principles are similar for other thread packages.

5.2.1 Review of Processes and Threads

Modern operating systems use *timesharing* to manage multiple running programs in such a way that they appear to the user to execute simultaneously.

Of course, if the machine has more than one CPU, more than one program actually can run simultaneously, but for simplicity we will assume just one processor, in which case the simultaneity is only apparent.

Each instance of a running program is represented by the OS as a *process* (in Unix terminology) or a *task* (in Windows). Thus, multiple invocations of a single program that execute at the same time (e.g., simultaneous sessions of the vi text editor) are distinct processes. Processes have to "take turns" on a machine with one CPU. For concreteness, let's assume that the "turns," called *timeslices*, are of length 30 milliseconds.

After a process has run for 30 milliseconds, a hardware timer emits an interrupt, which causes the OS to run. We say that the process has been *preempted*. The OS saves the current state of the interrupted process so it can be resumed later, then selects the next process to give a timeslice to. This is known as a *context switch*, because the CPU's execution environment has switched from one process to another. This cycle repeats indefinitely.

A turn may end early. For example, when a process needs to perform input/output, it ultimately calls a function in the OS that carries out low-level hardware operations; for instance, a call to the C library function scanf() results in a call to the Unix OS read() system call, which interfaces with the keyboard driver. In this manner the process relinquishes its turn to the OS, and the turn ends early.

One implication of this is that scheduling of timeslices for a given process is rather random. The time it takes for the user to think and then hit a key is random, so the time its next timeslice starts is unpredictable. Moreover, if you are debugging a threaded program, you do not know the order in which the threads will be scheduled; this may make debugging more difficult.

Here is a bit more detail: The OS maintains a *process table* that lists information about all current processes. Roughly speaking, each process is marked in the table as being in either the Run state or the Sleep state. Let's consider an example in which a running program reaches a point at which it needs to read input from the keyboard. As just noted, this will end the process's turn. Because the process is now waiting for the I/O to complete, the OS marks it as being in the Sleep state, making it ineligible for timeslices. Thus, being in Sleep state means that the process is blocked, waiting for some event to occur. When this event finally occurs later on, the OS will then change its state in the process table back to Run.

Non-I/O events can trigger a transition to Sleep state as well. For instance, if a parent process creates a child process and calls wait(), the parent will block until the child finishes its work and terminates. Again, exactly when this happens is usually unpredictable.

Furthermore, being in the Run state does not mean that the process is actually executing on the CPU; rather, it merely means that it is *ready* to run—that is, eligible for a processor timeslice. Upon a context switch, the OS chooses the process that is next given a turn on the CPU from among those currently in the Run state, according to the process table. The scheduling procedure used by the OS to select the new context guarantees that any given process will keep getting timeslices, and so eventually finish, but there is no promise of *which* timeslices it will receive. Thus, exactly when a sleeping process actually "awakens" once the event that it awaits has occurred is random, as is the exact rate of the process's progress toward completion.

A *thread* is much like a process, except that it is designed to occupy less memory and to take less time to create and switch between than processes do. Indeed, threads are sometimes called "lightweight" processes and, depending on the thread system and run-time environment, they may even be implemented as operating system processes. Like programs that spawn processes to get work done, a multithreaded application will generally execute a main() procedure that creates one or more child threads. The parent, main(), is also a thread.

A major difference between processes and threads is that although each thread has its own local variables, just as is the case for a process, the global variables of the parent program in a threaded environment are shared by all threads and serve as the main method of communication between the threads. (It is possible to share globals among Unix processes, but inconvenient to do so.)

On a Linux system, you can view all the processes and threads currently on the system by running the command ps axH.

There are nonpreemptive thread systems, but Pthreads uses a *preemptive* thread management policy, and a thread in a program can be interrupted at any time by another thread. Thus, the element of randomness described above for processes in a timeshared system also arises in the behavior of a threaded program. As a result, some bugs in applications developed using Pthreads are not readily reproducible.

5.2.2 Basic Example

We'll keep things simple and use the following code for finding prime numbers as an example. The program uses the classic Sieve of Eratosthenes. To find all the primes from 2 through *n*, we first list all the numbers, then cross out all the multiples of 2, then all the multiples of 3, and so on. Whatever numbers remain at the end are prime numbers.

```
1   // finds the primes between 2 and n; uses the Sieve of Eratosthenes,
2   // deleting all multiples of 2, all multiples of 3, all multiples of 5,
3   // etc.; not efficient, e.g. each thread should do deleting for a whole
4   // block of values of base before going to nextbase for more
5
6   // usage:  sieve nthreads n
7   // where nthreads is the number of worker threads
8
9   #include <stdio.h>
10  #include <math.h>
11  #include <pthread.h>
12
13  #define MAX_N 100000000
```

```
14    #define MAX_THREADS 100

15

16    // shared variables
17    int nthreads,  // number of threads (not counting main())
18        n,  // upper bound of range in which to find primes
19        prime[MAX_N+1],  // in the end, prime[i] = 1 if i prime, else 0
20        nextbase;  // next sieve multiplier to be used

21

22    int work[MAX_THREADS];  // to measure how much work each thread does,
23                            // in terms of number of sieve multipliers checked

24

25    // lock index for the shared variable nextbase
26    pthread_mutex_t nextbaselock = PTHREAD_MUTEX_INITIALIZER;

27

28    // ID structs for the threads
29    pthread_t id[MAX_THREADS];

30

31    // "crosses out" all multiples of k, from k*k on
32    void crossout(int k)
33    { int i;

34

35        for (i = k; i*k <= n; i++)  {
36            prime[i*k] = 0;
37        }
38    }

39

40    // worker thread routine
41    void *worker(int tn)  // tn is the thread number (0,1,...)
42    { int lim,base;

43

44        // no need to check multipliers bigger than sqrt(n)
45        lim = sqrt(n);

46

47        do  {
48            // get next sieve multiplier, avoiding duplication across threads
49            pthread_mutex_lock(&nextbaselock);
50            base = nextbase += 2;
51            pthread_mutex_unlock(&nextbaselock);
52            if (base <= lim)  {
53                work[tn]++;  // log work done by this thread
54                // don't bother with crossing out if base is known to be
55                // composite
56                if (prime[base])
57                    crossout(base);
58            }
59            else return;
60        } while (1);
```

```
61    }
62
63    main(int argc, char **argv)
64    {  int nprimes,  // number of primes found
65          totwork,   // number of base values checked
66          i;
67       void *p;
68
69       n = atoi(argv[1]);
70       nthreads = atoi(argv[2]);
71       for (i = 2; i <= n; i++)
72          prime[i] = 1;
73       crossout(2);
74       nextbase = 1;
75       // get threads started
76       for (i = 0; i < nthreads; i++)  {
77          pthread_create(&id[i],NULL,(void *) worker,(void *) i);
78       }
79
80       // wait for all done
81       totwork = 0;
82       for (i = 0; i < nthreads; i++)  {
83          pthread_join(id[i],&p);
84          printf("%d values of base done\n",work[i]);
85          totwork += work[i];
86       }
87       printf("%d total values of base done\n",totwork);
88
89       // report results
90       nprimes = 0;
91       for (i = 2; i <= n; i++)
92          if (prime[i]) nprimes++;
93       printf("the number of primes found was %d\n",nprimes);
94
95    }
```

There are two command-line arguments in this program, the upper bound n of the range to be checked for primes, and nthreads, the number of worker threads we wish to create.

Here main() creates the worker threads, each of which is an invocation of the function worker(). The workers share three data items: the upper bound variable, n; the variable specifying the next number whose multiples are to be eliminated from the range 2..n, nextbase; and the array prime[] that records, for each number in the range 2..n, whether or not it has been eliminated. Each invocation repeatedly fetches a yet-to-be-processed elimination multiplicand, base, and then eliminates all multiples of base from the range 2..n. After spawning the workers, main() uses pthread_join() to wait for all these threads to finish their work before resuming itself, at which point it counts the primes that are left and issues its report. The report includes not only the prime count, but also information on how much work each worker thread did. This assessment is useful for *load balancing* and performance optimization purposes on a multiprocessor system.

Each instance of worker() fetches the next value of base by executing the following code (lines 49–51):

```
pthread_mutex_lock(&nextbaselock);
base = nextbase += 2;
pthread_mutex_unlock(&nextbaselock);
```

Here, the global variable nextbase is updated and used to initialize the value of the worker() instance's local variable base; the worker then crosses out multiples of base in the array prime[]. (Note that we started by eliminating all multiples of 2 at the beginning of main(), and thereafter only need to consider odd values for base.)

Once the worker knows the value of base to use, it can safely cross out the multiples of base from the shared array prime[], because no other worker will use that value of base. However, we have to place *guard statements* around the update operation to the shared variable nextbase that base depends upon (line 26). Recall that any worker thread can be preempted, at an unpredictable time, by another worker thread, which will be at an unpredictable place in the code for worker(). In particular, it might just happen that the current worker is interrupted in the midst of the statement

```
base = nextbase += 2;
```

and the next timeslice is given to another thread that is also executing the same statement. In this case, there are two workers trying to modify the shared variable nextbase at once, which can lead to insidious and hard-to-reproduce bugs.

Bracketing the code that manipulates the shared variable—known as a *critical section*—with the guard statements prevents this from happening. The calls to pthread_mutex_lock() and pthread_mutex_unlock() ensure that there is at most only one thread executing the enclosed program fragment. They tell the OS to allow a thread to enter the critical section only if there is no other thread currently executing it, and to not preempt that thread until it completes the entire section. (The *lock variable* nextbaselock is used internally by the thread system to ensure this "mutual exclusion.")

Unfortunately, it's all too easy to fail to recognize and/or properly protect critical sections in threaded code. Let's see how GDB can be used to debug this sort of error in a Pthreads program. Suppose we had forgotten to include the unlock statement,

```
pthread_mutex_unlock(&nextbaselock);
```

This of course causes the program to hang once the critical section is first entered by a worker thread, as the other worker threads will wait forever for the lock to be relinquished. But let's pretend you don't already know this. How do you track down the culprit using GDB?

Compile the progam, making sure to include the flags -lpthread -lm in order to link in the Pthreads and math libraries (the latter is needed for thr call to sqrt()). Then run the code in GDB, with n = 100 and nthreads = 2:

```
(gdb) r 100 2
Starting program: /debug/primes 100 2
[New Thread 16384 (LWP 28653)]
[New Thread 32769 (LWP 28676)]
[New Thread 16386 (LWP 28677)]
[New Thread 32771 (LWP 28678)]
```

Each time a new thread is created, GDB announces it, as shown here. We'll look into which thread is which in a moment.

The program hangs, and you interrupt it by pressing CTRL-C. The GDB session now looks like this:

```
(gdb) r 100 2
Starting program: /debug/primes 100 2
[New Thread 16384 (LWP 28653)]
[New Thread 32769 (LWP 28676)]
[New Thread 16386 (LWP 28677)]
[New Thread 32771 (LWP 28678)]

Program received signal SIGINT, Interrupt.
[Switching to Thread 32771 (LWP 28678)]
0x4005ba35 in __pthread_sigsuspend () from /lib/i686/libpthread.so.0
```

At a point like this it's crucial to know what each thread is doing, which you can determine via GDB's info threads command:

```
(gdb) info threads
* 4 Thread 32771 (LWP 28678)  0x4005ba35 in __pthread_sigsuspend ()
   from /lib/i686/libpthread.so.0
  3 Thread 16386 (LWP 28677)  0x4005ba35 in __pthread_sigsuspend ()
   from /lib/i686/libpthread.so.0
  2 Thread 32769 (LWP 28676)  0x420db1a7 in poll () from
/lib/i686/libc.so.6
  1 Thread 16384 (LWP 28653)  0x4005ba35 in __pthread_sigsuspend ()
   from /lib/i686/libpthread.so.0
```

The asterisk means that you are currently in thread 4. Let's see what's going on with that thread:

```
(gdb) bt
#0  0x4005ba35 in __pthread_sigsuspend () from /lib/i686/libpthread.so.0
#1  0x4005adb8 in __pthread_wait_for_restart_signal ()
    from /lib/i686/libpthread.so.0
#2  0x4005d190 in __pthread_alt_lock () from /lib/i686/libpthread.so.0
#3  0x40059d77 in pthread_mutex_lock () from /lib/i686/libpthread.so.0
#4  0x0804855f in worker (tn=1) at Primes.c:49
#5  0x40059881 in pthread_start_thread () from /lib/i686/libpthread.so.0
#6  0x40059985 in pthread_start_thread_event () from
/lib/i686/libpthread.so.0
```

(This works under the LinuxThreads implementation of Pthreads but may not be possible on some other platforms.)

Aha—you see in frames 3 and 4 that this thread is on line 49 of the source code and is trying to acquire the lock and enter the critical section:

```
pthread_mutex_lock(&nextbaselock);
```

Note also from frame 0 above that the thread is apparently suspended pending the lock's being relinquished by another thread. It will not get any timeslices until this happens *and* the thread manager arranges for it to acquire the lock.

What are the other threads doing? You can inspect any thread's stack by switching to that thread and then issuing the bt command:

```
(gdb) thread 3
[Switching to thread 3 (Thread 16386 (LWP 28677))]#0  0x4005ba35 in
__pthread_sigsuspend () from /lib/i686/libpthread.so.0
(gdb) bt
#0  0x4005ba35 in __pthread_sigsuspend () from /lib/i686/libpthread.so.0
#1  0x4005adb8 in __pthread_wait_for_restart_signal ()
    from /lib/i686/libpthread.so.0
#2  0x4005d190 in __pthread_alt_lock () from /lib/i686/libpthread.so.0
#3  0x40059d77 in pthread_mutex_lock () from /lib/i686/libpthread.so.0
#4  0x0804855f in worker (tn=0) at Primes.c:49
#5  0x40059881 in pthread_start_thread () from /lib/i686/libpthread.so.0
#6  0x40059985 in pthread_start_thread_event () from
/lib/i686/libpthread.so.0
```

Recall that we created two worker threads. You saw above that thread 4 was one of them (frame 4 from its bt output), and now you see from frame 4 of the output here that thread 3 is the other one. You also see that thread 3 is trying to acquire the lock as well (frame 3).

There shouldn't be any other worker threads, but one of the fundamental principles of debugging is that nothing is taken on faith, and everything must be checked. We do this now by inspecting the status of the remaining threads. You'll find that the other two threads are nonworker threads, as follows:

```
(gdb) thread 2
[Switching to thread 2 (Thread 32769 (LWP 28676))]#0  0x420db1a7 in poll
()
    from /lib/i686/libc.so.6
(gdb) bt
#0  0x420db1a7 in poll () from /lib/i686/libc.so.6
#1  0x400589de in __pthread_manager () from /lib/i686/libpthread.so.0
#2  0x4005962b in __pthread_manager_event () from
/lib/i686/libpthread.so.0
```

So thread 2 is the threads manager. This is internal to the Pthreads package. It is certainly not a worker thread, partially confirming our expectation that there are only two worker threads. Checking thread 1,

```
(gdb) thread 1
[Switching to thread 1 (Thread 16384 (LWP 28653))]#0  0x4005ba35 in
__pthread_sigsuspend () from /lib/i686/libpthread.so.0
(gdb) bt
#0  0x4005ba35 in __pthread_sigsuspend () from /lib/i686/libpthread.so.0
#1  0x4005adb8 in __pthread_wait_for_restart_signal ()
    from /lib/i686/libpthread.so.0
#2  0x40058551 in pthread_join () from /lib/i686/libpthread.so.0
#3  0x080486aa in main (argc=3, argv=0xbfffe7b4) at Primes.c:83
#4  0x420158f7 in __libc_start_main () from /lib/i686/libc.so.6
```

you find it executes main() and can thus confirm that there are only two worker threads.

However, both of the workers are stalled, each waiting for the lock to be relinquished. No wonder the program is hanging! This is enough to pinpoint the location and nature of the bug, and we quickly realize that we forgot the call to the unlocking function.

5.2.3   A Variation

What if you hadn't realized the necessity of guarding the update of the shared variable nextbase in the first place? What would have happened in the previous example if you'd left out *both* the unlock and the lock operations?

A naive look at this question might lead to the guess that there would have been no harm in terms of correct operation of the program (i.e., getting an accurate count of the number of primes), albeit possibly with a slowdown due to duplicate work (i.e., using the same value of base more than once). It would seem that some threads may duplicate the work of others, namely when two workers happen to grab the same value of nextbase to initialize their local copies of base. Some composite numbers might then end up being crossed out twice, but the results (i.e., the count of the number of primes) would still be correct.

But let's take a closer look. The statement

```
base = nextbase += 2;
```

compiles to at least two machine language instructions. For instance, using the GCC compiler on a Pentium machine running Linux, the C statement above translates to the following assembly language instructions (obtained by running GCC with the -S option and then viewing the resulting .s file):

```
addl $2, nextbase
movl nextbase, %eax
movl %eax, -8(%ebp)
```

This code increments nextbase by 2, then copies the value of nextbase to the register EAX, and finally, copies the value of EAX to the place in the worker's stack where its local variable base is stored.

Suppose you have only two worker threads and the value of nextbase is, say, 9, and the currently running worker() invocation's timeslice ends just after it executes the machine instruction

```
addl $2, nextbase
```

which sets the shared global variable nextbase to 11. Suppose the next time-slice goes to another invocation of worker(), which happens to be executing those same instructions. The second worker now increments nextbase to 13, uses this to set its local variable base, and starts to eliminate all multiples of 13. Eventually, the first invocation of worker() will get another timeslice, and it will then pick up where it left off, executing the machine instructions

```
movl nextbase, %eax
movl %eax, -8(%ebp)
```

Of course, the value of nextbase is now 13. The first worker thus sets the value of its local variable base to 13 and proceeds to eliminate multiples of this value, not the value 11 that it set during its last timeslice. Neither worker does anything with the multiples of 11. You end up not only duplicating work unnecessarily, but also skipping necessary work!

How might you discover such an error using GDB? Presumably the "symptom" that surfaced was that the number of primes reported was too large. Thus you might suspect that values of base are somehow sometimes skipped. To check this hypothesis, you could place a breakpoint right after the line

```
base = nextbase += 2;
```

By repeatedly issuing the GDB continue (c) command and displaying the value of base, you might eventually verify that a value of base is indeed skipped.

The key word here is *might*. Recall our earlier discussion that threaded programs run in a somewhat random manner. In the context here, it may be the case that on some runs of the program the bug surfaces (i.e., too many primes are reported), but on other runs you may get correct answers!

There is, unfortunately, no good solution to this problem. Debugging threaded code often requires extra patience and creativity.

5.2.4   GDB Threads Command Summary

Here is a summary of the usage of GDB's thread-related commands:

- info threads (Gives information on all current threads)
- thread 3 (Changes to thread 3)
- break 88 thread 3 (Stops execution when thread 3 reaches source line 88)
- break 88 thread 3 if x==y (Stops execution when thread 3 reaches source line 88 and the variables x and y are equal)

5.2.5   Threads Commands in DDD

In DDD, select **Status | Threads**, and a window will pop up, displaying all threads in the manner of GDB's info threads, as seen in Figure 5-1. You can click a thread to switch the debugger's focus to it.

You will probably want to keep this pop-up window around, rather than using it once and then closing it. This way you don't have to keep reopening it every time you want to see which thread is currently running or switch to a different thread.

There appears to be no way to make a breakpoint thread-specific in DDD, as you did with the GDB command break 88 thread 3 above. Instead, you issue such a command to GDB via the DDD Console.

5.2.6   Threads Commands in Eclipse

Note first that the default makefile created by Eclipse will not include the -lpthread command-line argument for GCC (nor will it include the arguments for any other special libraries you need). You can alter the makefile directly if you wish, but it is easier to tell Eclipse to do it for you. While in the C/C++ perspective, right-click your project name, and select **Properties**; point the triangle next to C/C++ Build downward; select **Settings | Tool Settings**; point the triangle next to GCC C Linker downward and select **Libraries | Add** (the latter is the green plus sign icon); and fill in your library flags minus the -l (e.g., filling in m for -lm). Then build your project.

Recall from Chapter 1 that Eclipse constantly displays your thread list, as opposed to having to request it, as in DDD. Moreover, you do not need

Figure 5-1: Threads window

to ask for a backtrace kind of operation as you do in DDD; the call stack is shown in the thread list. This is depicted in Figure 5-2. As above, we ran the program for a while then interrupted it by clicking the Suspend icon to the right of *Resume*. The thread list is in the Debug view, which normally is in the upper-left portion of the screen but appears here in expanded form since we clicked Maximize in the Debug tab. (We can click Restore to return to the standard layout.)

We see that thread 3 had been running at the time of the interruption; it had received a SIGINT signal, which is the interruption (CTRL-C) signal. We see also that the associated system call had been invoked by pthread_join(), which in turn had been called by main(). From what we've seen about this program earlier, we know that this indeed is the main thread.

To view the information for another thread, we merely click the triangle next to the thread to point it downward. To change to another thread, we click its entry in the list.

We may wish to set a breakpoint that applies only to a specific thread. To do so, we must first wait until the thread is created. Then when execution

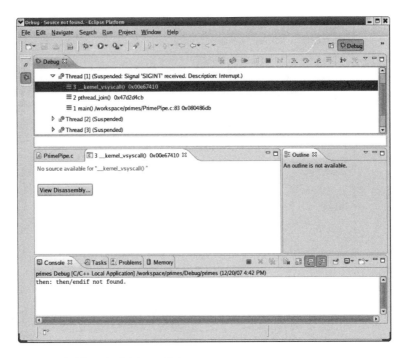

Figure 5-2: Threads display in Eclipse

pauses via a previous setting of a breakpoint, or an interruption as above, we right-click the breakpoint symbol in the same manner as we would to make a breakpoint conditional, but this time, select **Filtering**. A pop-up window like the one in Figure 5-3 will appear. We see that this breakpoint currently applies to all three threads. If we wish it to apply only to thread 2, for instance, we would uncheck the boxes next to the entries for the other two threads.

5.3 Debugging Parallel Applications

There are two main types of parallel programming architectures—shared memory and message passing.

The term *shared memory* means exactly that: Multiple CPUs all have access to some common physical memory. Code running on one CPU communicates with code running on the others by reading from and writing to this shared memory, much as threads in a multithreaded application communicate with one another through a shared address space. (Indeed, threaded programming has become the standard way to write application code for shared memory systems.)

By contrast, in a *message passing* environment, code running on each CPU can only access that CPU's local memory, and it communicates with the others by sending strings of bytes called *messages* over a communication medium. Typically this is some kind of network, running either a general-

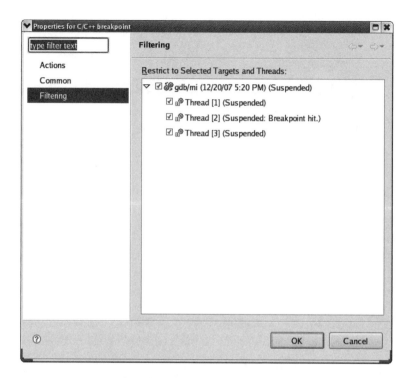

Figure 5-3: Setting a thread-specific breakpoint in Eclipse

purpose protocol like TCP/IP or a specialized software infrastructure that is tailored to message-passing applications.

5.3.1 Message-Passing Systems

We will discuss message passing first, using the popular Message Passing Interface (MPI) package as an example. We use the MPICH implementation here, but the same principles apply to LAM and other MPI implementations.

Let us again consider a prime-number finding program:

```
1   #include <mpi.h>
2
3   // MPI sample program; not intended to be efficient; finds and reports
4   // the number of primes less than or equal to n
5
6   // Uses a pipeline approach:  node 0 looks at all the odd numbers (i.e.,
7   // we assume multiples of 2 are already filtered out) and filters out
8   // those that are multiples of 3, passing the rest to node 1; node 1
9   // filters out the multiples of 5, passing the rest to node 2; node 2
10  // filters out the rest of the composites and then reports the number
11  // of primes
12
```

```
13    // the command-line arguments are n and debugwait
14
15    #define PIPE_MSG 0  // type of message containing a number to
16                        // be checked
17    #define END_MSG 1  // type of message indicating no more data will
18                        // be coming
19
20    int nnodes,  // number of nodes in computation
21        n,  // find all primes from 2 to n
22        me;   // my node number
23
24    init(int argc,char **argv)
25    {  int debugwait;  // if 1, then loop around until the
26                        // debugger has been attached
27
28       MPI_Init(&argc,&argv);
29       n = atoi(argv[1]);
30       debugwait = atoi(argv[2]);
31
32       MPI_Comm_size(MPI_COMM_WORLD,&nnodes);
33       MPI_Comm_rank(MPI_COMM_WORLD,&me);
34
35       while (debugwait) ;
36    }
37
38    void node0()
39    {  int i,dummy,
40           tocheck; // current number to check for passing on to next node
41       for (i = 1; i <= n/2; i++)  {
42          tocheck = 2 * i + 1;
43          if (tocheck > n) break;
44          if (tocheck % 3 > 0)
45             MPI_Send(&tocheck,1,MPI_INT,1,PIPE_MSG,MPI_COMM_WORLD);
46       }
47       MPI_Send(&dummy,1,MPI_INT,1,END_MSG,MPI_COMM_WORLD);
48    }
49
50    void node1()
51    {  int tocheck,  // current number to check from node 0
52           dummy;
53       MPI_Status status;  // see below
54
55       while (1)  {
56          MPI_Recv(&tocheck,1,MPI_INT,0,MPI_ANY_TAG,
57             MPI_COMM_WORLD,&status);
58          if (status.MPI_TAG == END_MSG) break;
59          if (tocheck % 5 > 0)
```

```
60              MPI_Send(&tocheck,1,MPI_INT,2,PIPE_MSG,MPI_COMM_WORLD);
61        }
62        // now send our end-of-data signal, which is conveyed in the
63        // message type, not the message itself
64        MPI_Send(&dummy,1,MPI_INT,2,END_MSG,MPI_COMM_WORLD);
65    }
66
67    void node2()
68    {  int tocheck,  // current number to check from node 1
69           primecount,i,iscomposite;
70       MPI_Status status;
71
72       primecount = 3;  // must account for the primes 2, 3 and 5, which
73                        // won't be detected below
74       while (1)  {
75          MPI_Recv(&tocheck,1,MPI_INT,1,MPI_ANY_TAG,
76             MPI_COMM_WORLD,&status);
77          if (status.MPI_TAG == END_MSG) break;
78          iscomposite = 0;
79          for (i = 7; i*i <= tocheck; i += 2)
80             if (tocheck % i == 0)  {
81                iscomposite = 1;
82                break;
83             }
84          if (!iscomposite) primecount++;
85       }
86       printf("number of primes = %d\n",primecount);
87    }
88
89    main(int argc,char **argv)
90    {  init(argc,argv);
91       switch (me)  {
92          case 0:  node0();
93             break;
94          case 1:  node1();
95             break;
96          case 2:  node2();
97       };
98       MPI_Finalize();
99    }
```

As explained in the comments at the beginning of the program, here our Sieve of Eratosthenes runs on three nodes of a parallel system and works in a pipelined manner. The first node starts with odd numbers and removes all multiples of 3, passing on the remaining values; the second node takes the output of the first and removes all multiples of 5; and the third node takes the output of the second, removes the rest of the nonprimes, and reports the number of primes that are left.

Here the pipelining is achieved by having each node pass one number at a time to the next. (Much greater efficiency could be attained by passing groups of numbers in each MPI message, thus reducing communications overhead.) When sending a number on to the next node, a node sends a message of type PIPE_MSG. When a node has no more numbers to send, it indicates this by sending a message of type END_MSG.

As a debugging example here, suppose we forget to include the latter notification at the first node—that is, we forget line 46 in the code for node0():

```
MPI_Send(&dummy,1,MPI_INT,1,END_MSG,MPI_COMM_WORLD);
```

The program will hang at the "downstream" nodes. Let's see how we can track down this bug. (Keep in mind that some line numbers in the GDB session below will differ by 1 from those in the above listing.)

You run an MPICH application program by invoking a script named mpirun on one node of the system. The script then starts the application program at each node, via SSH. Here we did this on a network of three machines, which we'll call Node 0, Node 1, and Node 2, with n equal to 100. The bug causes the program to hang at the latter two nodes. The program also hangs at the first node, because no instance of an MPI program will exit until all have executed the MPI_FINALIZE() function.

We would like to use GDB, but because we used mpirun to invoke the application at each of the three nodes, rather than running them directly on the nodes, we cannot run GDB directly. However, GDB allows you to dynamically *attach* the debugger to an already-running process, using the process number. So let's run ps on Node 1 to determine the number of the process that is executing our application there:

```
$ ps ax
...
 2755 ?       S    0:00 tcsh -c /home/matloff/primepipe node 1 3
 2776 ?       S    0:00 /home/matloff/primepipe node1 32812   4
 2777 ?       S    0:00 /home/matloff/primepipe node1 32812   4
```

The MPI program is running as process 2776, so we attach GDB to the program at Node 1:

```
$ gdb primepipe 2776
...
0xffffe002 in ?? ()
```

This is not very informative! So, let's see where we are:

```
(gdb) bt
#0  0xffffe002 in ?? ()
```

```
#1  0x08074a76 in recv_message ()
#2  0x080748ad in p4_recv ()
#3  0x0807ab46 in MPID_CH_Check_incoming ()
#4  0x08076ae9 in MPID_RecvComplete ()
#5  0x0806765f in MPID_RecvDatatype ()
#6  0x0804a29f in PMPI_Recv ()
#7  0x08049ce8 in node1 () at PrimePipe.c:56
#8  0x08049e19 in main (argc=8, argv=0xbffffb24) at PrimePipe.c:94
#9  0x420156a4 in __libc_start_main () from /lib/tls/libc.so.6
```

We see from frame 7 that the program is hanging at line 56, waiting to receive from Node 0.

Next, it would be useful to know how much work has been done by the function running at Node 1, node1(). Has it just started, or is it almost done? We can gauge the progress by determining the last value processed for the variable tocheck:

```
(gdb) frame 7
#7  0x08049ce8 in node1 () at PrimePipe.c:56
56              MPI_Recv(&tocheck,1,MPI_INT,0,MPI_ANY_TAG,
(gdb) p tocheck
$1 = 97
```

NOTE   *We needed to move to the stack frame for node1() first, using GDB's frame command.*

This indicates that Node 1 is at the end of execution, as 97 should be the last number that Node 0 passes to it for prime checking. So, currently we would be expecting a message from Node 0 of type END_MSG. The fact that the program is hanging would suggest that Node 0 might not have sent such a message, which would in turn lead us to check whether it had. In this manner, we hopefully would zero in quickly on the bug, which was the accidental omission of line 46.

By the way, keep in mind that when GDB is invoked with the command

```
$ gdb primepipe 2776
```

as we did above, GDB's command-line processing first checks for a core file named *2776*. In the unlikely event that such a file exists, GDB will load it instead of attaching to the intended process. Alternatively, GDB also has an attach command.

In this example, the bug caused the program to hang. The approach to debugging a parallel program like this one is somewhat different when the symptom is incorrect output. Suppose, for example, that in line 71 we incorrectly initialized primecount to 2 instead of 3. If we try to follow the same debugging procedure, the programs running on each node would finish execution and exit too quickly for you to attach GDB. (True, we could use a very large value of n, but it is usually better to debug with simple cases at first.) We need some device that can be used to make the programs wait and give you a chance to attach GDB. This is the purpose of line 34 in the init() function.

As can be seen in the source code, the value of debugwait is taken from the command line supplied by the user, with 1 meaning wait and 0 meaning no wait. If we specify 1 for the value of debugwait, then when each invocation of the program reaches line 34, it remains there. This gives us time to attach GDB. We can then break out of the infinite loop and proceed to debug. Here is what we do at Node 0:

```
node1:~$ gdb primepipe 3124
...
0x08049c53 in init (argc=3, argv=0xbfffe2f4) at PrimePipe.c:34
34          while (debugwait) ;
(gdb) set debugwait = 0
(gdb) c
Continuing.
```

Ordinarily, we dread infinite loops, but here we deliberately set one up in order to facilitate debugging. We do the same thing at Node 1 and Node 2, and at the latter we also take the opportunity to set a breakpoint at line 77 before continuing:

```
[matloff@node3 ~]$ gdb primepipe 2944
34          while (debugwait) ;
(gdb) b 77
Breakpoint 1 at 0x8049d7d: file PrimePipe.c, line 77.
(gdb) set debugwait = 0
(gdb) c
Continuing.

Breakpoint 1, node2 () at PrimePipe.c:77
77              if (status.MPI_TAG == END_MSG) break;
(gdb) p tocheck
$1 = 7
(gdb) n
78              iscomposite = 0;
(gdb) n
79              for (i = 7; i*i <= tocheck; i += 2)
(gdb) n
84              if (!iscomposite) primecount++;
(gdb) n
75              MPI_Recv(&tocheck,1,MPI_INT,1,MPI_ANY_TAG,
(gdb) p primecount
$2 = 3
```

At this point, we notice that primecount should be 4, not 3—the primes through 7 are 2, 3, 5, and 7—and thus we have found the location of the bug.

5.3.2   Shared-Memory Systems

Now, what about the shared-memory type of parallel programming? Here we have separate cases for true shared-memory machines and software-distributed shared-memory settings.

5.3.2.1   True Shared Memory

As mentioned earlier, in a true shared-memory environment, application programs are often developed using threads. Our material in Section 5.2 on debugging with GDB/DDD then applies.

OpenMP has become a popular programming environment on such machines. OpenMP supplies the programmer with high-level parallel programming constructs, which in turn make use of threads. The programmer still has thread-level access if needed, but for the most part the threaded implementation of the OpenMP directives is largely transparent to the programmer.

We present an extended example in Section 5.4 of debugging an OpenMP application.

5.3.2.2   Software Distributed Shared-Memory Systems

Prices of machines with dual-core CPUs are now within reach of ordinary consumers, but large-scale shared-memory systems with many processors still cost hundreds of thousands of dollars. A popular, inexpensive alternative is a *network of workstations (NOW)*. NOW architectures use an underlying library that gives the illusion of shared memory. The library, which is largely transparent to the application programmer, engages in network transactions that maintain consistency of copies of shared variables across the different nodes.

This approach is called *software distributed shared memory (SDSM)*. The most widely used SDSM library is Treadmarks, developed and maintained by Rice University. Another excellent package is JIAJIA, available from the Chinese Academy of Sciences (*http://www-users.cs.umn.edu/˜tianhe/paper/dist.htm*).

SDSM applications exhibit certain kinds of behavior that may baffle the unwary programmer. These are highly dependent on the particular system, so a general treatment cannot be given here, but we will briefly discuss a few issues common to many of them.

Many SDSMs are *page based*, meaning that they rely on the underlying virtual memory hardware at the nodes. The actions are complex, but we can give a quick overview. Consider a variable X that is to be shared among the NOW nodes. The programmer indicates this intention by making a certain call to the SDSM library, which in turn makes a certain Unix system call requesting the OS to replace its own seg fault handler with a function in the SDSM library for page faults involving the page containing X. The SDSM sets things up in such a way that only NOW nodes with valid copies of X have the corresponding memory pages marked as resident. When X is accessed at some other node, a page fault results, and the underlying SDSM software fetches the correct value from a node that has it.

Again, it's not essential to know the precise workings of the SDSM system; rather, the important thing is to simply understand that there *is* an underlying VM-based mechanism that's being used to maintain consistency of local copies of shared data across the NOW nodes. If you don't, you will be mystified when you try to debug SDSM application code. The debugger will *seem* to mysteriously stop for nonexistent seg faults, because the SDSM infrastructure deliberately generates seg faults, and when an SDSM application program is run under a debugging tool, the tool senses them. Once you realize this, there is no problem at all—in GDB, you'd merely issue a continue command to resume execution when one of these odd pauses occurs.

You may be tempted to order GDB not to stop or issue warning messages whenever any seg faults occur, using the GDB command

```
handle SIGSEGV nostop noprint
```

You should use this approach with caution, though, as it may result in your missing any genuine seg faults caused by bugs in the application program.

Yet another, related difficulty with debugging applications that run on page-based SDSMs arises as follows. If a node on the network changes the value of a shared variable, then any other node that needs the value of that variable must obtain the updated value through a network transaction. Once again, the details of how this happens depends on the SDSM system, but this means that if you are single-stepping through the code executing on one node, you may find that GDB mysteriously hangs because the node is now waiting for an update to its local copy of a variable that was recently modified by another node. If you happen to be running a separate GDB session to step through the code on that other node as well, the update will not occur on the first node until the debugging session on the second node progresses far enough. In other words, if the programmer is not alert and careful during the debugging of an SDSM application, he can cause his own deadlock situation through the debugging process itself.

The SDSM situation is similar to that of the message-passing case in one sense—the need to have a variable like debugwait in the MPI example above, which allows you to have the program pause at all nodes, giving you a chance to attach GDB at each node and step through the program from the beginning.

5.4 Extended Example

This section presents an example of debugging a shared-memory application developed using OpenMP. The necessary knowledge of OpenMP will be explained below. All that is needed is a basic understanding of threads.

5.4.1 OpenMP Overview

OpenMP is essentially a higher-level parallel programming interface to thread-management operations. The number of threads is set via the environment variable OMP_NUM_THREADS. In the C shell, for instance, you type

```
% setenv OMP_NUM_THREADS 4
```

at the shell prompt to arrange to have four threads.

Application code consists of C interspersed with OpenMP directives. Each directive applies to the block that follows it, delimited by left and right braces. The most basic directive is

```
#pragma omp parallel
```

This sets up `OMP_NUM_THREADS` threads, each of which concurrently executes the block of code following the pragma. There will typically be other directives embedded within this block.

Another very common OpenMP directive is

```
#pragma omp barrier
```

This specifies a "meeting point" for all the threads. When any thread reaches this point, it will block until all the other threads have arrived there.

You may often wish to have just one thread execute a certain block, while the other threads skip it. This is accomplished by writing

```
#pragma omp single
```

There is an implied barrier immediately following such a block.

There are many other OpenMP directives, but the only other one used in the example here is

```
#pragma omp critical
```

As the name implies, this creates a critical section, in which only one thread is allowed at any given time.

5.4.2 OpenMP Example Program

We implement the famous Dijkstra algorithm for determining minimum distances between pairs of vertices in a weighted graph. Say we are given distances between adjacent vertices (if two vertices are not adjacent, the distance between them is set to infinity). The goal is to find the minimum distances between vertex 0 and all other vertices.

Following is the source file, *dijkstra.c*. It generates random edge lengths among a specified number of vertices and then finds the minimum distances from vertex 0 to each of the other vertices.

```
1   // dijkstra.c
2
3   // OpenMP example program:  Dijkstra shortest-path finder in a
4   // bidirectional graph; finds the shortest path from vertex 0 to all
```

```
5    // others
6
7    // usage:  dijkstra nv print
8
9    // where nv is the size of the graph, and print is 1 if graph and min
10   // distances are to be printed out, 0 otherwise
11
12   #include <omp.h>  // required
13   #include <values.h>
14
15   // including stdlib.h and stdio.h seems to cause a conflict with the
16   // Omni compiler, so declare directly
17   extern void *malloc();
18   extern int printf(char *,...);
19
20   // global variables, shared by all threads
21   int nv,  // number of vertices
22       *notdone, // vertices not checked yet
23       nth,  // number of threads
24       chunk,  // number of vertices handled by each thread
25       md,  // current min over all threads
26       mv;  // vertex which achieves that min
27
28   int *ohd,  // 1-hop distances between vertices; "ohd[i][j]" is
29              // ohd[i*nv+j]
30       *mind;  // min distances found so far
31
32   void init(int ac, char **av)
33   {   int i,j,tmp;
34       nv = atoi(av[1]);
35       ohd = malloc(nv*nv*sizeof(int));
36       mind = malloc(nv*sizeof(int));
37       notdone = malloc(nv*sizeof(int));
38       // random graph
39       for (i = 0; i < nv; i++)
40         for (j = i; j < nv; j++)  {
41            if (j == i) ohd[i*nv+i] = 0;
42            else  {
43               ohd[nv*i+j] = rand() % 20;
44               ohd[nv*j+i] = ohd[nv*i+j];
45            }
46         }
47       for (i = 1; i < nv; i++)  {
48          notdone[i] = 1;
49          mind[i] = ohd[i];
50       }
51   }
```

```
52
53    // finds closest to 0 among notdone, among s through e; returns min
54    // distance in *d, closest vertex in *v
55    void findmymin(int s, int e, int *d, int *v)
56    {  int i;
57       *d = MAXINT;
58       for (i = s; i <= e; i++)
59          if (notdone[i] && mind[i] < *d)  {
60             *d = mind[i];
61             *v = i;
62          }
63    }
64
65    // for each i in {s,...,e}, ask whether a shorter path to i exists, through
66    // mv
67    void updatemind(int s, int e)
68    {  int i;
69       for (i = s; i <= e; i++)
70          if (notdone[i])
71             if (mind[mv] + ohd[mv*nv+i] < mind[i])
72                mind[i] = mind[mv] + ohd[mv*nv+i];
73    }
74
75    void dowork()
76    {
77       #pragma omp parallel
78       {  int startv,endv,  // start, end vertices for this thread
79                step,  // whole procedure goes nv steps
80                mymv,  // vertex which attains that value
81                me = omp_get_thread_num(),
82                mymd;  // min value found by this thread
83          #pragma omp single
84          {  nth = omp_get_num_threads();   chunk = nv/nth;
85             printf("there are %d threads\n",nth);  }
86          startv = me * chunk;
87          endv = startv + chunk - 1;
88          // the algorithm goes through nv iterations
89          for (step = 0; step < nv; step++)  {
90             // find closest vertex to 0 among notdone; each thread finds
91             // closest in its group, then we find overall closest
92             #pragma omp single
93             {  md = MAXINT;
94                mv = 0;
95             }
96             findmymin(startv,endv,&mymd,&mymv);
97             // update overall min if mine is smaller
98             #pragma omp critical
```

```
99      {   if (mymd < md)
100         {   md = mymd;   }
101     }
102     #pragma omp barrier
103     // mark new vertex as done
104     #pragma omp single
105     {   notdone[mv] = 0;   }
106     // now update my section of ohd
107     updatemind(startv,endv);
108         }
109     }
110  }
111
112  int main(int argc, char **argv)
113  {   int i,j,print;
114     init(argc,argv);
115     // start parallel
116     dowork();
117     // back to single thread
118     print = atoi(argv[2]);
119     if (print)  {
120        printf("graph weights:\n");
121        for (i = 0; i < nv; i++)  {
122           for (j = 0; j < nv; j++)
123              printf("%u  ",ohd[nv*i+j]);
124           printf("\n");
125        }
126        printf("minimum distances:\n");
127        for (i = 1; i < nv; i++)
128           printf("%u\n",mind[i]);
129     }
130  }
```

Let's review how the algorithm works. Start with all vertices except vertex 0, which in this case are vertices 1 through 5, in a "not done" set. In each iteration of the algorithm, do the following:

1. Find the "not done" vertex v that is closest to vertex 0, along paths known so far. This checking is shared by all the threads, with each thread checking an equal number of vertices. The function that does this work is findmymin().

2. Then move v to the "done" set.

3. For all remaining vertices i in the "not done" set, check whether going first from 0 to v along the best known path so far, and then from v to i in one hop, is shorter than the current shortest distance from 0 to i. If so, update that distance accordingly. The function that performs these actions is updatemind().

The iteration continues until the "not done" set is empty.

Since OpenMP directives require preprocessing, there is always the potential problem that we will lose our original line numbers and variable and function names. To see how to address this, we will discuss two different compilers. First we'll look at the Omni compiler (*http://www.hpcc.jp/Omni/*), and then at GCC (version 4.2 or later is required).

We compile our code under Omni as follows:

```
$ omcc -g -o dij dijkstra.c
```

After compiling the program and running it with four threads, we find that it fails to work properly:

```
$ dij 6 1
there are 4 threads
graph weights:
0   3   6   17  15  13
3   0   15  6   12  9
6   15  0   1   2   7
17  6   1   0   10  19
15  12  2   10  0   3
13  9   7   19  3   0
minimum distances:
3
6
17
15
13
```

Analyzing the graph by hand shows that the correct minimum distances should be 3, 6, 7, 8, and 11.

Next, we run the program in GDB. Here it is very important to understand the consequences of the fact that OpenMP works via directives. Although line numbers, function names, and so on are mostly retained by the two compilers discussed here, there are some discrepancies between them. Look at what happens when we try to set a breakpoint in the executable, dij, at the outset of the GDB session:

```
(gdb) tb main
Breakpoint 1 at 0x80492af
(gdb) r 6 1
Starting program: /debug/dij 6 1
[Thread debugging using libthread_db enabled]
[New Thread -1208490304 (LWP 11580)]
[Switching to Thread -1208490304 (LWP 11580)]
0x080492af in main ()
(gdb) l
```

```
1        /tmp/omni_C_11486.c: No such file or directory.
         in /tmp/omni_C_11486.c
```

We discover that the breakpoint is not in the source file. Instead, it is in Omni's OpenMP infrastructure code. In other words, main() here is Omni's main(), not your own. The Omni compiler mangled the name of our main() to _ompc_main().

To set a breakpoint at main(), we type

```
(gdb) tb _ompc_main
Breakpoint 2 at 0x80491b3: file dijkstra.c, line 114.
```

and check it by continuing:

```
(gdb) c
Continuing.
[New Thread -1208493152 (LWP 11614)]
[New Thread -1218983008 (LWP 11615)]
[New Thread -1229472864 (LWP 11616)]
_ompc_main (argc=3, argv=0xbfab6314) at dijkstra.c:114
114         init(argc,argv);
```

Okay, there's the familiar init() line. Of course, we could have issued the command

```
(gdb) b dijkstra.c:114
```

Note the creation of the three new threads, making four in all.

However we choose to set our breakpoints, we must do a bit more work here than normal, so it's particularly important to stay within a single GDB session between runs of the program, even when we change our source code and recompile, so that we retain the breakpoints, conditions, and so on. That way we only have to go to the trouble of setting these things up once.

Now, how do you track down the bug(s)? It is natural to approach the debugging of this program by checking the results at the end of each iteration. The main results are in the "not done" set (in the array notdone[]) and in the current list of best-known distances from 0 to the other vertices, that is, the array mind[]. For example, after the first iteration, the "not done" set should consist of vertices 2, 3, 4, and 5, vertex 1 having been selected in that iteration.

Armed with this information, let's apply the Principle of Confirmation and check notdone[] and mind[] after each iteration of the for loop in dowork().

We have to be careful as to exactly where we set our breakpoints. Although a natural spot for this seems to be line 108, at the very end of the algorithm's main loop, this may not be so good, as GDB will stop there for *each* thread. Instead, opt for placing a breakpoint inside an OpenMP single block, so that it will stop for only one thread.

So, instead we check the results after each iteration by stopping at the *beginning* of the loop, starting with the second iteration:

```
(gdb) b 92 if step >= 1
Breakpoint 3 at 0x80490e3: file dijkstra.c, line 92.
(gdb) c
Continuing.
there are 4 threads

Breakpoint 3, __ompc_func_0 () at dijkstra.c:93
93                  {  md = MAXINT;
```

Let's confirm that the first iteration did choose the correct vertex (vertex 1) to be moved out of the "not done" set:

```
(gdb) p mv
$1 = 0
```

The hypothesis is not confirmed, after all. Inspection of the code shows that on line 100 we forgot to set mv. We fix it to read

```
{  md = mymd;  mv = mymv;  }
```

So, we recompile and run the program again. As noted earlier in this section (and elsewhere in this book), it is very helpful to not exit GDB when you rerun the program. We could run the program in another terminal window, but just for variety let's take a different approach here. We temporarily disable our breakpoints by issuing the dis command, then run the recompiled program from within GDB, and then re-enable the breakpoints using ena:

```
(gdb) dis
(gdb) r
The program being debugged has been started already.
Start it from the beginning? (y or n) y
`/debug/dij' has changed; re-reading symbols.
Starting program: /debug/dij 6 1
[Thread debugging using libthread_db enabled]
[New Thread -1209026880 (LWP 11712)]
[New Thread -1209029728 (LWP 11740)]
[New Thread -1219519584 (LWP 11741)]
[New Thread -1230009440 (LWP 11742)]
there are 4 threads
graph weights:
0   3   6   17  15  13
3   0   15  6   12  9
6   15  0   1   2   7
17  6   1   0   10  19
```

```
15  12  2  10  0  3
13  9  7  19  3  0
minimum distances:
3
6
17
15
13

Program exited with code 06.
(gdb) ena
```

We're still getting wrong answers. Let's check things at that breakpoint again:

```
(gdb) r
Starting program: /debug/dij 6 1
[Thread debugging using libthread_db enabled]
[New Thread -1209014592 (LWP 11744)]
[New Thread -1209017440 (LWP 11772)]
[New Thread -1219507296 (LWP 11773)]
[New Thread -1229997152 (LWP 11774)]
there are 4 threads
[Switching to Thread -1209014592 (LWP 11744)]

Breakpoint 3, __ompc_func_0 () at dijkstra.c:93
93                { md = MAXINT;
(gdb) p mv
$2 = 1
```

At least mv now has the right value. Let's check mind[]:

```
(gdb) p *mind@6
$3 = {0, 3, 6, 17, 15, 13}
```

Note that because we constructed the mind[] array dynamically via malloc(), we could not use GDB's print command in its usual form. Instead, we used GDB's artificial array feature.

At any rate, mind[] is still incorrect. For instance, mind[3] should be 3 + 6 = 9, yet it is 17. Let's check the code that updates mind[]:

```
(gdb) b 107 if me == 1
Breakpoint 4 at 0x8049176: file dijkstra.c, line 107.
(gdb) r
The program being debugged has been started already.
Start it from the beginning? (y or n) y
Starting program: /debug/dij 6 1
[Thread debugging using libthread_db enabled]
```

```
[New Thread -1209039168 (LWP 11779)]
[New Thread -1209042016 (LWP 11807)]
[New Thread -1219531872 (LWP 11808)]
[New Thread -1230021728 (LWP 11809)]
there are 4 threads
[Switching to Thread -1230021728 (LWP 11809)]

Breakpoint 4, __ompc_func_0 () at dijkstra.c:107
107                 updatemind(startv,endv);
```

First, confirm that startv and endv have sensible values:

```
(gdb) p startv
$4 = 1
(gdb) p endv
$5 = 1
```

The chunk size is only 1? Let's see:

```
(gdb) p chunk
$6 = 1
```

After checking the computation for chunk, we realize that we need the number of threads to evenly divide nv. The latter has the value 6, which is not divisible by our thread count, 4. We make a note to ourselves to insert some error-catching code later, and reduce our thread count to 3 for now.

Once again, we do not want to exit GDB to do this. GDB inherits the environment variables when it is first invoked, but the values of those variables can also be changed or set within GDB, and that is what we do here:

```
(gdb) set environment OMP_NUM_THREADS = 3
```

Now let's run again:

```
(gdb) dis
(gdb) r
The program being debugged has been started already.
Start it from the beginning? (y or n) y
Starting program: /debug/dij 6 1
[Thread debugging using libthread_db enabled]
[New Thread -1208707392 (LWP 11819)]
[New Thread -1208710240 (LWP 11847)]
[New Thread -1219200096 (LWP 11848)]
there are 3 threads
graph weights:
0  3  6  17  15  13
3  0  15  6  12  9
6  15  0  1  2  7
```

```
17  6  1  0  10  19
15  12  2  10  0  3
13  9  7  19  3  0
minimum distances:
3
6
7
15
12


Program exited with code 06.
(gdb) ena
```

Aiyah, still the same wrong answers! We continue to check the updating process for mind[]:

```
(gdb) r
Starting program: /debug/dij 6 1
[Thread debugging using libthread_db enabled]
[New Thread -1208113472 (LWP 11851)]
[New Thread -1208116320 (LWP 11879)]
[New Thread -1218606176 (LWP 11880)]
there are 3 threads
[Switching to Thread -1218606176 (LWP 11880)]

Breakpoint 4, __ompc_func_0 () at dijkstra.c:107
107                updatemind(startv,endv);
(gdb) p startv
$7 = 2
(gdb) p endv
$8 = 3
```

All right, those are the correct values for startv and endv in the case of me = 1. So, we enter the function:

```
(gdb) s
[Switching to Thread -1208113472 (LWP 11851)]

Breakpoint 3, __ompc_func_0 () at dijkstra.c:93
93                 {  md = MAXINT;
(gdb) c
Continuing.
[Switching to Thread -1218606176 (LWP 11880)]
updatemind (s=2, e=3) at dijkstra.c:69
69         for (i = s; i <= e; i++)
```

Note that due to context switches among the threads, we did not enter updatemind() immediately. Now we check the case i = 3:

```
(gdb) tb 71 if i == 3
Breakpoint 5 at 0x8048fb2: file dijkstra.c, line 71.
(gdb) c
Continuing.
updatemind (s=2, e=3) at dijkstra.c:71
71                if (mind[mv] + ohd[mv*nv+i] < mind[i])
```

As usual, we apply the Principle of Confirmation:

```
(gdb) p mv
$9 = 0
```

Well, that's a big problem. Recall that in the first iteration, mv turns out to be 1. Why is it 0 here?

After a while we realize that those context switches should have been a big hint. Take a look at the GDB output above again. The thread whose system ID is 11851 was already on line 93—in other words, it was already in the next iteration of the algorithm's main loop. In fact, when we hit c to continue, it even executed line 94, which is

```
mv = 0;
```

This thread overwrote mv's previous value of 1, so that the thread that updates mind[3] is now relying on the wrong value of mv. The solution is to add another barrier:

```
updatemind(startv,endv);
#pragma omp barrier
```

After this fix, the program runs correctly.

The foregoing was based on the Omni compiler. As mentioned, beginning with version 4.2, GCC handles OpenMP code as well. All you have to do is add the -fopenmp flag to the GCC command line.

Unlike Omni, GCC generates code in such a way that GDB's focus is in your own source file from the beginning. Thus, issuing a command

```
(gdb) b main
```

at the very outset of a GDB session really will cause a breakpoint to be set in one's own main(), unlike what we saw for the Omni compiler.

However, at this writing, a major shortcoming of GCC is that the symbols for local variables that are inside an OpenMP parallel block (called *private* variables in OpenMP terminology) will not be visible within GDB. For example, the command

```
(gdb) p mv
```

that you issued for the Omni-generated code above will work for GCC-generated code, but the command

```
(gdb) p startv
```

will fail on GCC-generated code.

　　There are ways to work around this, of course. For instance, if you wish to know the value of startv, you can query the value of s within updatemind(). Hopefully this issue will be resolved in the next version of GCC.

6

SPECIAL TOPICS

 Various issues arise during debugging that do not deal with debugging tools. We'll cover some of these issues in this chapter.

6.1 What If It Doesn't Even Compile or Load?

Invaluable as GDB, DDD, and Eclipse are, they can't help you if your program doesn't even compile. In this section we'll give you some tips on dealing with this situation.

6.1.1 Phantom Line Numbers in Syntax Error Messages

Sometimes the compiler will tell you you've got a syntax error in line x, when in fact line x is perfectly correct, and the real error is in an earlier line.

For example, here is the source file *bintree.c* from Chapter 3, with a syntax error thrown in at a point which we will not disclose yet (well, it's fairly obvious if you want to look for it).

```
1   // bintree.c:  routines to do insert and sorted print of a binary tree
2
3   #include <stdio.h>
4   #include <stdlib.h>
```

```
5
6    struct node {
7      int val;              // stored value
8      struct node *left;    // ptr to smaller child
9      struct node *right;   // ptr to larger child
10   };
11
12   typedef struct node *nsp;
13
14   nsp root;
15
16   nsp makenode(int x)
17   {
18     nsp tmp;
19
20     tmp = (nsp) malloc(sizeof(struct node));
21     tmp->val = x;
22     tmp->left = tmp->right = 0;
23     return tmp;
24   }
25
26   void insert(nsp *btp, int x)
27   {
28     nsp tmp = *btp;
29
30     if (*btp == 0) {
31       *btp = makenode(x);
32       return;
33     }
34
35     while (1)
36     {
37       if (x < tmp->val) {
38
39         if (tmp->left != 0) {
40           tmp = tmp->left;
41         } else {
42           tmp->left = makenode(x);
43           break;
44         }
45
46       } else {
47
48         if (tmp->right != 0) {
49           tmp = tmp->right;
50         } else {
51           tmp->right = makenode(x);
```

```
52          break;
53        }
54
55    }
56  }
57
58  void printtree(nsp bt)
59  {
60    if (bt == 0) return;
61    printtree(bt->left);
62    printf("%d\n",bt->val);
63    printtree(bt->right);
64  }
65
66  int main(int argc, char *argv[])
67  {
68    int i;
69
70    root = 0;
71    for (i = 1; i < argc; i++)
72      insert(&root, atoi(argv[i]));
73    printtree(root);
74  }
```

Running this through GCC produces

```
$ gcc -g bintree.c
bintree.c: In function `insert':
bintree.c:75: parse error at end of input
```

Since line 74 is the end of the source file, the second error message is rather uninformative, to say the least. But the first message suggests that the problem is in insert(), so that's a clue, even though it doesn't say what or where the problem is.

In this kind of situation, the typical culprit is a missing closing brace or semicolon. You could check for this directly, but in a large source file this may be difficult. Let's take a different approach.

Recall the Principle of Confirmation from Chapter 1. Here, let's first confirm that the problem really is in insert(). To do so, temporarily comment out that function from the source code:

```
...
    tmp->val = x;
    tmp->left = tmp->right = 0;
    return tmp;
}

// void insert(nsp *btp, int x)
```

```
//  {
//     nsp tmp = *btp;
//
//     if (*btp == 0) {
//         *btp = makenode(x);
//         return;
//     }
//
//     while (1)
//     {
//         if (x < tmp->val) {
//
//             if (tmp->left != 0) {
//                 tmp = tmp->left;
//             } else {
//                 tmp->left = makenode(x);
//                 break;
//             }
//
//         } else {
//
//             if (tmp->right != 0) {
//                 tmp = tmp->right;
//             } else {
//                 tmp->right = makenode(x);
//                 break;
//             }
//
//         }
//     }
// }

void printtree(nsp bt)
{
   if (bt == 0) return;
...
```

NOTE   *Preferably, you will use a quick shortcut to do the commenting out, such as a block operation. Text editor shortcuts that are useful in debugging contexts will be discussed in Chapter 7.*

Save the file, and then re-run GCC:

```
$ gcc -g bintree.c
/tmp/ccgOLDCS.o: In function `main':
/home/matloff/public_html/matloff/public_html/Debug/Book/DDD/bintree.c:72:
undefined reference to `insert'
collect2: ld returned 1 exit status
```

Don't be distracted by the fact that the linker, LD, complained that it couldn't find insert(). After all, you knew that was coming, since you commented out that function. Instead, the point of interest is that there is no complaint of a syntax error, as you had before. So, you have indeed confirmed that the syntax error is somewhere in insert(). Now, uncomment the lines of that function (again, preferably using a text editor shortcut such as "undo") and save the file. Also, just to make sure you've restored things correctly, re-run GCC to confirm that the syntax error resurfaces (not shown here).

At this point you can apply another principle stated in Chapter 1: the Principle of Binary Search. Repeatedly narrow down your search area in the function insert(), cutting the area in half each time, until you obtain a sufficiently small area in which to spot the syntax error.

To that end, first comment out approximately half of the function. A reasonable way to do that would be to simply comment out the while loop. Then re-run GCC:

```
$ gcc -g bintree.c
$
```

Aha! The error message disappeared, so the syntax problem must be somewhere within the loop. So, you've narrowed down the problem to that half of the function, and now you'll cut that area in half, too. To do so, comment out the else code:

```
void insert(nsp *btp, int x)
{
   nsp tmp = *btp;

   if (*btp == 0) {
      *btp = makenode(x);
      return;
   }

   while (1)
   {
      if (x < tmp->val) {

         if (tmp->left != 0) {
            tmp = tmp->left;
         } else {
            tmp->left = makenode(x);
            break;
         }

      } // else {
//
//          if (tmp->right != 0) {
```

```
//            tmp = tmp->right;
//        } else {
//            tmp->right = makenode(x);
//            break;
//        }
//
//    }
}
```

Re-running GCC, you'll find that the problem reappears:

```
$ gcc -g bintree.c
bintree.c: In function `insert':
bintree.c:75: parse error at end of input
```

So, the syntax error is either in the if block or at the end of the function. By this time, you've narrowed the problem down to only seven lines of code, so you should probably be able to find the problem by visual inspection; it turns out that we had accidentally omitted the closing brace in the outer if-then-else.

The Principle of Binary Search can be very helpful in finding syntax errors of unknown locations. But in temporarily commenting out code, be sure not to create new syntax errors of your own! Comment out an entire function, an entire loop, and so on, as we did here.

6.1.2 Missing Libraries

Sometimes GCC—actually LD, the linker, which is invoked by GCC during the process of building your program—will inform you that it cannot find one or more functions called by your code. This is typically due to failure to inform GCC of the location of a function library. Many, if not most, readers of this book will be well versed on this topic, but for those who are not, we will provide a short introduction in this section. Note that our discussion here applies mainly to Linux and to various degrees to other Unix-family operating systems.

6.1.2.1 Example

Let's use the following very simple code as an example, consisting of a main program, in *a.c*,

```
// a.c

int f(int x);

main()
{
    int v;
```

```
    scanf("%d",&v);
    printf("%d\n",f(v));
}
```

and a subprogram, in *z/b.c*:

```
// b.c

int f(int x)
{
    return x*x;
}
```

If you try to compile *a.c* without any attempt to link in the code in *b.c*, then LD will of course complain:

```
$ gcc -g a.c
/tmp/ccIP5WHu.o: In function `main':
/debug/a.c:9: undefined reference to `f'
collect2: ld returned 1 exit status
```

We could go to *z*, compile *b.c* and then link in the object file:

```
$ cd z
$ gcc -g -c b.c
$ cd ..
$ gcc -g a.c z/b.o
```

However, if you had a lot of functions to link in, possibly from different source files, and if these functions were likely to be useful for future programs you might write, you could create a *library*, a single archive file. There are two kinds of library files. When you compile code that calls functions in a *static* library, those functions become part of the resulting executable file. On the other hand, if the library is *dynamic*, the functions are not physically attached to the calling code until the program is actually executed.

Here is how you could create a static library, say *lib88.a*, for the example here.

NOTE   *On Unix systems, it's customary to give static library filenames the suffix .a, with* a *standing for* archive. *Also, the custom is to give any library a name starting with* lib.

```
$ gcc -g -c b.c
$ ar rc lib88.a b.o
```

The ar command here creates the library *lib88.a* from whatever functions it finds in the file *b.o*. You would then compile your main program:

```
$ gcc -g a.c -l88 -Lz
```

The -l option here is a shortcut, having the same effect as

```
$ gcc -g a.c lib88.a -Lz
```

which directs GCC to tell LD that it will need to find functions in the library *lib88.a* (or a dynamic variant, as you'll see below).

The -L option directs GCC to tell LD to look in directories other than the current one (and the default search directories) when looking for your functions. In this case, it says that z is such a directory.

The disadvantage of this approach is that if many programs are using the same library, they each will contain space-wasting separate copies of it on disk. This problem is solved (at the expense of a little extra load time) by using dynamic libraries.

In the example here, you'd use GCC directly to create a dynamic library, rather than using *ar*. In z you would run

```
$ gcc -fPIC -c b.c
$ gcc -shared -o lib88.so b.o
```

This creates the dynamic library *lib88.so*. (Unix custom is to use the suffix *.so*, *shared object*, possibly followed by a version number, for naming dynamic libraries.) Link to it as you did for the static case:

```
$ gcc -g a.c -l88 -Lz
```

However, it now works a little differently. Whereas in the static case the functions called from the library would become part of our executable file *a.out*, now *a.out* will merely contain a notation that this program makes use of the library *lib88.so*. And significantly, that notation will not even state where that library is located. The only reason GCC (again, actually LD) wanted to take a peek at *lib88.so* at compile time was to get information about the library that it needs for the link.

The link itself will occur at run time. The operating system will search for *lib88.so*, and then link it into your program. That brings up the question of where the OS performs this search.

First of all, let's use the ldd command to check which libraries the program needs, and where, if anywhere, the OS finds them:

```
$ ldd a.out
        lib88.so => not found
        libc.so.6 => /lib/tls/libc.so.6 (0x006cd000)
        /lib/ld-linux.so.2 (0x006b0000)
```

The program needs the C library, which it finds in the directory */lib/tls*, but the OS fails to find *lib88.so*. The latter is in the directory */Debug/z*, but that directory is not part of the OS's normal search path.

One way to fix that would be to add */Debug/z* to that search path:

```
% setenv LD_LIBRARY_PATH ${LD_LIBRARY_PATH}:/Debug/z
```

If you want to add several directories, string their names together with colons as delimiters. (This is for the C shell or TC shell.) For bash, issue the commands

```
$ LD_LIBRARY_PATH=$LD_LIBRARY_PATH:/Debug/z
$ export LD_LIBRARY_PATH
```

Let's make sure it works:

```
$ ldd a.out
        lib88.so => /Debug/z/lib88.so (0xf6ffe000)
        libc.so.6 => /lib/tls/libc.so.6 (0x006cd000)
        /lib/ld-linux.so.2 (0x006b0000)
```

There are various other approaches, but they are beyond the scope of this book.

6.1.2.2 Library Usage in Open Source Software

Open source software has become quite popular, especially among Linux users. A problem that sometimes arises, though, is that the build script, typically named *configure*, that comes with the source code cannot find some necessary libraries. Attempts to solve the problem by setting the LD_LIBRARY_PATH environment variable may fail. As this falls under the "missing libraries" topic under discussion here, and it is usually not documented in the source packages, a brief note about it may be of value.

Often, the root of the problem will lie in a program invoked by *configure*, named *pkgconfig*. The latter will retrieve information about libraries from certain metadata files, which have the suffix *.pc*, with the prefix being the name of the library. For example, the file *libgcj.pc* would contain the location of the library files *libgcj.so**.

The default directory that *pkgconfig* searches for the *.pc* files depends on the location of *pkgconfig* itself. For instance, if the program resides in */usr/bin*, it will search */usr/lib*. That won't be enough if the needed library is */usr/local/lib*. To fix that problem, set the environment variable PKG_CONFIG_PATH. In the C or TC shell, you would issue the shell command

```
% setenv PKG_CONFIG_PATH /usr/lib/pkgconfig:/usr/local/lib/pkgconfig
```

6.2   Debugging GUI Programs

These days, users are accustomed to having their application programs come with graphical user interfaces (GUIs). They are, of course, just programs, so general debugging principles apply, but special considerations do come into play.

GUI programming consists largely of calls to a library to perform various operations on the screen. There are many, many such libraries in widespread use. We obviously can't cover them all, and in any case the principles are similar.

Accordingly, we've chosen the simplest example, the curses library. It's so simple that many people might not consider it a GUI at all—one student called it "a text-based GUI"—but it will get the point across.

6.2.1   Debugging Curses Programs

The curses library enables the programmer to write code that will move the cursor around the screen, change colors of characters or change them to reverse video, insert and delete text, and so on.

For example, text editors such as Vim and Emacs are programmed in curses. In Vim, hitting the j key will make the cursor move down one line. Typing dd will result in the current line being erased, the lines below it moving up one line each, and the lines above it remaining unchanged. These actions are achieved by calls to the functions in the curses library.

In order to use curses, you must include this statement in your source code

```
#include <curses.h>
```

and you must link in the curses library:

```
gcc -g sourcefile.c -lcurses
```

Let's take the code below as an example. It runs the Unix ps ax command to list all the processes. At any given time, the line at which the cursor currently lies will be highlighted. You can move the cursor up and down by hitting the u and d keys, and so on. See the comments in the code for a full list of commands.

Don't worry if you haven't used curses before, as the comments tell what that library does.

```
// psax.c; illustration of curses library

// read this code in a "top-down" manner:  first these comments and the global
// variables, then main(), then the functions called by main()

// runs the shell command 'ps ax' and saves the last lines of its output,
// as many as the window will fit; allows the user to move up and down
```

```
// within the window, with the option to kill whichever process is
// currently highlighted

// usage:  psax

// user commands:

//    'u':  move highlight up a line
//    'd':  move highlight down a line
//    'k':  kill process in currently highlighted line
//    'r':  re-run 'ps ax' for update
//    'q':  quit

// possible extensions:  allowing scrolling, so that the user could go
// through all the 'ps ax' output, not just the last lines; allow
// wraparound for long lines; ask user to confirm before killing a
// process

#define MAXROW 1000
#define MAXCOL 500

#include <curses.h>  // required

WINDOW *scrn; // will point to curses window object

char cmdoutlines[MAXROW][MAXCOL];  // output of 'ps ax' (better to use
                                   // malloc())
int ncmdlines,  // number of rows in cmdoutlines
    nwinlines,  // number of rows our "ps ax" output occupies in the
                // xterm (or equiv.) window
    winrow,  // current row position in screen
    cmdstartrow,  // index of first row in cmdoutlines to be displayed
    cmdlastrow;  // index of last row in cmdoutlines to be displayed

// rewrites the line at winrow in bold font
highlight()
{
   int clinenum;
   attron(A_BOLD);  // this curses library call says that whatever we
                    // write from now on (until we say otherwise)
                    // will be in bold font
   // we'll need to rewrite the cmdoutlines line currently displayed
   // at line winrow in the screen, so as to get the bold font
   clinenum = cmdstartrow + winrow;
   mvaddstr(winrow,0,cmdoutlines[clinenum]);
   attroff(A_BOLD);  // OK, leave bold mode
   refresh();  // make the change appear on the screen
```

```
}

// runs "ps ax" and stores the output in cmdoutlines
runpsax()
{
    FILE *p; char ln[MAXCOL]; int row,tmp;
    p = popen("ps ax","r");  // open UNIX pipe (enables one program to read
                             // output of another as if it were a file)
    for (row = 0; row < MAXROW; row++)  {
        tmp = fgets(ln,MAXCOL,p);  // read one line from the pipe
        if (tmp == NULL) break;  // if end of pipe, break
        // don't want stored line to exceed width of screen, which the
        // curses library provides to us in the variable COLS, so truncate
        // to at most COLS characters
        strncpy(cmdoutlines[row],ln,COLS);
        cmdoutlines[row][MAXCOL-1] = 0;
    }
    ncmdlines = row;
    close(p);  // close pipe
}

// displays last part of command output (as much as fits in screen)
showlastpart()
{
    int row;
    clear();  // curses clear-screen call
    // prepare to paint the (last part of the) 'ps ax' output on the screen;
    // two cases, depending on whether there is more output than screen rows;
    // first, the case in which the entire output fits in one screen:
    if (ncmdlines <= LINES)  { // LINES is an int maintained by the curses
                               // library, equal to the number of lines in
                               // the screen
        cmdstartrow = 0;
        nwinlines = ncmdlines;
    }
    else  { // now the case in which the output is bigger than one screen
        cmdstartrow = ncmdlines - LINES;
        nwinlines = LINES;
    }
    cmdlastrow = cmdstartrow + nwinlines - 1;
    // now paint the rows to the screen
    for (row = cmdstartrow, winrow = 0; row <= cmdlastrow; row++,winrow++)
        mvaddstr(winrow,0,cmdoutlines[row]);  // curses call to move to the
                                              // specified position and
                                              // paint a string there
    refresh();  // now make the changes actually appear on the screen,
                // using this call to the curses library
```

```
    // highlight the last line
    winrow--;
    highlight();
}

// moves cursor up/down one line
updown(int inc)
{
    int tmp = winrow + inc;
    // ignore attempts to go off the edge of the screen
    if (tmp >= 0 && tmp < LINES)  {
        // rewrite the current line before moving; since our current font
        // is non-BOLD (actually A_NORMAL), the effect is to unhighlight
        // this line
        mvaddstr(winrow,0,cmdoutlines[winrow]);
        // highlight the line we're moving to
        winrow = tmp;
        highlight();
    }
}

// run/re-run "ps ax"
rerun()
{
    runpsax();
    showlastpart();
}

// kills the highlighted process
prockill()
{
    char *pid;
    // strtok() is from C library; see man page
    pid = strtok(cmdoutlines[cmdstartrow+winrow]," ");
    kill(atoi(pid),9);  // this is a UNIX system call to send signal 9,
                        // the kill signal, to the given process
    rerun();
}

main()
{
    char c;
    // window setup; next 3 lines are curses library calls, a standard
    // initializing sequence for curses programs
    scrn = initscr();
    noecho();  // don't echo keystrokes
    cbreak();  // keyboard input valid immediately, not after hit Enter
```

```
    // run 'ps ax' and process the output
    runpsax();
    // display in the window
    showlastpart();
    // user command loop
    while (1)  {
        // get user command
        c = getch();
        if (c == 'u') updown(-1);
        else if (c == 'd') updown(1);
        else if (c == 'r') rerun();
        else if (c == 'k') prockill();
        else break;  // quit
    }
    // restore original settings
    endwin();
}
```

Running the program, you'll find that the picture looks all right, but when you hit the u key to make the cursor go up a line, it doesn't work correctly, as you see in Figure 6-1.

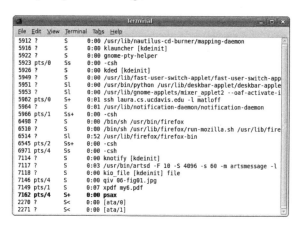

Figure 6-1: The program running in a terminal window

The output of ps ax is in ascending order by process number, yet suddenly you see process 2270 being displayed after 7162. Let's track down the bug.

A curses program is a debugging book author's dream, because it forces the programmer to use a debugging tool. The programmer cannot use printf() calls or cout statements to print out debugging information, because that output would be mixed in with the program output itself, causing hopeless chaos.

6.2.1.1 Using GDB

So start up GDB, but there is one extra thing we must do, related to that last point. We must tell GDB to have the program execute in a different terminal window than the one that GDB is running in. We can do that with GDB's tty command. First, we go to another window, in which the program I/O will be done, and run the Unix tty command there to determine the ID for that window. In this case, the output of that command tells us that the window is terminal number /dev/pts/8, so we type

```
(gdb) tty /dev/pts/8
```

in the GDB window. From now on, all keyboard input and screen output for the program will be in the execution window.

One last thing before we start: We must type something like

```
sleep 10000
```

in the execution window, so that our keyboard input to that window will go to the program, rather than to the shell.

NOTE   *There are other ways we could handle the problem of separating GDB output from the program's output. For instance, we could start the program's execution first, then fire up GDB in another window, attaching it to the running program.*

Next, set a breakpoint at the beginning of the function updown(), since the error occurs when we try to move the cursor up. We then type run, and the program will begin to execute in the execution window. Hit the u key in that window, and GDB will stop at the breakpoint.

```
(gdb) r
Starting program: /Debug/psax
Detaching after fork from child process 3840.

Breakpoint 1, updown (inc=-1) at psax.c:103
103        {  int tmp = winrow + inc;
```

First, let's confirm that the variable tmp has the right value.

```
(gdb) n
105            if (tmp >= 0 && tmp < LINES)  {
(gdb) p tmp
$2 = 22
(gdb) p LINES
$3 = 24
```

The variable winrow shows the current location of the cursor within the window. That location should be the very end of the window. LINES has the value 24, so winrow should be 23, since the numbering starts at 0. With inc equal to -1 (since we were moving the cursor up, not down), the value of tmp shown here, 22, is confirmed.

Now let's go to the next line.

```
(gdb) n
109             mvaddstr(winrow,0,cmdoutlines[winrow]);
(gdb) p cmdoutlines[winrow]
$4 = " 2270 ?       Ss      0:00 nifd -n\n", '\0' <repeats 464 times>
```

Sure enough, there it is, the line for process 2270. We quickly realize that the line

```
mvaddstr(winrow,0,cmdoutlines[winrow]);
```

in the source code should be

```
mvaddstr(winrow,0,cmdoutlines[cmdstartrow+winrow]);
```

Once we fix that, the program runs fine.

When we are done, press CTRL-C in the execution window, so as to kill the sleep command and make the shell usable again.

Note that if something goes wrong and the program finishes prematurely, that execution window may retain some of the nonstandard terminal settings—for example, cbreak mode. To fix this, go to that window and press CTRL-J, then type the word reset, then press CTRL-J again.

6.2.1.2 Using DDD

What about DDD? Again, you'll need a separate window for execution of the program. Arrange this by choosing **View | Execution Window**, and DDD will pop up an execution window. Note that you don't type the sleep command into that window, as DDD does that for you. The screen will now appear as in Figure 6-2.

Set breakpoints as usual, but remember to type the program input in the execution window.

6.2.1.3 Using Eclipse

First note that in building your project, you need to tell Eclipse to use a -lcurses flag in the makefile, the procedure for which was shown in Chapter 5.

Here too you will need a separate execution window. You can do this when you set up your debug dialog. After setting up a run dialog as usual and selecting Run | Open Debug Dialog, we'll take a slightly different path from what we've done up to now. In Figure 6-3, note that in addition to the usual choice, C/C++ Local Application, there is also the option C/C++ Attach to Local Application. The latter means that you want Eclipse to make use of GDB's ability to attach itself to an already running process (discussed

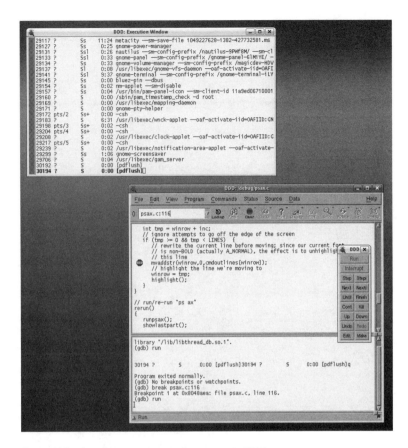

Figure 6-2: Attaching to a running program in DDD

in Chapter 5). Right-click **C/C++ Attach to Local Application**, select **New**, and proceed as before.

When you start an acual debug run, first start your program in a separate shell window. (Don't forget that the program probably resides in your Eclipse workspace directory.) Then select **Run | Open Debug Dialog** as you usually do the first time you go through a debug run; in this case, Eclipse will pop up a window listing processes and asking you to choose the one to which you wish GDB to attach. This is shown in Figure 6-4, which shows that your psax process has ID 12319 (notice the program running in another window, partially hidden here). Click that process, then click **OK**, leading to the situation depicted in Figure 6-5.

In that figure, you can see that we stopped during a system call. Eclipse informs you that it does not have source code for the current instruction, but this is to be expected and is no problem. Actually, this is a good time to set breakpoints in the source file, *psax.c*. Do so, and then click the Resume icon. Eclipse will run until it hits the first breakpoint, and then you can debug as usual.

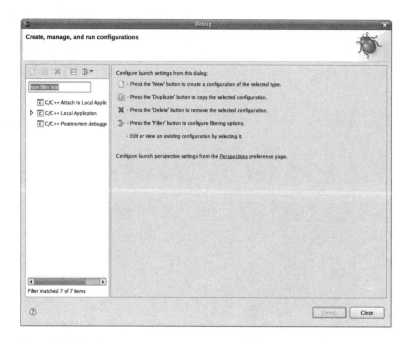

Figure 6-3: Attaching to a running program in Eclipse

Figure 6-4: Choosing the process to attach GDB to

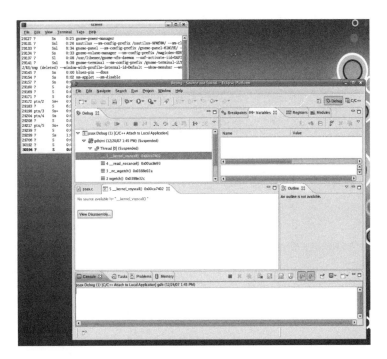

Figure 6-5: Stopped in the kernel

7

OTHER TOOLS

Becoming proficient at debugging code doesn't end with learning to use a debugger like GDB—it *begins* there. There are a variety of other tools, both free and commercial, that also help to prevent, detect, and eliminate bugs in code. The savvy programmer keeps several of them in his or her bag of tricks, understands what each is good for, and recognizes when to use one of them to save time and effort if bugs appear.

So far we've focused our attention on using symbolic debuggers, but now we'd like to broaden our coverage to other aspects of debugging, including defensive programming. This chapter is devoted to some of the tools and techniques *other than* GDB that you may find useful, both to prevent bugs from arising in the first place and to find and fix them when they do.

7.1 Making Good Use of a Text Editor

The best debugging method is to not make programming errors to begin with! Simply making good use of an editor that has support for programming is one of the most overlooked aspects of "pre-debugging."

If you spend a lot of time coding, we urge you to think carefully about your choice of editor and to learn as much as you possibly can about the editor you will use. There are two main reasons. First, becoming proficient with a powerful editor decreases the time it takes you to write code. Editors that have specialized features, like automatic indentation, word completion, and global symbol lookup are a boon for programmers, and there are several to choose from. Second, a good editor can actually help the coder catch certain kinds of bugs as the code is being written. That's what this section is all about.

Both authors of this book use Vim for programming, so that's what we'll focus on. However, all the popular editors have similar, if not identical, feature sets. If Vim is enhanced to provide a useful feature not currently in Emacs, the community of Emacs developers would quickly rectify the situation, and vice versa. Therefore, although we give specifics for Vim, most of what we talk about applies to other excellent editors like Emacs as well.

7.1.1   Syntax Highlighting

Vim employs *syntax highlighting* to display portions of a program file with different colors or fonts, so that code elements like keywords, type identifiers, local variables, and preprocessor directives each have their own color and font scheme. The editor selects the color and font scheme by looking at the filename extension to determine the language you're using. For instance, if the filename ends with *.pl* (indicating a Perl script), occurrences of the word *die* (which is the name of a Perl function) are highlighted, whereas if the filename ends in *.c*, they are not.

A better name for syntax highlighting would be *lexical highlighting*, because the editor generally doesn't analyze syntax too closely. It can't tell you that you've provided the wrong number of arguments or arguments of the wrong type in a function call. Instead, it only understands (for example) that words like *bless* and *foreach* are Perl keywords and that *fmt* and *dimension* are Fortran keywords and displays them accordingly.

Even so, syntax highlighting is still very useful for catching simple but easy-to-make errors. For instance, on our computer the default color for type identifiers, like the FILE or float keywords in C, is green. Once your eye becomes trained to the font and color scheme, you'll catch the color inconsistency that arises when a type name is misspelled and automatically correct the mistake without having to go through a needless compile cycle.

An example of using syntax highlighting to check keywords that we (the authors) enjoy occurs with makefiles. The patsubst keyword is a very useful text search-and-replace command for makefiles. One of its most common uses is to generate a list of *.o* files from the *.c* files of a project's source code:

```
TARGET = CoolApplication
OBJS = $(patsubst %.c, %.o, $(wildcard *.c))


$(TARGET): $(OBJS)
```

One of the authors can never remember whether it's patsubst, pathsubst, or patsub. Knowing that makefile keywords are displayed in a light color (yellow), can you figure out which version of the line shown below is incorrect? Even if you don't know how to write makefiles, syntax highlighting alone should make it clear![1]

```
OBJS = $(patsub %.c, %.o $(wildcard *.c))
OBJS = $(patsubst %.c, %.o $(wildcard *.c))
```

Figure 7-1: Syntax highlighting finds my makefile mistake.

Furthermore, here's an example where syntax highlighting is a bit smarter. The figure below has an honest-to-goodness syntax error. Try to find, without thinking too much, what (or at least where) the error is, based on the colors alone:

```
if (fp == NULL) {
    puts("This was a "bad" file pointer.");
    exit(1);
}
```

Figure 7-2: Syntax highlighting reveals a common error.

and here's another illustration of a similar error. Try to let the color guide your eye to the error.

```
fprintf(fp, "argument %d is \"%s\".\n, i, argv[i]);
printf("I just wrote \"%s\" which is argument %d\n", argv[i], i);
```

Figure 7-3: Syntax highlighting reveals another common error.

You may find that certain colors in the syntax highlighting scheme are hard to read. If so, you can turn off the highlighting by typing the following:

```
: syntax off
```

---

[1] This figure needed to be converted to grayscale for the book. In practice, identifying the error would be even easier.

The command to turn it back on again is of course

```
: syntax on
```

A better option would be to modify the syntax file to use a different, better color for that type of keyword, but that's beyond the scope of our discussion here.

7.1.2 Matching Brackets

Unbalanced bracket errors are extremely common and can be very difficult to catch. Consider the following code:

```
mytype *myvar;
if ((myvar = (mytype *)malloc(sizeof(mytype))) == NULL) {
    exit(-1);
}
```

NOTE   *In this section, the word* bracket *refers to parentheses, square brackets, and braces (or curly brackets):* (), [], *and* {}, *respectively.*

Quickly: Are the parentheses balanced?[2] Have you ever had to track down unbalanced brackets in long blocks of code with lots of conditionals? Or tried to use TeX? (We shudder to think of some of our past LaTeX files with missing braces!) Then you must agree with us that that's exactly what computers are for—to relieve us of such tedious work! Vim has some great features that can help.

- Whenever you type a bracket at the keyboard, Vim's showmatch option makes Vim momentarily place the cursor over the matching bracket (if the matching bracket exists and is visible on the screen). You can even control how long the cursor lingers on the matching bracket by setting the matchtime variable, which specifies this duration in tenths of seconds.

- Typing the percent symbol when the cursor is on a bracket will move the cursor to the bracket's mate. This command is a great way to track down unbalanced brackets.

- When you place the cursor on a bracket, Vim will highlight its mate, as shown in Figure ??. This is also a great way to track down unbalanced bracket problems.

The showmatch option is useful when you're programming, but it can otherwise be annoying. You can use autocommands to set this option only when you program. For example, to set showmatch only for editing sessions with C/C++ source code files, you can put lines like these in your *.vimrc* file (see the Vim helpfiles for more information):

---

[2] Admit it. You were expecting them not to balance. Our point is not that you were wrong, but that it probably took you longer than it should have to answer the question!

```
au BufNewFile,BufRead *.c set showmatch
au BufNewFile,BufRead *.cc set showmatch
```

What if an unbalanced bracket enters your code, or worse, you need to catch unbalanced brackets in someone else's spaghetti code? The previously mentioned % editor command searches for balanced grouping characters. For example, if you place the cursor over a left square bracket, [, and type % from command mode, Vim will reposition the cursor to the next] character. If you place the cursor on a right curly brace, }, and invoke %, then Vim repositions the cursor on the previous matching { character. In this way, you can verify not only that any given round, curly, or square bracket has a corresponding matching partner, but also that the partner matches semantically. You can even define other matching pairs of "brackets," like the HTML comment delimiters <!-- and -->, using Vim's matchpair command. See the Vim help pages for more information.

7.1.3 Vim and Makefiles

The make utility manages the compilation and building of executables on Linux/Unix systems, and a little bit of effort in learning how to use it can pay great dividends to the programmer. However, this also introduces new opportunities for errors. Vim has a few features that can really help in the debugging process if you use make. Consider the following makefile snippet:

```
all: yerror.o main.o
    gcc -o myprogram yerror.o main.o

yerror.o: yerror.c yerror.h
    gcc -c yerror.c

main.o: main.c main.h
    gcc -c main.c
```

There's an error in this makefile, but it's hard to see. make is very picky about formatting. The command line of a target must start with a tab character—not with spaces. If you issue the set list command from within Vim, you can see what's wrong immediately:

```
all: yerror.o main.o$
^Igcc -o myprogram yerror.o main.o$
$
yerror.o: yerror.c yerror.h$
^Igcc -c yerror.c$
$
main.o: main.c main.h$
    gcc -c main.c$
```

In `list` mode, Vim displays nonprintable characters. By default, the end-of-line character shows up as $, and control characters are displayed with the caret symbol (^); thus, the tab character, which is CTRL-I, is displayed as ^I. Hence you can distinguish spaces from tabs, and the mistake is clear to see: The command line for the *main.o* make target begins with spaces.

You can control what is displayed by using Vim's `listchars` option. For example, if you want to change the end-of-line character to be = instead of $, you can use `:set listchars=eol:=`.

7.1.4 Makefiles and Compiler Warnings

Invoking `make` from within Vim can be very handy. For instance, instead of manually saving your file and typing `make clean` in another window, all you need to do is type `:make clean` from command mode. (Make sure `autowrite` is set, so that Vim automatically saves the file before running the `make` command.) In general, whenever you type

```
:make arguments
```

from command mode, Vim will run `make` and pass *arguments* to it.

It gets even better. When you make your program from within Vim, the editor captures all the messages that the compiler issues. It understands the syntax of GCC's output and knows when a compiler warning or error occurs. Let's take a look at this in action. Consider the following code:

```
#include <stdio.h>

int main(void)
{
    printf("There were %d arguments.\n", argc);

    if (argc .gt. 5) then
      print *, 'You seem argumentative today';
    end if

    return 0;
}
```

Listing 7-1: main.c

It looks like somebody's been doing a little concurrent Fortran and C coding! Suppose you're currently editing *main.c* and want to build the program. Issue the `:make` command from within Vim and see all the error messages (Figure 7-4).

Now if you press ENTER or the spacebar, you return to editing the program, but with the cursor positioned on the line that generated the first warning or error (in this case, the message that `argc` was undeclared) as shown in Figure 7-5.

```
:!make  2>&1| tee /tmp/v243244/1
gcc -std=c99 -W -Wall    main.c   -o main
main.c: In function 'main':
main.c:12: error: 'argc' undeclared (first use in this function)
main.c:12: error: (Each undeclared identifier is reported only once
main.c:12: error: for each function it appears in.)
main.c:14: error: expected identifier before numeric constant
main.c:14: error: 'then' undeclared (first use in this function)
main.c:15: error: expected ';' before 'print'
main.c:15:18: warning: character constant too long for its type
main.c:16: error: 'end' undeclared (first use in this function)
main.c:16: error: expected ';' before 'if'
make: *** [main] Error 1
(3 of 12): error: 'argc' undeclared (first use in this function)
Press ENTER or type command to continue█
```

Figure 7-4: The error messages

```
#include <stdio.h>

int main(void)
{
   █rintf("There were %d arguments.\n", argc);

   if (argc .gt. 5) then
      print *, 'You seem argumentative today';
   end if

   return 0;
}
```

Figure 7-5: The cursor is positioned at the first error.

After you fix the error, there are two ways to proceed to the next error:

- You could remake the program, and Vim will again display the remaining warnings and errors and reposition the cursor on the first one. This makes sense if the build time is negligible, especially if you map a single keystroke to build the program, for example, with:

```
au BufNewFile,BufRead *.c map <F1> :make<CR>
```

- You could also use :cnext, which displays the next error or warning. Similarly, :cprevious displays the *last* error or warning, and :cc displays the *current* error or warning. All three commands conveniently reposition the cursor to the location of the "active" error or warning.

7.1.5   Final Thoughts on a Text Editor as an IDE

Becoming proficient with your chosen editor is so self-evident that it's often neglected, but it is really the first step in learning to program in a particular environment. At the risk of overstating things, editors are to programmers as musical instruments are to musicians. Even the most creative composers need to know the basics of how to play an instrument in order to realize their ideas so that other people can benefit from them. Learning to use your editor to its fullest extent enables you to program more quickly, figure out other people's code more effectively, and reduce the number of compile cycles you need to perform when debugging code.

If you use Vim, we recommend Steve Oualline's *Vi IMproved—Vim* (New Riders, 2001). The book is thorough and well written. (Unfortunately, it was written for Vim 6.0, and Vim 7.0 and later features like folding are not covered.) Our purpose here was just to give a taste of the things that Vim can do for the programmer, but Steve's book is a great resource for learning the details.

Vim has many features that the authors find obscenely useful. For example, we would have liked to cover

- Using `K` to look up functions in the man pages
- Finding variable declarations with `gd` and `gD`
- Jumping to macro definitions with `[^D` and `]^D`
- Displaying macro definitions with `]d`, `]d`, `[D`, and `]D`
- Window splitting to view *.c* and *.h* files concurrently to check prototypes
- . . . and much more

But this is a book on debugging, not on Vim, and we need to get back to discussing additional software tools.

7.2 Making Good Use of the Compiler

If your editor is your first weapon in the battle against bugs, then your compiler is your second. All compilers have the ability to scan code and find common errors, but you usually have to enable this error checking by invoking the appropriate option.

Many of the compiler warning options, like GCC's `-Wtraditional` switch, are probably overkill except in special situations. However, don't even *think* about using GCC without using `-Wall` each and every time. For example, one of the most common mistakes that new C programmers make is illustrated by the following statement:

```
if (a = b)
    printf("Equality for all!\n");
```

This is valid C code, and GCC will merrily compile it. The variable a is assigned the value of b, and that value is used in the conditional. However, this is almost certainly not what the programmer meant to do. Using GCC's `-Wall` switches, you'll at least get a warning alerting you that this code might be a mistake:

```
$ gcc try.c
$ gcc -Wall try.c
   try.c: In function `main':
   try.c:8: warning: suggest parentheses around assignment used as truth value
```

GCC suggests that you parenthesize the assignment a = b before using it as a truth value, in the same way that you do when you assign a value and perform a comparison: if ((fp = fopen("myfile", "w")) == NULL). GCC is essentially asking, "Are you *sure* you want the assignment a = b here, instead of the test for equality a == b?"

You should always use your compiler's error-checking options, and if you teach programming, you should require your students to use them, too, in order to instill good habits. GCC users should *always* use -Wall, even for the smallest "Hello, world!" program. We've found that it is prudent to use -Wmissing-prototypes and -Wmissing-declarations, as well. Indeed, if you have a spare 10 minutes, scanning the GCC man page and reading the compiler warning section is a great way to spend the time, especially if you're going to be programming under Unix to any significant extent.

7.3 Error Reporting in C

Error reporting in C is accomplished through the use of an old mechanism named errno. Although errno shows its age and has some deficiencies, it generally gets the job done. You may wonder why you need an error-reporting mechanism at all, since most C functions have a handy return value that tells whether the call succeeded or failed. The answer is that a return value can warn you that a function didn't do what you wanted it to, but it may or may not tell you why. To make this more concrete, consider this code snippet:

```
FILE *fp
fp = fopen("myfile.dat", "r");
retval = fwrite(&data, sizeof(DataStruct), 1, fp);
```

Suppose you inspect retval and find it to be zero. From the man page, you see that fwrite() should return the number of items (not bytes or characters) written, so retval should be 1. How many different ways can fwrite() fail? Lots! For starters, the filesystem may be full, or you might not have write permissions on the file. In this case, however, there's a bug in the code that causes fwrite() to fail. Can you find it?[3] An error-reporting system like errno can provide diagnostic information to help you figure out what happened in cases like this. (The operating system may announce certain errors, as well.)

7.3.1 Using errno

System and library calls that fail usually set a globally defined integer variable named errno. On most GNU/Linux systems errno is declared in */usr/include/errno.h*, so by including this header file, you don't have to declare extern int errno in your own code.

---

[3] We opened the file in read mode and then tried to write to it.

When a system or library call fails, it sets errno to a value that indicates the type of failure. It's up to you to check the value of errno and take the appropriate action. Consider the following code:

```c
#include <stdio.h>
#include <errno.h>
#include <math.h>

int main(void)
{
    double trouble = exp(1000.0);
    if (errno) {
        printf("trouble: %f (errno: %d)\n", trouble, errno);
        exit(-1);
    }

    return 0;
}
```

Listing 7-2: double-trouble.c

On our system, exp(1000.0) is larger than what a *double* can store, so the assignment results in a floating-point overflow. From the output, you see that an errno value of 34 indicates a floating-point overflow error:

```
$ ./a.out
trouble: inf (errno: 34)
```

This pretty much illustrates how errno works. By convention, when a library function or system call fails, it sets errno to a value that describes why the call failed. You just saw that the value 34 means the result of exp(1000.0) was not representable by a double, and there are lots of other codes that indicate underflow, permission problems, file not found, and other error conditions. However, before you start using errno in your programs, there are some issues you need to be aware of.

First, code that uses errno may not be completely portable. For example, the ISO C standard only defines a few error codes, and the POSIX standard defines quite a few more. You can see which error codes are defined by which standards in the errno man page. Moreover, the standards don't specify numeric values, like 34, for the error codes. They prescribe *symbolic error codes*, which are macro constants whose names are prefixed by E and which are defined in the errno header file (or in files included by the errno header). The only thing about their values that is consistent across platforms is that they are nonzero. Thus, you can't assume that a particular value always indicates the same error condition.[4] You should always use the symbolic names to refer to errno values.

In addition to the ISO and POSIX errno values, specific implementations of the C library, like GNU's glibc, can define even more errno values. On GNU/Linux, the errno section of the of libc info pages[5] is the canonical source for all the available errno values on that platform: ISO, POSIX, and glibc. Here are some error code defines we pulled from */usr/include/asm/errno.h* off of a GNU/Linux machine:

```
#define EPIPE        32 /* Broken pipe */
#define EDOM         33 /* Math arg out of domain of func */
#define ERANGE       34 /* Math result not representable */
#define EDEADLK      35 /* Resource deadlock would occur */
#define ENAMETOOLONG 36 /* File name too long */
#define ENOLCK       37 /* No record locks available */
#define ENOSYS       38 /* Function not implemented */
```

Next, there are some important facts to remember about how errno is used. errno can be set by any library function or system call, whether it fails or succeeds! Because even successful function calls can set errno, you cannot rely on errno to tell you *whether* an error occurs. You can only rely on it to tell you *why* an error happened. Therefore, the safest way to use errno is as follows:[6]

1. Perform the call to the library or system function.

2. Use the function's return value to determine whether or not an error occured.

3. If an error occured, use errno to determine why.

In pseudocode:

```
retval = systemcall();

if (retval indicates an error) {
   examine_errno();
   take_action();
}
```

This brings us to man pages. Suppose you're coding and you want to throw in some error checking after a call to ptrace(). Step two says to use ptrace()'s return value to determine if an error has occured. If you're like us,

---

[4] For example, some systems differentiate between EWOULDBLOCK and EAGAIN, but GNU/Linux does not.

[5] In addition to the libc info pages, you can look around in your system header files to examine the errno values. Not only is this a safe and natural thing to do, it's actually an encouraged practice!

[6] Our use of errno in Listing 7-2 was not good practice.

you don't have the return values of ptrace() memorized. What can you do? Every man page has a section named "Return Value." You can quickly go to it by typing man *function name* and searching for the string return value.

Although errno has some drawbacks, there is good news as well.

There's extensive work underway in the GNU C library to save errno when a function is entered and then restore it to the original value *if* the function call succeeds. It looks like glibc tries very hard not to write over errno for successful function calls. However, the world is not GNU (yet), so portable code should not rely on this fact.

Also, although going through documentation every time you want to see what a particular error code means gets tiresome, there are two functions that make it easier to interpret error codes: perror() and strerror(). They do the same thing, but in different ways. The perror() function takes a string argument and has no return value:

```
#include <stdio.h>
void perror(const char *s);
```

The argument of perror() is a user-supplied string. When perror() is called, it prints this string, followed by a colon and space, and then a description of the type of error based on the value of errno. Here's a simple example of how to use perror():

```
int main(void)
{
    FILE *fp;

    fp = fopen("/foo/bar", "r");

    if (fp == NULL)
        perror("I found an error");

    return 0;
}
```

Listing 7-3: perror-example.c

If there's no file */foo/bar* on your system, the output looks like this:

```
$ ./a.out
I found an error: No such file or directory
```

The output of perror() goes to standard error. Remember this if you want to redirect your program's error output to a file.

Another function that helps you translate errno codes into descriptive messages is strerror():

```
#include <string.h>
char *strerror(int errnum);
```

This function takes the value of errno as its argument and returns a string that describes the error. Here's an example of how to use strerror():

```
int main(void)
{
    close(5);
    printf("%s\n", strerror(errno));
    return 0;
}
```

Listing 7-4: strerror-example.c

Here is the output of this program:

```
$ ./a.out
Bad file descriptor
```

7.4   Better Living with strace and ltrace

It is important to understand the difference between library functions and system calls. Library functions are higher level, run completely in user space, and provide a more convenient interface for the programmer to the functions that do the real work—system calls. System calls do work in kernel mode on the user's behalf and are provided by the kernel of the operating system itself. The library function printf() may look like a very general printing function, but all it really does is format the data you give it into strings and write the string data using the low-level system call write(), which then sends the data to a file associated with your terminal's standard output.

The strace utility prints out each system call that your program makes, along with its arguments and return value. Would you like to see what system calls are made by printf()? It's easy! Write a "Hello, world!" program, but run it like this:

```
$ strace ./a.out
```

Aren't you impressed by how hard your computer works just to print something to the screen?

Each line of the strace output corresponds to one system call. Most of the strace output shows calls to mmap() and open() with filenames like *ld.so* and *libc*. This has to do with system-level things like mapping disk files into memory and loading shared libraries. You most likely don't care about all of that. For our purposes, there are exactly two lines of interest, toward the end of the output:

```
write(1, "hello world\n", 12hello world) = 12
_exit(0) = ?
```

These lines illustrate the general format of strace output:

- The name of the system function that is being called
- The arguments to the system call between parentheses
- The return value of the system call[7] following the = symbol

That's all there is to it, but what a wealth of information! You also may see errors. On our system, for example, we get the following lines:

```
open("/etc/ld.so.preload", O_RDONLY) = -1 ENOENT (No such file or directory)
open("/etc/ld.so.cache", O_RDONLY)   = 3
```

The first call to open() tries to open a file named *etc/ld.so.preload*. The return value of the call to open() (which should be a non-negative file descriptor) is -1, indicating an error of some sort. strace helpfully tells us that the error that caused open() to fail is ENOENT: the file *etc/ld.so.preload* doesn't exist.

strace tells us that the second call to open() returned the value 3. This is a valid file descriptor, so apparently the call to open the file *etc/ld.so.cache* succeeded. Accordingly, there are no error codes on the second line of the strace output.

By the way, don't worry about errors like this. What you see is related to dynamic library loading and is not really an error *per se*. The file *ld.so.preload* can be used to override the system's default shared libraries. Since I have no desire to fiddle with such things, the file simply doesn't exist on my system. As you gain experience with strace, you'll get better and better at filtering out this kind of "noise" and concentrating on the parts of the output you're really interested in.

strace has a few options which you'll need to use at some point or another, so we'll describe them briefly here. If you looked at the complete strace output of a "Hello, world!" program, you might have noticed that strace can be a bit . . . verbose. It's much more convenient to save all that output in a file than to try to look at it on the screen. One way, of course, is to redirect stderr, but you can also use the -o *logfile* switch to make strace write all its output to a logfile. Also, strace normally truncates strings to 32 characters. This can sometimes hide important information. To force strace to truncate strings at N characters, you can use the -s *N* option. Lastly, if you're running strace on a program that forks child processes, you can capture strace output for the individual children to a file named *LOG.*xxx with the -o LOG -ff switch, where *xxx* is the child's process ID.

---

[7] You may be surprised by the question mark return value of exit(). All strace is saying here is that _exit returns a void.

There's also a utility named ltrace which is like strace, but shows library calls rather than system calls. ltrace and strace have many options in common, so knowing how to use one of them will take you far toward learning the other.

The strace and ltrace utilities are very useful when you want to send bug reports and diagnostic information to maintainers of programs for which you don't have the source code, and even if you do have the source files, using these tools can sometimes be faster than digging through the code.

One of the authors first stumbled across the usefulness of these tools when trying to install and run a poorly documented proprietary application on his system. When launched, the application immediately returned to the shell, apparently without doing anything. He wanted to send the company something more informative than just the observation, "Your program immediately exits." Running strace on the application yielded a clue:

```
open(umovestr: Input/output error 0, O_RDONLY) = -1 EFAULT (Bad address)
```

and running ltrace yielded even more clues:

```
fopen(NULL, "r")                                    = 0
```

According to the output, this was the very first call to fopen(). The application presumably wanted to open some kind of configuration file, but fopen() was passed NULL. The application had some kind of internal fault handler that exited but produced no error message. The author was able to write a detailed bug report to the company, and as it turned out, the problem was that the application shipped with a faulty global configuration file that pointed to a non-existent local configuration file. A patch was issued the next day.

Since then the authors have found strace and ltrace to be immensely useful for tracking down bugs and figuring out stubborn, mysterious program behavior that can cause lots of head scratching.

7.5 Static Code Checkers: lint and Friends

There are a number of free and commercial tools that scan your code without compiling it and warn you about errors, possible errors, and deviations from strict C coding standards. They are appropriately named *static code checkers*. The canonical static code checker for C, written by S.C. Johnson in the late 1970s, was called lint. It was written mainly to check function calls, as early versions of C didn't support prototyping. lint spawned many derivative static checkers. One such checker, written by Dave Evans of the University of Virginia's computer science department, was named lclint and was popular on modern systems like Linux. In January 2002, Dave renamed lclint to splint to emphasize the increased focus on *secure programming* (and because *splint* is easier to pronounce than *lclint*).

The aim of splint is to help you write the most defensive, secure, and error-free program possible. splint, like its predecessors, can be very picky about what constitutes good code.[8] As an exercise, try to find anything in the following code that might cause a warning:

```
int main(void)
{
    int i;

    scanf("%d", &i);

    return 0;
}
```

Listing 7-5: scan.c

When this code is run through splint, it warns that you're discarding the return value of scanf().[9]

```
$ splint test.c
Splint 3.0.1.6 --- 11 Feb 2002

test.c: (in function main)
test.c:8:2: Return value (type int) ignored: scanf("%d", &i)
    Result returned by function call is not used. If this is intended, can cast
    result to (void) to eliminate message. (Use -retvalint to inhibit warning)

Finished checking --- 1 code warning
```

All splint warnings have a fixed format. The first line of a splint warning tells you the filename and function where the warning occurs. The next line gives the line number and position of the warning. After that is a description of the warning, along with instructions on how to go about suppressing this kind of warning. As you can see here, invoking splint -retvalint test.c turns off all warnings about discarding integer function return values. Alternatively, if you don't want to turn off *all* reports about discarded int return values, you can suppress the warning for just this call to scanf() by typecasting scanf() to void. That is, replace scanf("%d", &i); with (void) scanf("%d", &i);. (There's yet another way to suppress this warning, by using *annotations*, which the interested reader can learn about from the splint documentation.)

---

[8] Many programmers consider it a badge of honor when splint reports no warnings. When this happens, the code is declared *lint free*.
[9] The return value of scanf() is the number of input items that were assigned.

7.5.1 How to Use splint

splint comes with a staggering number of switches, but as you use it, you'll get a feel for which ones typically suit your needs. Many switches are Boolean in nature—they turn a feature on or off. These types of switches are preceded by a + to turn them on or a - to turn them off. For example, -retvalint turns off reporting of discarded int return values, and +retvalint turns this reporting on (which is the default behavior).

There are two ways to use splint. The first is informal and is used mainly when you're running splint on someone else's code or on code that's mostly final:

```
$ splint +weak *.c
```

Without the +weak switch, splint is typically too picky to be useful. There are three levels of checking in addition to +weak. You can get more details about them from the splint manual, but they are, briefly, as follows:

+weak   Weak checking, typically for unannotated C code

+standard   The default mode

+checks   Moderately strict checking

+strict   Absurdly strict checking

The more formal use of splint involves documenting your code specifically for use with splint. This splint-specific documentation is called an *annotation*. Annotation is a large topic, and it would take us too far afield to include it in this book, but it is well covered in the splint documentation.

7.5.2 Last Words

splint supports many, but not all, of the C99 library extensions. It also doesn't support some of the C99 language changes. For instance, splint doesn't know about complex data types or about defining an int variable in the initializer of a for loop.

splint is released under the GNU GPL. Its homepage is at *http://www.splint.org/*.

7.6 Debugging Dynamically Allocated Memory

As you may know, *dynamically allocated memory (DAM)* is memory that a program requests from the heap with functions like malloc() and calloc().[10] Dynamically allocated memory is typically used for data structures like binary trees and linked lists, and it is also at work behind the scenes when you create an object in object-oriented programming. Even the standard C library

---

[10] For the rest of this section, we'll refer only to malloc(), but we really mean malloc() and friends, like calloc() and realloc().

uses DAM for its own internal purposes. You may also recall that dynamic memory must be freed when you're done with it.[11]

DAM problems are notoriously difficult to find and fall into a few general categories:

- Dynamically allocated memory is not freed.
- The call to malloc() fails (this is easy to detect by checking the return value of malloc()).
- A read or write is performed to an address outside the DAM segment.
- A read or write is performed to memory within a DAM region after the segment has been freed.
- free() is called twice on the same segment of dynamic memory.

These errors may not cause your program to crash in an obvious way. Let's discuss this a bit further. To make the discussion more concrete, here's an example illustrating these problems:

```
int main( void )
{
   int *a = (int *) malloc( 3*sizeof(int) ); // malloc return not checked
   int *b = (int *) malloc( 3*sizeof(int) ); // malloc return not checked

   for (int i = -1; i <= 3; ++i)
     a[i] = i; // a bad write for i = -1 and 3

   free(a);
   printf("%d\n", a[1]); // a read from freed memory
   free(a); // a double free on pointer a

   return 0; // program ends without freeing *b.
}
```

Listing 7-6: memprobs.c

The first problem is called a *memory leak*. For example, consider the following code:

```
int main( void )
{
       ... lots of previous code ...

       myFunction();
```

---

[11] One notable exception is the alloca() function, which requests dynamic memory from the current stack frame rather than from the heap. The memory in the frame is automatically freed when the function returns. Thus, you don't have to free memory allocated by alloca().

```
        ... lots of future code ...
}


void myFunction( void )
{
        char *name = (char *) malloc( 10*sizeof(char) );
}
```

Listing 7-7: Example of a memory leak

When myFunction() executes, you allocate memory for 10 char values. The only way you can refer to this memory is by using the address returned by malloc(), which you've stored in the pointer variable name. If, for some reason, you lose track of the address—for example, name goes out of scope when myFunction() exits, and you haven't saved a copy of its value elsewhere—then you have no way to access the allocated memory, and, in particular, you have no way to free it.

But this is exactly what happens in the code. Dynamically allocated memory doesn't simply disappear or go out of scope, the way that a storage for a stack-allocated variable like name does, and so each time myFunction() is called, it gobbles up memory for 10 chars, which then is never released. The net result is that the available heap space gets smaller and smaller. That's why this bug is called a *memory leak*.

Memory leaks decrease the amount of memory available to the program. On most modern systems, like GNU/Linux, this memory is reclaimed by the operating system when the application with the memory leak terminates. On ancient systems, like Microsoft DOS and Microsoft Windows 3.1, leaked memory is lost until the operating system is rebooted. In either case, memory leaks cause degradation in system performance due to increased paging. Over time, they can cause the program with the leak, or even the entire system, to crash.

The second problem encountered with dynamically allocated memory is that the call to malloc() may fail. There are lots of ways this can happen. For example, a bug in a computation might cause a request for an amount of DAM that is too large or is negative. Or perhaps the system really is out of memory. If you don't realize this has happened and continue to try to read and write to what you mistakenly believe to be valid DAM, complications develop in an already unpleasant situation. This is a type of access violation that we'll discuss shortly. However, to avoid it, you should *always* check whether or not malloc() returns a non-NULL pointer, and try to exit the program gracefully if it does not.

The third and fourth problems are called *access errors*. Both are basically versions of the same thing: The program tries to read from or write to a memory address that is not available to it. The third problem involves accessing a memory address above or below the DAM segment. The fourth problem involves accessing a memory address that used to be available, but was freed prior to the access attempt.

Calling free() on the same segment of DAM twice is colloquially known as a *double free*. The C library has internal memory management structures that describe the boundaries of each allocated DAM segment. When you call free() twice on the same pointer to dynamic memory, the program's memory management structure becomes corrupted, which can lead to the program crashing, or in some cases, can allow a malicious programmer to exploit the bug to produce a buffer overflow. In a sense, this is also an access violation, but for the C library itself, rather than the program.

Access violations cause one of two things to happen: The program can crash, possibly writing a core file[12] (usually after receiving the segmentation fault signal), or, much worse, it can continue to execute, leading to data corruption.

Of these two consequences, the former is infinitely more desirable. In fact, there are a number of tools available that will cause your program to seg fault and dump core whenever *any* problem with DAM is detected, rather than risk the alternative!

You may wonder, "Why in the world would I *want* my program to seg fault?" You should get comfortable with the idea that if your code's handling of DAM is buggy, it is a Very Good Thing[TM] when it crashes, because the other option is intermittent, puzzling, and irreproducible bad behavior. Memory corruption can go unnoticed for a long time before its effects are felt. Often, the problem manifests itself in parts of your program that are quite far from the bug, and tracking it down can be a nightmare. If that weren't bad enough, memory corruption can give rise to breaches of security. Applications known to cause buffer overruns and double frees can, in some instances, be exploited by malicious crackers to run arbitrary code and are responsible for many operating system security vulnerabilities.

On the other hand, when your program seg faults and dumps core, you can perform a postmortem on the core file and learn the precise source file and line number of the code that caused the seg fault. And that, dear reader, is preferable to bug hunting.

In short, catching DAM problems *as soon as possible* is of extreme importance.

7.6.1 Strategies for Detecting DAM Problems

In this section we'll discuss Electric Fence, a library that enforces a "fence" around allocated memory addresses. Access to memory outside of these fences typically results in a seg fault and core dump. We'll also discuss two GNU tools, mtrace() and MALLOC_CHECK_, that add hooks into the standard libc allocation functions to keep records about currently allocated memory. This allows libc to perform checks on memory you're about to read, write, or free. Keep in mind that care is needed when using several software tools, each

---

[12] This is colloquially known as *dumping core*.

of which uses hooks to heap-related function calls, because one facility may install one of its hooks over a previously installed hook.[13]

7.6.2 Electric Fence

Electric Fence, or *EFence*, is a library written by Bruce Perens in 1988 and released under the GNU GPL license while he worked at Pixar. When linked into your code, it causes the program to immediately seg fault and dump core[14] when any of the following occur:

- A read or write is performed outside the boundary of DAM.
- A read or write is performed to DAM that has already been freed.
- A free() is performed on a pointer that doesn't point to DAM allocated by malloc() (this includes double frees as a special case).

Let's see how to use Electric Fence to track down malloc() problems. Consider the program *outOfBound.c*:

```
int main(void)
{
   int *a = (int *) malloc( 2*sizeof(int) );

   for (int i=0; i<=2; ++i) {
     a[i] = i;
     printf("%d\n ", a[i]);          .
   }

   free(a);
   return 0;
}
```

Listing 7-8: outOfBound.c

Although the program contains an archetypal malloc() bug, it will probably compile without warnings. Chances are, it will even run without problems:[15]

```
$ gcc -g3 -Wall -std=c99 outOfBound.c -o outOfBound_without_efence -lefence
$ ./outOfBound_without_efence
```

---

[13] Actually, you *can* use mtrace() and MALLOC_CHECK_ together safely, because mtrace() is careful to preserve any existing hooks it finds.

[14] If you run a program linked with EFence from within GDB, rather than invoking it on the command line, the program will seg fault without dumping core. This is desirable because core files of executables linked to EFence can be quite large, and you don't need the core file anyway, because you'll already be inside of GDB and staring at the source code file and line number where the seg fault occured.

[15] That doesn't mean malloc() overruns won't wreak havoc with your code! This example is contrived to show how you use EFence. In a *real* program, writing beyond an array's bounds can cause some serious problems!

```
0
1
2
```

We were able to write beyond the last element of the array a[]. Everything looks fine now, but that just means this bug manifests itself unpredictably and will be difficult to nail down later on.

Now we'll link outOfBound with EFence and run it. By default, EFence only catches reads or writes *beyond the last element* of a dynamically allocated region. That means outOfBound should seg fault when you try to write to a[2]:

```
$ gcc -g3 -Wall -std=c99 outOfBound.c -o outOfBound_with_efence -lefence
$ ./outOfBound_with_efence
  Electric Fence 2.1 Copyright (C) 1987-1998 Bruce Perens.
0
1
Segmentation fault (core dumped)
```

Sure enough, EFence found the write operation past the last element of the array.

Accidentally accessing memory *before the first element* of an array (for example, specifying the "element" a[-1]) is less common, but it can certainly occur as a result of buggy index calculations. EFence provides a global int named EF_PROTECT_BELOW. When you set this variable to 1, EFence catches only array underruns and does not check for array overruns:

```
extern int EF_PROTECT_BELOW;


double myFunction( void )
{
   EF_PROTECT_BELOW = 1;   // Check from below

       int *a = (int *) malloc( 2*sizeof(int) );

       for (int i=-2; i<2; ++i) {
               a[i] = i;
               printf("%d\n", a[i]);
       }


   ...
}
```

Because of the way EFence works, you can catch *either* attempts to access memory beyond dynamically allocated blocks *or* attempts to access memory before allocated blocks, but not both types of access errors at the same time.

To be thorough, you should run your program *twice* using EFence: once in the default mode to check for dynamic memory overruns and a second time with `EF_PROTECT_BELOW` set to 1 to check for underruns.[16]

In addition to `EF_PROTECT_BELOW`, EFence has a few other global integer variables that you can set in order to control its behavior:

`EF_DISABLE_BANNER` Setting this variable to 1 hides the banner that is displayed when you run a program linked with EFence. Doing this is not recommended, because the banner warns you that EFence is linked into the application and that the executable should not be used for a production release, because executables linked to EFence are larger, run more slowly, and produce very large core files.

`EF_PROTECT_BELOW` As discussed, EFence checks for DAM overruns by default. Setting this variable to 1 will cause EFence to check for memory underruns.

`EF_PROTECT_FREE` By default, EFence will not check for access to DAM that has already been freed. Setting this variable to 1 enables protection of freed memory.

`EF_FREE_WIPES` By default, Efence will not change the values stored in memory that is freed. Setting this variable to a nonzero value causes EFence to fill segments of dynamically allocated memory with `0xbd` before they are released. This makes improper accesses to freed memory easier to detect by EFence.

`EF_ALLOW_MALLOC_0` By default, EFence will trap any call to `malloc()` you make that has an argument of 0 (i.e., any request for zero bytes of memory). The rationale is that writing something like `char *p = (char *) malloc(0);` is probably a bug. However, if for some reason you really do mean to pass zero to `malloc()`, then setting this variable to a nonzero value will cause EFence to ignore such calls.

As an exercise, try writing a program that accesses DAM that has already been freed, and use EFence to catch the error.

Whenever you change one of these global variables, you need to recompile the program, which can be inconvenient. Thankfully, there's an easier way. You can also set shell environment variables with the same names as EFence's global variables. EFence will detect the shell variables and take the appropriate action.

As a demonstration, we'll set the environment variable `EF_DISABLE_BANNER` to supress the printing of the EFence banner page. (As mentioned before, you shouldn't do this; do as I say, not as I do!) If you use Bash, execute

```
$ export EF_DISABLE_BANNER=1
```

C shell users should execute

---

[16] If you want to be *really* careful, read the "Word-Alignment and Overrun Detection" and "Instructions for Debugging Your Program" sections of the EFence man page.

```
% setenv EF_DISABLE_BANNER 1
```

Then re-run Listing 7-8, and verify that the banner is disabled.

Another trick is to set the EFence variables from within GDB during a debugging session. This works because the EFence variables are global; however, it also means that the program needs to be executing, but paused.

7.6.3   Debugging DAM Problems with GNU C Library Tools

If you're working on a GNU platform, such as GNU/Linux, there are some GNU C library-specific features, similar to EFence, that you can use to catch and recover from dynamic memory problems. We'll discuss them briefly here.

7.6.3.1   The MALLOC_CHECK_ Environment Variable

The GNU C library provides a shell environment variable named MALLOC_CHECK_ that can be used, like EFence, to catch DAM access violations, but you don't need to recompile your program to use it. The settings and their effects are as follows:

0   All DAM checking is turned off (this is also the case if the variable is undefined).

1   A diagnostic message is printed on stderr when heap corruption is detected.

2   The program aborts immediately and dumps core when heap corruption is detected.

3   The combined effects of 1 and 2.[17]

Since MALLOC_CHECK_ is an environment variable, using it to find heap-related problems is as simple as typing:

```
$ export MALLOC_CHECK_=3
```

Although MALLOC_CHECK_ is more convenient to use than EFence, it has a few serious drawbacks. First, MALLOC_CHECK_ only reports a dynamic memory problem upon the next execution of a heap-related function (such as malloc(), realloc(), or free(), for example) *following* an illegal memory access. This means that not only do you not know the source file and line number of the problematic code, you often don't even know which pointer is the problem variable. To illustrate, consider this code:

```
1   int main(void)
2   {
```

---

[17] This is undocumented on the authors' system. Thanks to Gianluca Insolvibile for reading the glibc sources and finding this option!

```
3    int *p = (int *) malloc(sizeof(int));
4    int *q = (int *) malloc(sizeof(int));
5
6    for (int i=0; i<400; ++i)
7      p[i] = i;
8
9    q[0] = 0;
10
11   free(q);
12   free(p);
13   return 0;
14 }
```

Listing 7-9: malloc-check-0.c

The program aborts at line 11 when the problem really occurs on line 7. Examining the core file might lead you to believe the problem lies with q, not p:

```
$ MALLOC_CHECK_=3 ./malloc-check-0
malloc: using debugging hooks
free(): invalid pointer 0x8049680!
Aborted (core dumped)
$ gdb malloc-check-0 core
Core was generated by `./malloc-check-0'.
Program terminated with signal 6, Aborted.
Reading symbols from /lib/libc.so.6...done.
Loaded symbols for /lib/libc.so.6
Reading symbols from /lib/ld-linux.so.2...done.
Loaded symbols for /lib/ld-linux.so.2
#0  0x40046a51 in kill () from /lib/libc.so.6
(gdb) bt
#0  0x40046a51 in kill () from /lib/libc.so.6
#1  0x40046872 in raise () from /lib/libc.so.6
#2  0x40047986 in abort () from /lib/libc.so.6
#3  0x400881d2 in _IO_file_xsputn () from /lib/libc.so.6
#4  0x40089278 in free () from /lib/libc.so.6
#5  0x080484bc in main () at malloc-check-0.c:13
```

You might be able to live with this drawback when debugging 14-line programs, but it can be a serious issue when working with a real application. Nevertheless, knowing that a DAM problem exists at all is useful information.

Second, this implies that if no heap-related function is called after an access error occurs, MALLOC_CHECK_ will not report the error at all.

Third, the MALLOC_CHECK_ error messages don't seem to be very meaningful. Although the previous program listing had an array overrun error, the error message was simply "invalid pointer." Technically true, but not useful.

Finally, MALLOC_CHECK_ is disabled for setuid and setgid programs, because this combination of features could be used in a security exploit. It can be re-enabled by creating the file */etc/suid-debug*. The contents of this file aren't important, only the file's existence matters.

In conclusion, MALLOC_CHECK_ is a convenient tool to use during code development to catch heap-related programming blunders. However, if you suspect a DAM problem or want to carefully scan your code for possible DAM problems, you should use another utility.

7.6.3.2 Using the mcheck() Facility

An alternative to the MALLOC_CHECK_ facility for catching DAM problems is the mcheck() facility. We've found this method to be more satisfactory than MALLOC_CHECK_. The prototype for mcheck() is

```
#include <mcheck.h>
int mcheck (void (*ABORTHANDLER) (enum mcheck_status STATUS))
```

You must call mcheck() before calling any heap-related functions, otherwise the call to mcheck() will fail. Therefore, this function should be invoked very early in your program. A call to mcheck() returns a 0 upon success and a -1 if it is called too late.

The argument, *ABORTHANDLER, is a pointer to a user-supplied function that's called when an inconsistency in DAM is detected. If you pass NULL to mcheck(), then the default handler is used. Like MALLOC_CHECK_, this default handler prints an error message to stdout and calls abort() to produce a core file. Unlike MALLOC_CHECK_, the error message is useful. For instance, trampling past the end of a dynamically allocated segment in the following example:

```
int main(void)
{
  mcheck(NULL);
  int *p = (int *) malloc(sizeof(int));
  p[1] = 0;
  free(p);
  return 0;
}
```

Listing 7-10: mcheckTest.c

produces the error message shown here:

```
$ gcc -g3 -Wall -std=c99 mcheckTest.c -o mcheckTest -lmcheck
$ ./mcheckTest
memory clobbered past end of allocated block
Aborted (core dumped)
```

Other types of problems have similarly descriptive error messages.

7.6.3.3 Using mtrace() to Catch Memory Leaks and Double Frees

The mtrace() facility is part of the GNU C library and is used to catch memory leaks and double frees in C and C++ programs. Using it involves five steps:

1. Set the environment variable MALLOC_TRACE to a valid filename. This is the name of the file in which mtrace() places its messages. If this variable isn't set to a valid filename or write permissions are not set for the file, mtrace() will do nothing.

2. Include the *mcheck.h* header file.

3. Call mtrace() at the top of your program. Its prototype is

```
#include <mcheck.h>
void mtrace(void);
```

4. Run the program. If any problems are detected, they'll be documented, in a non human-readable form, in the file pointed to by MALLOC_TRACE. Also, for security reasons, mtrace() won't do anything for setuid or setgid executables.

5. The mtrace() facility comes with a Perl script called mtrace that's used to parse the log file and print the contents to standard output in human-readable form.

Note that there's also a muntrace() call, which is used to stop memory tracing, but the glibc info page recommends not using it. The C library, which may also use DAM for your program, is notified that your program has terminated only after main() has returned or a call to exit() has been made. Memory that the C library uses for your program is not released until this happens. A call to muntrace() before this memory is released may lead to false positives.

Let's take a look at a simple example. Here's some code that illustrates both of the problems that mtrace() catches. In the following code, we never free the memory allocated on line 6 and pointed to by p, and on line 10 we call free() on the pointer q, even though it doesn't point to dynamically allocated memory.

```
1   int main(void)
2   {
3       int *p, *q;
4
5       mtrace();
6       p = (int *) malloc(sizeof(int));
7       printf("p points to %p\n", p);
8       printf("q points to %p\n", q);
9
10      free(q);
11      return 0;
```

}

Listing 7-11: mtrace1.c

We compile this program and run it, after setting the `MALLOC_TRACE` variable.

```
$ gcc -g3 -Wall -Wextra -std=c99 -o mtrace1 mtrace1.c
$ MALLOC_TRACE="./mtrace.log" ./mtrace1
p points to 0x8049a58
q points to 0x804968c
```

If you look at the contents of *mtrace.log*, it makes no sense at all. However, running the Perl script `mtrace()` produces understandable output:

```
$ cat mtrace.log
= Start
@ ./mtrace1:(mtrace+0x120)[0x80484d4] + 0x8049a58 0x4
@ ./mtrace1:(mtrace+0x157)[0x804850b] - 0x804968c
p@satan$ mtrace mtrace.log
- 0x0804968c Free 3 was never alloc'd 0x804850b

Memory not freed:
-----------------
   Address     Size     Caller
0x08049a58      0x4  at 0x80484d4
```

However, this is only slightly helpful, because although `mtrace()` found the problems, it reported them as pointer addresses. Fortunately, `mtrace()` can do better. The `mtrace()` script also takes the executable's filename as an optional argument. Using this option, you get line numbers along with the associated problems.

```
- 0x0804968c Free 3 was never alloc'd
/home/p/codeTests/mtrace1.c:15

Memory not freed:
-----------------
   Address     Size     Caller
0x08049a58      0x4  at /home/p/codeTests/mtrace1.c:11
```

Now this is what we wanted to see!

Like the `MALLOC_CHECK_` and `mcheck()` utilities, `mtrace()` won't prevent your program from crashing. It simply checks for problems. If your program crashes, some of the output of `mtrace()` may become lost or garbled, which could produce puzzling error reports. The best way to cope with this is to catch and handle seg faults in order to give `mtrace()` a shot at shutting down gracefully. The following example illustrates how to do so.

```
void sigsegv_handler(int signum);

int main(void)
{
    int *p;

    signal(SIGSEGV, sigsegv_handler);
    mtrace();
    p = (int *) malloc(sizeof(int));


    raise(SIGSEGV);
    return 0;
}

void sigsegv_handler(int signum)
{
    printf("Caught sigsegv: signal %d. Shutting down gracefully.\n", signum);
    muntrace();
    abort();
}
```

Listing 7-12: mtrace2.c

8

USING GDB / DDD / ECLIPSE FOR OTHER LANGUAGES

GDB and DDD are commonly known as debuggers for C/C++ programs, but they can be used for development in other languages, as well. Eclipse was originally designed for Java development, but it has plug-ins for many other languages. This chapter will show you how to use this multilanguage capability.

GDB/DDD/Eclipse are not necessarily the "best" debuggers for any particular language. A large number of excellent debugging tools are available for specific languages. What we are saying, though, is that it would be nice to be able use the same debugging interface no matter which language you are writing in, whether it be C, C++, Java, Python, Perl, or other languages/debuggers that these tools can be used with. DDD has been "ported" to all of them.

For example, consider Python. The Python interpreter includes a simple, text-based debugger of its own. Again, a number of excellent Python-specific GUI debuggers and IDEs do exist, but another option is to use DDD as an interface to Python's built-in debugger. This enables you to achieve the convenience of a GUI while still using the interface that you are familiar with from your C/C++ coding (DDD).

How does the multilanguage versatility of these tools come about?

- Though GDB was originally created as a debugger for C/C++, the GNU people later offered a Java compiler too, GCJ.

- Recall that DDD is not a debugger in its own right, but rather a GUI through which you can issue commands to an underlying debugger. For C and C++, that underlying debugger is typically GDB. However, DDD can be, and often is, used as a frontend for debuggers specific to other languages.

- Eclipse is also just a frontend. The plug-ins for various languages give it the power to manage the development and debugging of code in those languages.

In this chapter, we'll give an overview of debugging in Java, Perl, Python, and assembly language with these tools. It should be noted that in each case there are additional features not covered here, and we urge you to explore the details for the language you are using.

8.1 Java

As an example, let's consider an application program that manipulates a linked list. Here objects of class Node represent the nodes in a linked list of numbers, which are maintained in order of ascending key value. The list itself is an object of class LinkedList. The test program *TestLL.java* reads in numbers from the command line, builds up a linked list consisting of those numbers in sorted order, and then prints out the sorted list. Here are the source files:

TestLL.java

```
1   // usage:  [java] TestLL list_of_test_integers
2
3   // simple example program; reads integers from the command line,
4   // storing them in a linear linked list, maintaining ascending order,
5   // and then prints out the final list to the screen
6
7   public class TestLL
8   {
9       public static void main(String[] Args) {
10          int NumElements = Args.length;
11          LinkedList LL = new LinkedList();
12          for (int I = 1; I <= NumElements; I++)  {
13              int Num;
14              // do C's "atoi()", using parseInt()
15              Num = Integer.parseInt(Args[I-1]);
16              Node NN = new Node(Num);
```

```
17        LL.Insert(NN);
18      }
19      System.out.println("final sorted list:");
20      LL.PrintList();
21    }
22  }
```

LinkedList.java

```
1   // LinkedList.java, implementing an ordered linked list of integers
2
3   public class LinkedList
4   {
5      public static Node Head = null;
6
7      public LinkedList()  {
8         Head = null;
9      }
10
11     // inserts a node N into this list
12     public void Insert(Node N)  {
13        if (Head == null)  {
14           Head = N;
15           return;
16        }
17        if (N.Value < Head.Value)  {
18           N.Next = Head;
19           Head = N;
20           return;
21        }
22        else if (Head.Next == null)  {
23           Head.Next = N;
24           return;
25        }
26        for (Node D = Head; D.Next != null; D = D.Next)  {
27           if (N.Value < D.Next.Value)  {
28              N.Next = D.Next;
29              D.Next = N;
30              return;
31           }
32        }
33     }
34
35     public static void PrintList()  {
36        if (Head == null) return;
37        for (Node D = Head; D != null; D = D.Next)
38           System.out.println(D.Value);
```

```
39        }
40    }
```

Node.java

```
1    // Node.java, class for a node in an ordered linked list of integers
2
3    public class Node
4    {
5       int Value;
6       Node Next;  // "pointer" to next item in list
7
8       // constructor
9       public Node(int V)  {
10         Value = V;
11         Next = null;
12      }
13   }
```

There is a bug in the code. Let's try to find it.

8.1.1   Direct Use of GDB for Debugging Java

Java is ordinarily thought of as an interpreted language, but with GNU's GCJ compiler, you can compile Java source to native machine code. This enables your Java applications to run much faster, and it also means you can use GDB for debugging. (Make sure you have GDB version 5.1 or later.) GDB, either directly or via DDD, is more powerful than JDB, the debugger that comes with the Java Development Kit. For instance, JDB does not allow you to set conditional breakpoints, which is a basic GDB debugging technique, as you have seen. Thus you not only gain by having to learn one fewer debugger, but you also have better functionality.

First compile the application into native machine code:

```
$ gcj -c -g Node.java
$ gcj -c -g LinkedList.java
$ gcj -g --main=TestLL TestLL.java Node.o LinkedList.o -o TestLL
```

These lines are analogous to the usual GCC commands, except for the -main=TestLL option, which specifies the class whose function main() is to be the entry point for execution of the program. (We compiled the two source files one at a time. We found this to be necessary in order to ensure that GDB keeps track of the source files correctly.) Running the program on test input gives the following:

```
$ TestLL 8 5 12
final sorted list:
```

Somehow the input 12 disappeared. Let's see how to use GDB to find the bug. Start GDB as usual, and first tell it not to stop or print announcements to the screen when Unix signals are generated by Java's garbage collection operations. Such actions are a nuisance and may interfere with your ability to single-step using GDB.

```
(gdb) handle SIGPWR nostop noprint
Signal       Stop      Print    Pass to program Description
SIGPWR       No        No       Yes              Power fail/restart
(gdb) handle SIGXCPU nostop noprint
Signal       Stop      Print    Pass to program Description
SIGXCPU      No        No       Yes              CPU time limit exceeded
```

Now, since the first apparent casualty of the bug was the number 12 in the input, let's set a breakpoint at the beginning of the Insert() method, conditional on the node's key value being equal to 12:

```
(gdb) b LinkedList.java:13 if N.Value == 12
Breakpoint 1 at 0x8048bb4: file LinkedList.java, line 13.
```

As an alternative, you might think to try the command

```
(gdb) b LinkedList.java:Insert if N.Value == 12
```

However, although this would work later on, at this point, the LinkedList class has not yet been loaded.

Now run the program in GDB:

```
(gdb) r 8 5 12
Starting program: /debug/TestLL 8 5 12
[Thread debugging using libthread_db enabled]
[New Thread -1208596160 (LWP 12846)]
[New Thread -1210696800 (LWP 12876)]
[Switching to Thread -1208596160 (LWP 12846)]

Breakpoint 1, LinkedList.Insert(Node) (this=@47da8, N=@11a610)
    at LinkedList.java:13
13              if (Head == null)  {
Current language:  auto; currently java
```

Recalling the Principle of Confirmation, let's confirm that the value about to be inserted is 12:

```
(gdb) p N.Value
$1 = 12
```

Now let's step through the code:

```
(gdb) n
17              if (N.Value < Head.Value)  {
(gdb) n
22              else if (Head.Next == null)  {
(gdb) n
26              for (Node D = Head; D.Next != null; D = D.Next)  {
(gdb) n
27                  if (N.Value < D.Next.Value)  {
(gdb) p D.Next.Value
$2 = 8
(gdb) n
26              for (Node D = Head; D.Next != null; D = D.Next)  {
(gdb) n
12          public void Insert(Node N)  {
(gdb) n
33          }
(gdb) n
TestLL.main(java.lang.String[]) (Args=@ab480) at TestLL.java:12
12              for (int I = 1; I <= NumElements; I++)  {
```

Hmm, that's not good. We went through all of `Insert()` without inserting the 12.

Looking a bit more closely, you'll see that in the loop starting at line 26 of *LinkedList.java*, we compared the value to be inserted, 12, to the two values currently in the list, 5 and 8, and found that in both cases the new value was larger. That in fact is where the error lies. We didn't deal with the case in which the value to be inserted is larger than all of the values already in the list. We need to add code after line 31 to handle that situation:

```
else if (D.Next.Next == null)  {
   D.Next.Next = N;
   return;
}
```

After making that correction, you'll find that the program works as it should.

8.1.2   Using DDD with GDB to Debug Java

These steps are much easier and more pleasant if you use DDD as your interface to GDB (again assuming the source code is compiled using GCJ). Start up DDD as usual:

```
$ ddd TestLL
```

(Ignore the error message about a temporary file.)

The source code does not immediately appear in DDD's Source Text window, so you can begin by using DDD's Console:

```
(gdb) handle SIGPWR nostop noprint
(gdb) handle SIGXCPU nostop noprint
(gdb) b LinkedList.java:13
Breakpoint 1 at 0x8048b80: file LinkedList.java, line 13.
(gdb) cond 1 N.Value == 12
(gdb) r 8 5 12
```

At this point the source code appears, and you are at the breakpoint. You can then proceed with DDD operations as usual.

8.1.3 Using DDD as a GUI for JDB

DDD can be used directly with the Java Development Kit's JDB debugger. The command

```
$ ddd -jdb TestLL.java
```

will start DDD, which then invokes JDB.

However, we have found that it then becomes quite cumbersome, so we do not recommend this usage of DDD.

8.1.4 Debugging Java in Eclipse

If you originally downloaded and installed a version of Eclipse that is tailored to C/C++ development, you'll need to get the JDT (Java Development Tools) plug-in.

The basic operations are as we described before for C/C++, but note the following:

- When creating your project, make sure to choose **Java Project**. Also, we recommend that you check **Use Project Folder As Root for Sources and Classes**.

- Use the Package Explorer view for your navigator.

- Source files will be compiled to *.class* as soon as they are saved (or imported).

- When you create a run dialog, right-click **Java Application** and select **New**. In the space labeled Main Class, fill in the class in which main() is defined.

- When you create a debug dialog, check **Stop in Main**.

- In debug runs, Eclipse will stop before main(). Just click the **Resume** button to continue.

Figure 8-1 shows a typical Java debugging scene in Eclipse. Note that as with C/C++, in the Variables view we have displayed the values of the node N by pointing the triangle next to N downward.

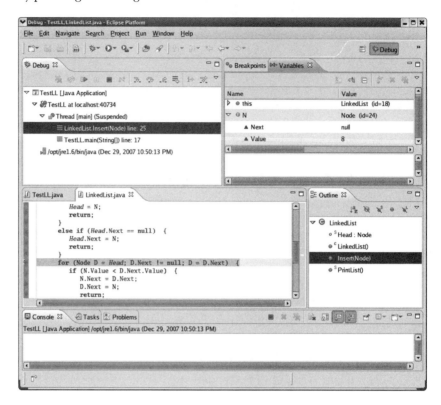

Figure 8-1: Java debugging in Eclipse

8.2   Perl

We will use the following example, *textcount.pl*, which computes statistics on text files:

```perl
1   #! /usr/bin/perl
2
3   # reads the text file given on the command line, and counts words,
4   # lines, and paragraphs
5
6   open(INFILE,@ARGV[0]);
7
8   $line_count = 0;
9   $word_count = 0;
10  $par_count = 0;
11
```

```
12  $now_in_par = 0;  # not inside a paragraph right now
13
14  while ($line = <INFILE>) {
15     $line_count++;
16     if ($line ne "\n")  {
17        if ($now_in_par == 0)  {
18           $par_count++;
19           $now_in_par = 1;
20        }
21        @words_on_this_line = split(" ",$line);
22        $word_count += scalar(@words_on_this_line);
23     }
24     else  {
25        $now_in_par = 0;
26     }
27  }
28
29  print "$word_count $line_count $par_count\n";
```

The program counts the number of words, lines, and paragraphs in the text file specified on the command line. As a test case, let's use the file *test.txt* shown below (you may recognize this as similar to text from Chapter 1):

```
In this chapter we set out some basic principles of debugging, both
general and also with regard to the GDB and DDD debuggers.  At least one
of our ``rules'' will be formal in nature, The Fundamental Principle of
Debugging.


Beginners should of course read this chapter carefully, since the
material here will be used throughout the remainder of the book.

Professionals may be tempted to skip the chapter.  We suggest, though,
that they at least skim through it.  Many professionals will find at
least some new material, and in any case it is important that all
readers begin with a common background.
```

There is one blank line at the top, two after *Debugging* and one before *Professionals*. The output from running our Perl code on this file should be as shown below:

```
$ perl textcount.pl test.txt
102 14 3
```

Now, suppose we had forgotten the else clause:

```
else {
   $now_in_par = 0;
}
\end{Code}
```

The output would then be

```
\begin{Code}
$ perl textcount.pl test.txt
102 14 1
```

The word and line counts are correct, but the paragraph count is wrong.

8.2.1   Debugging Perl via DDD

Perl has its own built-in debugger, which is invoked via the -d option on the command line:

```
$ perl -d myprog.pl
```

One drawback of the built-in debugger is that it does not have a GUI, but that can be remedied by running the debugger through DDD. Let's see how we could use DDD to find the bug. Invoke DDD by typing

```
$ ddd textcount.pl
```

DDD automatically notices that this is a Perl script, invokes the Perl debugger, and sets the green "you are here" arrow at the first executable line of code.

Now we specify the command-line argument, test.txt, by clicking **Program | Run** and filling in the Run with Arguments section of the pop-up window, as seen in Figure 8-2. (You may get a message in the DDD Console along the lines of ". . . do not know how to create a new TTY . . ." Just ignore it.) Alternatively, we could set the argument "manually" by simply typing the Perl debugger command

```
@ARGV[0] = "test.txt"
```

in the DDD Console.

Since the error is in the paragraph count, let's see what happens when the program reaches the end of the first paragraph. This will occur right after the condition

```
$words_on_this_line[0] eq "Debugging."
```

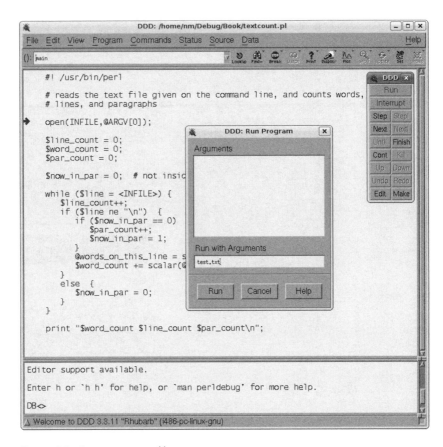

Figure 8-2: Setting command-line arguments

becomes true. Let's put a breakpoint near the beginning of the while loop. We do this in exactly the same manner as we have seen for C/C++ programs, by right-clicking the line and choosing **Set Breakpoint**.

We should also impose the above condition on this breakpoint. Again, click **Source | Breakpoints**, making sure the given breakpoint is highlighted in the Breakpoints and Watchpoints pop-up window, and then we click the Props icon. Then we fill in the desired condition. See Figure 8-3.

We then select **Program | Run**. (We do not choose Run Again, as this seems to take one into the Perl internals.) We move the mouse pointer to an instance of the variable $words_on_this_line, and DDD's usual yellow box pops up displaying the value of that variable. Thus we confirm that the breakpoint condition holds, as it should. See Figure 8-4.

After pressing Next a few times to skip over the blank lines in the text file, you'll notice that we also skip over the line

```
$par_count++;
```

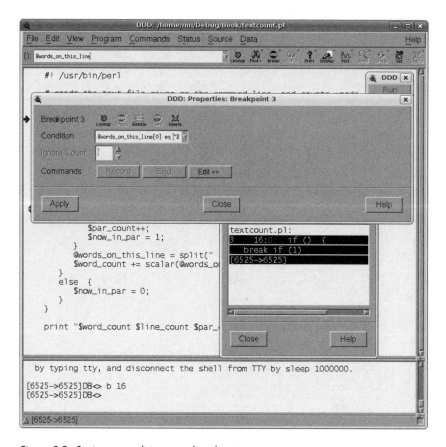

Figure 8-3: Setting a condition on a breakpoint

which was supposed to increment the paragraph count. Working backwards, we see that this was caused by the variable $now_in_par being 0, and by following up on this observation we soon realize how to repair the bug.

A breakpoint can also be disabled, enabled, or deleted in DDD by selecting **Source | Breakpoints**, highlighting the breakpoint, and then clicking the desired choice.

If you change the source file, you have to notify DDD to update itself by selecting **File | Restart**.

8.2.2   Debugging Perl in Eclipse

To develop Perl code in Eclipse, you'll need the PadWalker Perl package, which you can downloaded from CPAN, and the EPIC Eclipse plug-in for Perl.

Again, the basic operations are the same as what we described before for C/C++, but note the following:

*   When creating a project, choose **Perl Project**.

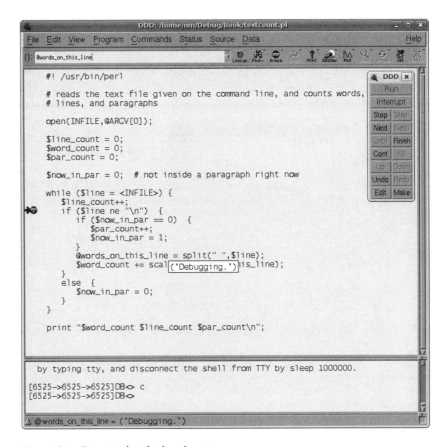

```
#! /usr/bin/perl

# reads the text file given on the command line, and counts words,
# lines, and paragraphs

open(INFILE,@ARGV[0]);

$line_count = 0;
$word_count = 0;
$par_count = 0;

$now_in_par = 0;   # not inside a paragraph right now

while ($line = <INFILE>) {
    $line_count++;
    if ($line ne "\n") {
        if ($now_in_par == 0)  {
            $par_count++;
            $now_in_par = 1;
        }
        @words_on_this_line = split(" ",$line);
        $word_count += scal('Debugging.')his_line);
    }
    else {
        $now_in_par = 0;
    }
}

print "$word_count $line_count $par_count\n";
```

```
by typing tty, and disconnect the shell from TTY by sleep 1000000.

[6525->6525->6525]DB<> c
[6525->6525->6525]DB<>
```

△ @words_on_this_line = ('Debugging.')

Figure 8-4: On arrival at the breakpoint

- Use Navigator as your navigator view.
- There is no build phase, as Perl does not produce byte code.
- In the Debug perspective, the values of the variables are accessible only in the Variables view, not by mouse action in the source code view, and only for local variables.

  You'll need to use the Perl my keyword in the first instance of each variable in your source code in order to see the global variables (this is where the PadWalker package comes in).

Figure 8-5 show a typical Perl debug screen. Note that we've added the my keyword to the global variables.

8.3 Python

Let's take as our example *tf.py*, which counts words, lines, and paragraphs in a text file, as with our Perl example above.

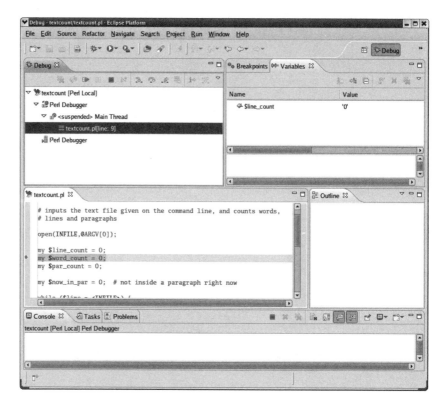

Figure 8-5: Perl debugging screen

```
1   class textfile:
2       ntfiles = 0  # count of number of textfile objects
3       def __init__(self,fname):
4           textfile.ntfiles += 1
5           self.name = fname   # name
6           self.fh = open(fname)
7           self.nlines = 0   # number of lines
8           self.nwords = 0   # number of words
9           self.npars = 0  # number of words
10          self.lines = self.fh.readlines()
11          self.wordlineparcount()
12      def wordlineparcount(self):
13          "finds the number of lines and words in the file"
14          self.nlines = len(self.lines)
15          inparagraph = 0
16          for l in self.lines:
17              w = l.split()
18              self.nwords += len(w)
19              if l == '\n':
```

```
20          if inparagraph:
21              inparagraph = 0
22          elif not inparagraph:
23              self.npars += 1
24              inparagraph = 1
25
26      def grep(self,target):
27          "prints out all lines in the file containing target"
28          for l in self.lines:
29              if l.find(target) >= 0:
30                  print l
31          print i
32
33  def main():
34      t = textfile('test.txt')
35      print t.nwords, t.nlines, t.npars
36
37  if __name__ == '__main__':
38      main()
```

Be sure to include in your source code the two lines shown at the end of the program:

```
if __name__ == '__main__':
    main()
```

NOTE   *If you are an experienced Python programmer, you are probably well aware of this pattern. If you are unfamiliar with Python, a brief explanation of these lines is that you need to test whether your Python program is being invoked on its own or being imported as a module into some other program. This is an issue that arises when running the program via a debugger.*

8.3.1   Debugging Python in DDD

Python's basic debugger is PDB (*pdb.py*), a text-based tool. Its utility is greatly enhanced by using DDD as a GUI frontend.

There is a bit of business to take care of before starting, though. In order to enable DDD to access PDB properly, Richard Wolff wrote PYDB (*pydb.py*), a slightly modified version of PDB. You would then run DDD with the -pydb option. But Python evolved, and the original PYDB stopped working correctly.

A nice solution has been developed by Rocky Bernstein. As of this writing, in summer 2007, his modified (and greatly extended) PYDB is slated to be included in the next release of DDD. Alternatively, you can use the patch that Richard Wolff kindly provided. You will need the following files:

- *http://heather.cs.ucdavis.edu/~matloff/Python/DDD/pydb.py*
- *http://heather.cs.ucdavis.edu/~matloff/Python/DDD/pydbcmd.py*

- *http://heather.cs.ucdavis.edu/~matloff/Python/DDD/pydbsupt.py*

Place the files in some directory, say */usr/bin*, give them execute permission, and create a file named *pydb* consisting of a single line

```
/usr/bin/pydb.py
```

Make sure you give the file *pydb* execute permission too. Once this has been done, you can use DDD for Python programs. Then fire up DDD:

```
$ ddd --pydb
```

NOTE   *If an error window pops up saying, "PYDB couldn't start," you may have path problems—for example, you may have another file named* pydb. *Just make sure the one for DDD will be encountered first in your search path.*

Then bring in the source file *tf.py*, either by selecting **File** | **Open Source** and double-clicking the filename or by typing

```
file tf.py
```

in the Console. The (Pdb) prompt may not show up initially, but type your command anyway.

Your source code will appear in the Source Text window, and you can then set breakpoints as usual. Suppose that you set a breakpoint at the line

```
w = l.split()
```

To run the program, click **Program** | **Run**, set any command-line arguments in the Run pop-up window, and then click **Run**. After clicking Run, you will need to click **Continue** twice. This is due to the workings of the underlying PDB/PYDB debugger. (If you forget to do this, PDB/PYDB will remind you in the DDD Console.)

If you make a change to the source code, issue the `file` command in the Console, or select Source | Reload Source. Your breakpoints from the last run will be retained.

8.3.2   Debugging Python in Eclipse

Once again, the procedures for Python are similar to those of the other languages. This of course illustrates the value of having a single tool to use on multiple languages—once you learn how to use the tool in one language, it is quite easy to use it for another one. The main Python-specific points to keep in mind are:

- You need to install the Pydev plug-in. After you do so, select **Window** | **Preferences** | **Pydev**, and inform Eclipse as to the location of your Python interpreter, for example, */usr/bin/python*.

- Use Pydev Package Explorer as your navigator perspective.

- No permanent byte code files are created, so there is no build procedure.

- In setting up a run/debug dialog, note the following: Fill in Main Module with the name of the source file in which you wish execution to start. In the Arguments tab, fill in Base Directory to be the one in which you have input files (or the root of a tree of such directories), and put your command-line arguments in Program Arguments.

- In the Debug perspective, the values of the variables are accessible only in the Variables view, and only for local variables.

One major advantage of Eclipse over DDD is that PDB, the underlying debugging engine used by DDD, does not work on threaded programs, whereas Eclipse does.

8.4 Debugging SWIG Code

SWIG (Simplified Wrapper and Interface Generator) is a popular open source tool for interfacing Java, Perl, Python, and a number of other interpreted languages with C/C++. It is included with most Linux distributions and can also be downloaded from the Web. It allows you to write most of an application's code in an interpreted language and incorporate specific sections that you have written in C/C++, for example, to enhance performance.

The question arises of how to run GDB/DDD on such code. Here we will present a small example using Python and C. The C code will manage a first in, first out (FIFO) queue:

```
1  // fifo.c, SWIG example; manages a FIFO queue of characters
2
3  char *fifo; // the queue
4
5  int nfifo = 0, // current length of the queue
6     maxfifo; // max length of the queue
7
8  int fifoinit(int spfifo) // allocate space for a max of spfifo elements
9  { fifo = malloc(spfifo);
10    if (fifo == 0) return 0; // failure
11    else {
12       maxfifo = spfifo;
13       return 1; // success
14    }
15 }
16
17 int fifoput(char c) // append c to queue
18 { if (nfifo < maxfifo) {
19      fifo[nfifo] = c;
20      return 1; // success
```

```
21    }
22    else return 0; // failure
23  }
24
25  char fifoget() // delete head of queue and return
26  { char c;
27    if (nfifo > 0) {
28      c = fifo[0];
29      memmove(fifo,fifo+1,--nfifo);
30      return c;
31    }
32    else return 0; // assume no null characters ever in queue
33  }
```

Besides the *.c* file, SWIG also requires an *interface file*, in this case *fifo.i*. It consists of the global symbols, listed once in SWIG style and once in C style:

```
%module fifo

%{extern char *fifo;
extern int nfifo,
           maxfifo;
extern int fifoinit(int);
extern int fifoput(char);
extern char fifoget(); %}

extern char *fifo;
extern int nfifo,
           maxfifo;
extern int fifoinit(int);
extern int fifoput(char);
extern char fifoget();
```

To compile the code, first run swig, which generates an extra *.c* file and a Python file. Then use GCC and ld to produce a *.so* shared object dynamic library. Here is the Makefile:

```
_fifo.so:  fifo.o fifo_wrap.o
        gcc -shared fifo.o fifo_wrap.o -o _fifo.so

fifo.o fifo_wrap.o:  fifo.c fifo_wrap.c
        gcc -fPIC -g -c fifo.c fifo_wrap.c -I/usr/include/python2.4

fifo.py fifo_wrap.c:  fifo.i
        swig -python fifo.i
```

The library is imported into Python as a module, as shown in the test program:

```
# testfifo.py

import fifo

def main():
    fifo.fifoinit(100)
    fifo.fifoput('x')
    fifo.fifoput('c')
    c = fifo.fifoget()
    print c
    c = fifo.fifoget()
    print c

if __name__ == '__main__': main()
```

The output of this program should be "x" and "c," but we come up empty:

```
$ python testfifo.py


$
```

To use GDB, remember that the actual program you are running is the Python interpreter, python. So run GDB on the interpreter:

```
$ gdb python
```

Now, we'd like to set a breakpoint within the attached FIFO library, but the library has not been loaded yet. The loading won't occur until the import line

```
import fifo
```

is executed by the Python interpreter. Fortunately, we can ask GDB to stop at a function in the library anyway:

```
(gdb) b fifoput
Function "fifoput" not defined.
Make breakpoint pending on future shared library load? (y or [n]) y

Breakpoint 1 (fifoput) pending.
```

Now run the interpreter, whose argument is the test program, *testfifo.py*:

```
(gdb) r testfifo.py
Starting program: /usr/bin/python testfifo.py
Reading symbols from shared object read from target memory...(no debugging
symbols found)...done.
Loaded system supplied DSO at 0x164000
(no debugging symbols found)
(no debugging symbols found)
(no debugging symbols found)
[Thread debugging using libthread_db enabled]
[New Thread -1208383808 (LWP 15912)]
(no debugging symbols found)
(no debugging symbols found)
(no debugging symbols found)
(no debugging symbols found)
Breakpoint 2 at 0x3b25f8: file fifo.c, line 18.
Pending breakpoint "fifoput" resolved
[Switching to Thread -1208383808 (LWP 15912)]

Breakpoint 2, fifoput (c=120 'x') at fifo.c:18
18        {  if (nfifo < maxfifo)  {
```

You can now do what you already know so well:

```
(gdb) n
19              fifo[nfifo] = c;
(gdb) p nfifo
$1 = 0
(gdb) c
Continuing.

Breakpoint 2, fifoput (c=99 'c') at fifo.c:18
18        {  if (nfifo < maxfifo)  {
(gdb) n
19              fifo[nfifo] = c;
(gdb) p nfifo
$2 = 0
```

Well, there's the problem. Each time you attempt to add a character
to the queue, you simply overwrite the previously added character. Line 19
should be

```
fifo[nfifo++] = c;
```

Once you make that change, the code works fine.

8.5 Assembly Language

GDB and DDD can be extremely useful in debugging assembly language code. There are a number of special considerations to keep in mind, which will be described in this section.

Take as an example the code in file *testff.s*:

```
1   # the subroutine findfirst(v,w,b) finds the first instance of a value v
2   # in a block of w consecutive words of memory beginning at b, returning
3   # either the index of the word where v was found (0, 1, 2, ...) or -1 if
4   # v was not found; beginning with _start, we have a short test of the
5   # subroutine
6
7   .data  # data segment
8   x:
9         .long   1
10        .long   5
11        .long   3
12        .long   168
13        .long   8888
14  .text  # code segment
15  .globl _start  # required
16  _start:  # required to use this label unless special action taken
17        # push the arguments on the stack, then make the call
18        push $x+4  # start search at the 5
19        push $168  # search for 168 (deliberately out of order)
20        push $4  # search 4 words
21        call findfirst
22  done:
23        movl %edi, %edi  # dummy instruction for breakpoint
24  findfirst:
25        # finds first instance of a specified value in a block of words
26        # EBX will contain the value to be searched for
27        # ECX will contain the number of words to be searched
28        # EAX will point to the current word to search
29        # return value (EAX) will be index of the word found (-1 if not found)
30        # fetch the arguments from the stack
31        movl 4(%esp), %ebx
32        movl 8(%esp), %ecx
33        movl 12(%esp), %eax
34        movl %eax, %edx  # save block start location
35        # top of loop; compare the current word to the search value
36  top:  cmpl (%eax), %ebx
37        jz found
38        decl %ecx  # decrement counter of number of words left to search
39        jz notthere  # if counter has reached 0, the search value isn't there
40        addl $4, %eax  # otherwise, go on to the next word
41        jmp top
```

```
42   found:
43       subl %edx, %eax  # get offset from start of block
44       shrl $2, %eax  # divide by 4, to convert from byte offset to index
45       ret
46   notthere:
47       movl $-1, %eax
48       ret
```

This is Linux Intel assembly language, using the AT&T syntax, but users familiar with other Intel syntaxes should find the code easy to follow. (The GDB command set disassembly-flavor intel will cause GDB to display all output of its disassemble command in Intel syntax, which is like the syntax used by the NASM compiler, for example. By the way, since this is a Linux platform, the program runs in the Intel CPU's 32-bit flat mode.)

As indicated by the comments, the subroutine findfirst finds the first occurrence of a specified value within a specified block of consecutive words of memory. The return value of the subroutine is the index (0, 1, 2, ...) of the word in which the value was found, or -1 if it was not found.

The subroutine expects the arguments to be placed on the stack, so that the stack looks like this upon entry:

```
address of the start of the block to be searched
number of words in the block
value to be searched
return address
```

NOTE   *Intel stacks grow downward, that is, toward address 0 in memory. Words with smaller addresses appear further down in the picture.*

To introduce a bug that we can use GDB to find, we deliberately scrambled the elements in the calling sequence in the "main" program:

```
push $x+4  # start search at the 5
push $168  # search for 168 (deliberately out of order)
push $4  # search 4 words
```

The instructions preceding the call should instead be

```
push $x+4  # start search at the 5
push $4  # search 4 words
push $168  # search for 168
```

Just as you use the -g option when compiling C/C++ code for use with GDB/DDD, here at the assembly level you use -gstabs:

```
$ as -a --gstabs -o testff.o testff.s
```

This produces an object file *testff.o* and prints out a side-by-side comparison of the assembly source code and the corresponding machine code. It also shows offsets of data items and other information that is potentially useful for the debugging process.

We then link:

```
$ ld testff.o
```

This produces an executable with the default name *a.out*.
Let's run this code under GDB:

```
(gdb) b done
Breakpoint 1 at 0x8048085: file testff.s, line 18.
(gdb) r
Starting program: /debug/a.out
Breakpoint 1, done () at testff.s:18
18              movl %edi, %edi  # dummy for breakpoint
Current language:  auto; currently asm
(gdb) p $eax
$1 = -1
```

As you can see here, the registers can be referred to via dollar sign prefixes, in this case $eax for the EAX register. Unfortunately, the value in that register is -1, indicating that the desired value, 168, was not found in the specified block.

When debugging assembly language programs, one of the first things to do is to check the stack for accuracy. So, let's set a breakpoint at the subroutine and then inspect the stack when you get there:

```
(gdb) b findfirst
Breakpoint 2 at 0x8048087: file testff.s, line 25.
(gdb) r
The program being debugged has been started already.
Start it from the beginning? (y or n) y
Starting program: /debug/a.out
Breakpoint 2, findfirst () at testff.s:25
25              movl 4(%esp), %ebx
(gdb) x/4w $esp
0xbfffd9a0:    0x08048085    0x00000004    0x000000a8    0x080490b4
```

The stack is of course part of memory, so to inspect it you must use the GDB x command, which examines memory. Here, we asked GDB to display the four words starting at the location indicated by the stack pointer ESP (note that the picture of the stack above shows four words). The x command will display memory in order of increasing addresses. That is exactly what you want, since on the Intel architecture, as on many others, the stack grows toward 0.

You see from the picture of the stack shown above that the first word should be the return address. This expectation could be checked in various ways. One approach would be to use GDB's disassemble command, which lists assembly language instructions (reverse-translated from the machine code) and their addresses. Stepping into the subroutine, you could then check whether contents of the first word on the stack matches the address of the function that follows the call.

You'll see that it does. However, you'll find that the second number, 4, which ought to be the value to be searched for (168), is in fact the size of the search block (4). From this information you'll quickly realize that we accidentally switched the two push instructions before the call.

INDEX